The History of Marley

To my parents

The History of Marley

Fred Wellings

WOODHEAD PUBLISHING LIMITED

Cambridge, England

Published by Woodhead Publishing Limited, Abington Hall, Abington, Cambridge, CB1 6AH, England

First published 1994, Woodhead Publishing Limited

British Library Cataloguing in Publication Data
A catalogue record for this book is available from the British Library

ISBN 1 85573 159 2

Designed by Andrew Jones (text) and Chris Feely (jacket).
Typeset by BookEns Ltd, Baldock, Herts.
Printed by St Edmundsbury Press, Suffolk, England.

Contents

Acknowledgements

The history of Marley was commissioned in 1988 by Sir George Russell and Mike Armstrong, then Chief Executive and Finance Director respectively; to both I owe a debt for providing me with the opportunity to write the history of one of the country's most interesting building materials companies. Colin James, Company Secretary until his retirement in 1993, unerringly guided me through the Marley cast list, past and present, helping to secure me a wide range of interviews. Throughout, I have been given unrestricted access to all Marley minutes, board papers and other archive material up to 1985, events thereafter being touched on only briefly. I am grateful to the Marley Board, which has given me every support and encouragement throughout this venture, yet leaving me to present the text in my own style and with my own conclusions. The text and conclusions remain, of course, the author's responsibility.

Sir Owen Aisher, who sadly died in 1993 before he could see this work published, dominated Marley for half a century. I first interviewed him when he was 88, and had many meetings with him over the succeeding years. The depth of his knowledge of the affairs of the company and the industries it served was fascinating and invaluable. Sir Owen also made some of his private archive available to me, and the contemporary typed "diaries" of his overseas trips would have made a book in their own right. Sir Owen did read a late draft of the book and I had the benefit of his opinions, delivered, as everyone who knew him would expect, in forthright style.

Many of the directors and senior executives who have worked for Marley over the years gave of their time. Apart from those already mentioned, I wish to record my thanks to Jack Aisher (Chairman from 1982 to 1985), Owen Aisher, Robin Aisher, Richard Aisher, Trevor Aisher, Peter Amsden, Geoff Barrett, Bill Borgia, Sir Robert Clark (non-executive Chairman from 1985 to 1989), Bill Courtney, John Dewar, Mike Evans, Fred Hardy (to whom I must give special thanks), Jim Hobbs, Denis Hunt, Geoff Marsh, Bill Moffatt, Denis Moss, Mike Moxon, David Musgrave, John Pollard, Denis Rigden, Tom O'Sullivan, Archie Orme, Bill Richardson, Colin Somerville, Denis Stoker, David Trapnell, Alistair Vearonelly and Peter Wilson.

Documentation relating to the period before the flotation (1936) and to the relationship between the Aishers and Arthur Blackman (who was the controlling shareholder until 1934) is limited. I am grateful for information and material from Arthur Blackman's original coal merchanting business which still exists as Blackman Pavie & Ladden; F G Beckett, a retired member of Blackman's solicitors, Menneer, Idle & Brackett; Alex Thomson of Gibbons & Mannington who was able to find early Blackman minute books; A R Holliman of BAT's Dean Finance who supplied minutes relating to the period when Dean Finance briefly controlled Marley; and Frank Cooper who was Assistant Secretary of Dean Finance at the time of flotation. Duncan McDowall and Nancy Sample of Ottawa's Carleton University were also able to direct me to the James Dunn Papers in the Canadian National Archive and obtain copies of correspondence between Sir James Dunn and Sir Owen Aisher that related to the flotation and the associated legal action.

Contributions from directors of other companies have helped to provide a breadth to the discussion of the industries in which Marley operates and have given additional insights into the nature of the competition; I hope they do not feel that I have leaned too far in favour of the home team. I was helped on the early years of the roof tile industry by Sir Colin Corness, then Chairman of Redland and the two "founders" of Redland, Alex Young and Tony White. Len Griffiths, the retired chief chemist of Dunlop Semtex gave me considerable help on the technical aspects of the early floor tiles and the relations between the three leaders. G Halstead of the Halstead Group and Roger Strugnell of Forbo-Nairn both gave me written comments on more recent developments. Michael Collins, the founder of Key Plastics and later Chairman of Reed Building Products, gave me similar help on the early years of plastic extrusions.

In writing about the early years of Marley Foam (as it then was) I owe much to Paul Casey, ex-President of Davidson Rubber. His 'tapes across the Atlantic' contained original material on the early history of Davidson and the development of plastics for the motor industry. I was also greatly assisted in describing Marley's various partnerships with Eternit, one of the more secretive continental companies, by Fritz Hatschek, of Eternit Austria and the grandson of Ludwig Hatschek, the founder of the original Eternit company.

Finally, Lord Taylor and Phyllis Reed (daughter of Charles Daniels) gave me interesting personal reminiscences.

I have left until last an especial thank you to Dr David Jeremy, currently Reader in Business History at Manchester Metropolitan University and past Editor of the *Dictionary of Business Biography*. David's experience and guidance have been available to me throughout the preparation of this history and I have benefited considerably from his broader perspective.

Fred Wellings

Foreword

I joined Marley at the end of 1985, not many years after Sir Owen Aisher had retired as Chairman of the business he had built. His influence was still strong in the company and is to this day. He was Marley – and he epitomised it all over the world.

I was conscious that Sir Owen and his achievements were unique, and that to have a company approaching 70 years of age with its founder still alive and full of vitality presented an unrivalled opportunity to commission a definitive book about Marley. In 1989 Fred Wellings took on the task and with his special knowledge of both the building industry and Marley has brought a rare insight into our company. His knowledge, coupled with Sir Owen's views and the memories of many Marley people, past and present, have enabled the work to be completed.

Marley is publishing it as a memorial to Sir Owen Aisher. He remained spendidly active to the last. Two days before his death on 26th September 1993 he was urging a hapless Marley factory manager to make faster progress in developing a new product, and earlier in the year had continued to catch trout on the Test. His final twenty-four hours 'above ground' (his phrase) were spent at his request in the old factory building at Lenham, where the first Marley tiles were made 70 years ago. A large proportion of the plant

workforce filed past to pay their respects. Many lined the route of the Marley lorry which then took him to his final resting place in Harrietsham churchyard – a most moving tribute to a truly remarkable man.

Sir George Russell CBE
Chairman, Marley plc.

January 1994

Part 1

The early days: capital and labour in concrete roof tiles

The Aisher family

The friendship of two families in the neighbouring Wiltshire villages of Amesbury and Shipton Bellinger provides the link between the two founding families of the Marley business – the Aishers and the Blackmans. It proved the classic partnership between labour and capital, with Arthur Blackman supplying all the early finance, and the Aishers the labour, knowledge and, above all, the drive and determination which was to make Marley one of the most influential firms in the development of the building materials industry. Although the partnership was to survive barely a decade before Blackman was bought out in 1934, without it, Marley could not have achieved its pre-war domination of the concrete roof tile industry.

Owen Aisher, Sir Owen's father, laid the foundations of the present Marley business when he began building houses in Kent after the First World War. He was born at Godshill on the Isle of Wight in January 1876. The Aisher or Asher family can be traced back to John Asher of Amesbury in the mid-eighteenth century. Little information is available on the occupations or place in society of the early Aishers but Owen's grandfather John (died 1841) and his father George were both dairymen. George Aisher (1802–1876), one of eight children, clearly managed to improve his position for the 1851 Census records him as farming the 140 acre Turners Farm at Ringwood in Hampshire – we presume as a tenant.

Following the death of his first wife, George Aisher remarried at the age of 60 (though admitting only to 59), to Emily Cherrett, some 31 years his junior; this marriage produced further four sons, the youngest being Owen. Owen Aisher was born on the 28th of January 1876, by which time the family had moved to Godshill on the Isle of Wight, the birthplace of George Aisher's first wife. Unfortunately, George Aisher was to survive his youngest son but two years, dying in 1878; Emily died a few years later, at the age of 44, leaving Owen a 10-year-old orphan.

As his elder brothers had already moved back to the mainland to find work, Owen Aisher was first taken care of by a local grocer and Baptist lay preacher, Mr Holdaway. The experience does not appear to have imbued a religious ethos into the Marley business in the manner of John Laing's Brethren upbringing. Asked about the influence of religion, his son (Sir Owen) remarked 'I always remember what my Father said about the Boer War: "the Boers were practically unbeatable because they had the best pony between their legs in South Africa; the best rifles, the Mauser; and they had a bible under the other arm." I think the same thing applies to business – beware of chaps with bibles under their arms!'

Mr Holdaway looked after Owen Aisher for about two years. The dates are unclear but according to Charles Dobson, a close family friend of the Aishers (writing in *Marley News*), Owen had crossed to Hampshire at the age of 12, working first for a blacksmith at Boscombe. This is confirmed by Owen Aisher's army service records. In January 1894, shortly before his 18th birthday, Owen attested at Poole for six years' reserve service with the 3rd Battalion Dorset Regiment. He gave his trade as 'shoeing smith', stating that he was no longer an apprentice and that his former master was a Mr Jackson of Bournemouth.

For whatever reason, Owen must have abandoned the smith's trade for Dobson records him joining his brother, who was already established as a journeyman plasterer, at Boscombe. Together they plastered houses being built in the expansion of the seaside towns. At that time, plasterers would often involve themselves in slating work, and this would have represented Owen Aisher's first experience of the trade which was later to form the basis of the Marley Tile Company. 'Slating, in England, in the absence of a Union, ceased to be a special trade, and became the prey of jobbing plasterers or bricklayers... Till quite recently, a slater was regarded as a type of plasterer'.[1]

As work became more difficult to find on the South Coast, Owen appears to have headed for London, settling in the Kingston area where he continued in

---

1   *R W Postgate, The Builders' History, London, 1923.*

the plastering trade. However, he must still have been making regular visits back to the coast for his militia attendances. That does not seem to have been the only call on his time for, at the turn of the century, he married Emily Charlotte Willis at Portsea Island, Portsmouth; by then he was able to describe himself as a 'Plasterer (master)'. As Owen and Emily were being married, Mafeking, Kimberley and Ladysmith were all under siege. In January 1900, Owen's six year reserve service was due to end but in the previous May he had re-engaged, this time as a corporal. Promotion to sergeant followed in February, and in October he was called up for full-time service, sailing for South Africa in March 1901.

After serving for a year in South Africa Owen Aisher, now 26, returned to England, though not to resume his old craft of plastering. Instead, he moved to the army camp at Bulford on the Salisbury Plain with his wife and 'Young Owen'. As a civilian, he took up a clerical appointment in the Fuel and Light Department. Where Owen acquired the necessary educational skills is unclear. His early schooling would have been limited, though his brief period under the care of a lay preacher after his mother died may have helped. Charles Dobson wrote 'one wonders how much formal education he could have had... Yet in later life he was a well read man, and he wrote a good legible hand that many might envy... The truth is that in the main he was self-educated.'

Owen Aisher worked at Bulford Camp until the end of the First World War, as the senior clerk in the Fuel and Light Office, supervising the issue of supplies to the units stationed at the camp and keeping the accounts. However, in 1915 the family moved their home a few miles to Amesbury. While they

Owen Aisher Senior

The house where Owen Aisher Senior was born

lived in Amesbury, Owen's Aisher's eldest son, now Sir Owen, ran a taxi business for the family, first with a Ford and then progressing to a Daimler. Within eighteen months, that had made enough money to enable Owen Aisher to buy a smallholding, called Ingleside, at Andover. The farming was not a success, hardly surprising given the small scale of the enterprise, and for a brief period after the First World War, Owen Aisher returned to the Isle of Wight. In 1919, Owen Aisher moved to Charing Heath in Kent to try his hand again with a smallholding but apparently with little more success. After a gap of twenty years, Owen Aisher was ready to return to the building trade; in the aftermath of Lloyd George's 'a fit country for heroes to live in', this time it was to be as a housebuilder.

According to Charles Dobson, writing in *Marley News*, the decision was carefully researched; the 'study of certain building and related statistics had led him to think that Kent was going to be ahead of most southern counties in the matter of building development, and his judgement proved to be sound'. The first land was bought at Harrietsham, some four miles down the road from Charing Heath: the substance of the Marley business had not yet arrived but its physical location was now established. Dobson describes the Harrietsham purchase. 'In October 1920, while he was on holiday with his family in the Isle of Wight, he happened to see in a Kent newspaper an advertisement of building land for sale. Something about the wording of the advertisement aroused their interest and without more ado they cut short their holiday, went to Harrietsham, saw the land and the agents, and after a short period of negotiation bought in an area of about ten acres' at a price of £20 an acre.

Enter the coal merchant

Dobson's account suggests that Owen Aisher was no longer a tradesman but a man with some capital, however modest, and the confidence and experience to start a small entrepreneurial venture. But neither can his capital have been substantial for it was around this time that he turned to Arthur Blackman for financial backing. Whether it was to finance the original purchase of the Harrietsham land, the subsequent building work, or to support Owen when the housing market later became more difficult, is not known. What we do know is that by 1923, when the manufacture of concrete roof tiles was first considered, Arthur Blackman was already an equal partner with Owen Aisher in his building business; and for the first decade of Marley Tile's existence, Arthur Blackman was to be the majority shareholder in a venture run by the Aisher family.

Arthur Blackman was the archetypal self-made Victorian businessman, starting from nothing to become one of the dominant political and business figures in Hastings before and after the First World War. Blackman was born in July 1868 at Netherfield, near Battle in Sussex; his father, David Blackman, was an agricultural labourer and his mother, Mary, kept a small shop (according to the 1871 Census). Arthur was one of a large family, having eight surviving brothers; he attended the village school until he was nine and then started what was clearly an arduous working childhood. In giving £25,000 to a Trust for the education and training of young people Arthur Blackman later said 'I had no education, and every day of my life I realise how much I missed by having to leave school so young. My six shillings a week was good pay, only a shilling less than my father was earning at the time. But I don't want other children to go through what I went through'.[2] That early work appears to have been in a woodchopper's yard where charcoal was burnt. His father was described on Arthur's birth certificate as an agricultural labourer but at some point he must have tried coal delivery for Blackman's obituary reported that while in his teens 'he had taken over a small coal business in Hastings from his Father. There was only a horse and cart and no business premises'[3] there are certainly local memories handed down of Arthur as a child sweeping up the coal dust after his father had delivered the coal. Anyway, that was the start of Arthur Blackman's coal merchanting business, based at the Coal Exchange London and at Hastings. By the turn of the century he was ready to go into local politics and was elected to the Hastings Council in 1905, serving with a break of only one

2 Sussex Express, *September 1938.*
3 Hastings & St Leonards Observer, *2nd November 1957.*

Arthur Blackman (reproduced by kind permission of Hastings Borough Council)

year until 1952. He was a JP, a Baron of the Cinque Ports and Mayor of Hastings five times, the second occasion being in 1923, just as the partnership with Owen Aisher was being extended. Usefully, his other business interests included a directorship of the Hastings & Thanet Building Society.

There are conflicting versions of how Owen Aisher and Arthur Blackman came together. There is no doubt that there was a common Wiltshire link. In 1892 Blackman had married Elizabeth Miles, who came from Shipton Bellinger, a village near Andover. It was there that the Aisher family had its roots and young Owen remembers them knowing Elizabeth Miles' brother. Perhaps what had been a loose acquaintance helped Owen Aisher decide which building society to approach for finance. Indeed, writing in 1963 in *Marley News*, Charles Dobson suggested that it was in the normal course of business with the building society that the two men first met, only discovering later that they had a common link in the Andover area of Wiltshire. However reminiscences from Blackman's own solicitors suggest that the two men had dealt with each other in the First World War when Owen Aisher was a contracts officer; one of his suppliers was the coal merchant Arthur Blackman.

Whatever its origins, the Aisher/Blackman partnership was formed in the early 1920s and we can now return to Owen Aisher building on his newly acquired Harrietsham land. The early signs were encouraging; he started by building a bungalow for his own occupation, sold it before it was completed and then repeated the exercise. After the first three bungalows had been sold for around £1,000 each, Owen Aisher bought another five acres of land and began to build more substantial properties selling for £1,850 each – a very high price then. Sir Owen remembers their distinctive character: 'Most of them had a veranda, he conceived the idea of advertising in the colonial papers, and people would write from all parts of the world for particulars because many of them had been stuck in the Colonies all through the War and were now coming home in retirement. Of the houses that Dad built at Harrietsham I would think more than half of them were sold to people who came home retiring from the Colonial Service.' They sold well, to be followed by more land and more houses; one year produced profits of £10,000, but suddenly Owen Aisher ran into sales problems. Although the mid-1920s was a period of steady demand for private housing, 1923 proved a hard exception for Owen Aisher who found himself with a poor market and half a dozen unsold bungalows. What now looks a relatively minor cash flow problem had far reaching significance: when the concrete roofing tile business came to be capitalised, the Aisher family had to rely more extensively on Arthur Blackman for funds than they would have liked; it was to take a full decade before effective financial control returned to the Aishers.

The Marley name

After the First World War, it was still common for housebuilders to make many of their own materials, often on site. Owen Aisher had made all the joinery for his own houses 'with a shed, an engine and a little bit of machinery'. Sir Owen remembers the foreman saying 'we must go out and sell it' and under the name of 'O Aisher, Builder and Contractor' the firm began selling windows and doors into the local market. From this stemmed the adoption of the Marley name. Sir Owen remembers:

> we discovered that builders, or architects didn't like buying things from a builder to sell to another builder. So we asked a man from Maidstone, who worked for Kenrick & Jefferson, from whom we bought our notepaper, to come out. Walking up and down the Pilgrims Way, he said "Well, what do you want to call it?" I said I didn't think I knew, what could he suggest? He asked the name of the road and I told him Pilgrims Way. He said "that isn't very good", then he asked the name of the other road and I told him Dickley Lane but he said "that's no good"; then he asked the name of the farm and I told him it's Marley Farm and Marley Court. He said "that's a good name", so we became The Marley Joinery Works.

As coincidence would have it, Arthur Blackman's charcoal burning operation was situated down a Marley Lane in Battle, Sussex which has not surprisingly given rise to an alternative derivation of the Marley name.[4]

---

4   Blackman, Pavie & Ladden *still operate on the same site.*

Early Winget machine

At some point during 1923/24, Owen Aisher had problems obtaining sufficient roofing tiles for his houses. When he began to build more expensive houses, he wanted to replace the cheaper asbestos slate with the traditional clay roofing tile but the aftermath of the War, combined with the local authority building boom, had left many materials in short supply. Sir Owen remembers: 'as Dad couldn't get tiles locally from either Hollingbourne where there was a small works or Westwell where there was another small works, he heard that a firm called Burtenshaw & Green at Hailsham had some tiles. When he got there to see them they were concrete, probably some of the first that were ever made on the Winget machine, and he bought them and put them on the house.'

That brief incursion into substitute materials might have been the end of it had it not been for a chance meeting at the next Building Exhibition. Again, Sir Owen: 'Dad actually saw a chap on the Winget stand who knew him in the South African War. They had a chat and the fellow said we have got this tile machine, and Dad thought that was good, it's £27.10s and he bought it. When I went down on my holiday (in 1924) they were just starting to make tiles. I helped to make the very first tiles we ever made at the garage and then they moved it into the shed.' The mixing – indeed everything – was done by hand and the Aishers employed two men. The output was more than their own modest housebuilding would absorb and the first sales to outside customers became a possibility.

Enter "young Owen"

Sir Owen himself now enters more directly into the story. Known for many years as 'young Owen', we use the convenience of his current title to distinguish Owen Arthur Aisher not only from his father but also from his eldest son Owen Arthur Allingham Aisher. Sir Owen was born on the 28th of May 1900, the eldest of six children; his younger brothers Richard and Jack were later to become actively involved in Marley. Young Owen was brought up on the army camp at Bulford. Although his father worked as a civilian, his son was able to benefit from an education at the army school; there he formed a lifelong friendship with Charles Dobson, later to become the Director in charge of roofing at Hall & Co., merchants, and author of a number of books on roof tiling. Sundays fell into a routine not untypical of the time. 'I was never confirmed but you went to church in the morning, went to Sunday school in the afternoon and went to church in the evening and sang in the choir – that was it.' Sir Owen's father appeared more of an influence: 'Dad could write extraordinarily well and he read well, and he taught me to read.' Sir Owen remembers his father's early aphorisms: 'to read much is to learn much', 'to learn much is to know much' and 'knowledge is power'. The message clearly had an impact for one of the things on which everybody agreed was that Sir Owen himself was an extraordinarily widely read man and it was the breadth of his reading, as well as his travelling and, of course, his limitless energy that lay behind Marley's unremitting adoption of new ideas.

After the First World War, in which he had served towards the end as a motor cycle dispatch rider, Sir Owen had joined the Metropolitan Police as a constable on the beat. 'In addition you could go to night school at Burlington House, in order to take the Civil Service examination so that you could become a Sergeant, etc.' In 1920 he was called up to Scotland Yard, serving in the motorised section as one of the first motor cycle policemen. In April 1921, he married Annie Allingham and they lived off the Caledonian Road, within walking distance of Kings Cross police station. Soon after, with their first child, Clare, on the way, they were able to move into a new police flat in Ironmonger Row, just off Old Street. The 30 shilling bicycle which Sir Owen bought to get to the police station also enabled him to cycle down to Harrietsham on his days off, both helping and observing his father develop the embryonic Marley business. Owen was already beginning to have doubts about his long term future in the police. It was going to take a long time before he could become a Sergeant or Inspector and 'the best you could hope for was one day to become a Superintendent, but one had to work 30 years for a full pension'.

Eventually, the inevitable happened: 'the idea was in my mind that I should leave the police and come and help Dad, the business was thought to be big enough. So one day I went to the Superintendent and said I wanted to leave and he said "What are you going to do?" I told him and he said "What do you know about business?" I said "Very little Sir but I am going to learn". I said I would like to go at once rather than give a month's notice and he said "Why?" and I said "They want me to go to York to an Exhibition and demonstrate making concrete roofing tiles" '.[5] The next day, Sir Owen was in York in civilian clothes 'demonstrating the making of concrete roofing tiles as if I was the only chap in England who knew how to do it'. However, there was to be a rude shock, when Sir Owen returned from York, he discovered that the houses had not been selling and the business was losing money. The concrete tile market was there to be developed but not the capital to finance the operation.

From Germany to Harrietsham: the early history of the concrete roof tile

Marley Tile and the Aisher family can be properly credited with pioneering the commercial development of concrete roof tiling in Britain, but it was the development of a product whose antecedents stretched back into the 1890s in this country, and some fifty years before that in Germany. For a full description of the German period the reader should refer to *The History of the Concrete Roofing Tile – Its Origin and Development in Germany*[6] by Charles Dobson and sponsored by Marley; a brief summary is given in Appendix A. The concrete roof tile had its origins in Southern Bavaria in the 1840s where its diamond shape replicated the traditional shape of the local slates. Despite the wide availability of the technology, the concrete roof tile was never widely adopted in Germany and it is ironic that it was a British firm, Redland, which resurrected the concrete roof tile in Germany after the Second World War to the point where it substantially replaced clay and asbestos-cement.

During the 1890s the technology of the German diamond-pattern concrete tiles began to find its way into England. Charles Dobson identified tiles on roofs at Caterham and Minehead, made on German machines introduced into England about 1895. In the thirty or so years before the Aisher family appeared on the scene, the industry saw a variety of small local producers, most of whom have left little trace and none of more than minor local significance. Names remembered from before the First World War include Cousins of Canterbury, Pepper of Amberley, and Sharp Jones of Poole, all of

---

5 *The Yorkshire Agricultural Show was held at Knavesmere, July 23rd to 25th 1924.*
6 *Charles Dobson,* The History of the Concrete Roofing Tile – Its Origin and Development in Germany, *London, 1959.*

whom made the diamond-pattern tile. Immediately after the War, a concern called The Concrete Tile Syndicate promoted a number of separate concrete tile companies, e.g. Leighton Buzzard Tile, Everlasting Tile and the Redhill Tile Company. Although doing little more than hanging on to its existence in that inter-war period, Redhill developed into Marley's strongest, even bitterest, competitor; renamed Redland after the Second World War, it developed into the only other national producer, eventually rivalling Marley in size.

Thus, by the time Owen Aisher started making roof tiles, as no more than incidental to his main business, the concrete product had been available in England for thirty years: tried, tested but unloved and little used. How the Aisher family developed their back garden business to be the largest roofing tile manufacturer and the largest roofing contractor in the country within a decade, and promoted the concrete roofing tile to the point where it accounted for 90% of pitched roofing in Britain by 1965, is one of the more remarkable achievements in the twentieth century history of the building materials industry. There is a tendency to accept the development of the concrete roofing tile as an inevitable progression of modern technology, but we have to remember that it did not happen in Germany, the home of the concrete roof tile, and it was only the strength of the British industry that provided the base for Redland successfully to reintroduce the concrete tile back into Germany in 1954. Indeed, Marley and Redland between them have led the promotion of the concrete tile across Europe, Australasia, South Africa and more recently the USA.

The way is open for concrete

The reasons for Marley's success will become apparent in later chapters: the sheer drive of the Aisher family, particularly young Owen, a low-cost production base and a revolution in marketing (the supply and fix concept) feature large. But the time and the structure of the existing roofing industry provided the ideal background. Before the First World War, high transport costs, the lack of manufacturing economies of scale and the fragmented nature of the housebuilding industry would have precluded the establishment of a national tile business. This had its parallels in clay tiles, bricks and joinery, for example, although the development of larger scale process units had facilitated the emergence of national firms in the cement and flat glass industries.

The First World War had left the traditional building materials industry poorly placed to meet the demands of the inter-war housebuilding boom. Nowhere was this more evident than in roofing where the slate industry had problems peculiar to its own geography and cost structure. Before the First War, slate was the dominant medium for pitched roofing, some 90% of the indigenous production controlled by The North Wales Slate Quarries

Association: 'one has to reconcile oneself to the inevitability of Welsh slate'.[7] Precise market shares are hard to discern but it appears that slate had around 60% of the market.[8] The collapse in the housing market in the first decade of the century (from an average of around 150,000 a year, completions fell to only 53,000 in 1912); a decline in the export trade exacerbated by the imposition of tariffs; and increased competition from imports, all combined to create a severe depression in the North Wales slate industry. 'The depression in the slate industry resulted in "hundreds" emigrating in 1906 from Blaenau Ffestiniog to the USA, where they hoped to find employment in the American slate quarries. In addition, about 200 quarrymen from the Ffestiniog district went to South Wales; and others had gone to Australia and Patagonia. In September 1908 "painful scenes" were enacted in the Ffestiniog district "owing to the departure of batches of slate quarrymen to the coalfields in South Africa." Work was so scarce that hundreds had left the area.'[9] That then was the state of the country's principal roofing material industry when war arrived; apart from the natural call of the armed services, many of the miners went to the coalfields, never to return.

When the war ended, and building activity began to gather momentum in the mid-1920s, the slate industry found it difficult to respond and, despite the housing boom, output never regained the levels achieved even in the years immediately preceding the war. The quarries were in poor financial state, transport costs were high and the quarrying nature of the business made it difficult to bring down manufacturing costs. 'It is generally contended that owing to the loss of skilled men... the output per hour has decreased compared with before the War'.[10]

It should have been a heaven-sent opportunity for the clay roof tile industry. Yet the clay tile manufacturers themselves seemed to have been harder hit by the war than most. According to the *Committee on the High Cost of Working Class Dwellings*,[11] the output of cement in 1918 was little more than half the average output before the war; bricks only one third and clay tiles less than 10%. By the time of writing in 1921, the Committee estimated that both the brick and cement industries were producing in excess of their pre-war levels but clay tiles were still more than 10% below. 'This branch of the building materials trade has, perhaps, been more seriously affected by the war than any

---

7   Martin S Briggs, A Short History of the Building Crafts, *Oxford, 1925.*

8   *The 1912 Census of Production gives production of both roofing slates and clay roofing tiles though by tonnage for the former and number for the latter.*

9   Slate Trade Gazette, quoted in Jean Lindsay, A History of the North Wales Slate Industry, *Newton Abbot, 1974.*

10   Profiteering Acts 1919–1920, *Central Committee Report on Slates, Cmd 1338, 1921.*

11   *Cmd 1447, 1921.*

The original Marley building at Harrietsham

other branch, and it has been stated that during the war, 90 per cent of tile manufacturers in the country closed down their works entirely'.[12]

It is difficult to see why, given the disarray of the slate trade, the clay industry should have been so slow to respond, but it may have reflected the profusion of very small producers unwilling to regard themselves as anything more than local enterprises. Perhaps if Sir Owen had lived in the Potteries, we would now be housed under clay roofs. The *1924 Census of Production*, conveniently timed to coincide with the start of the Marley story, showed the continued decline of slate at only three-quarters of its pre-war production levels and clay had risen to 60% of the combined clay/slate market. Although clay tile production did steadily rise through the inter-war period, the industry was unable to replace the slate trade and cope with the housing boom at the same time. The way was open for a substitute material.

Harrietsham: the Aishers are in business

We left young Owen in July 1924, returning from the Building Exhibition in York to discover that the housebuilding business he had joined was losing money. 'Dad had lost thousands of pounds; houses were not selling as they had been. We then had to do something quite different.' One of the first things that

---

12   Final Report on the Stone, Brick and Clayware Trades, *Cmd 1209, 1921*.

Owen did do was to try to increase the sales of his father's joinery. 'I started off with the Builders Manager, if you could call him that, on a motorbike and sidecar, to sell joinery. Not very successfully but at least it kept them going, and the next step was that I had to go out by train and bus to sell windows and stairs in the South London area.' That seemed no more profitable but it gave Owen some early, and invaluable, exposure to selling into the building industry.

At the same time as the Aishers were selling their joinery, they were aware that they were also selling modest amounts of their new concrete tile in the local market. The response had been encouraging and the decision was made to take the tile business, probably still the smallest of their three operations, and expand it. For that, capital was required; the losses that had been made on housing had not helped. Once again Owen Aisher turned to Arthur Blackman. 'How we were able to persuade Mr Blackman that making roof tiles might be a good thing I don't really know but the fact was that he agreed.' There was to be a cost, however. In return for providing the additional finance, Blackman's share of the tile business rose to two-thirds; it was to increase still further as the business expanded and proved a growing source of friction between the two families.

The capital outlay amounted to no more than £15,000. Sir Owen: 'I went and bought a small engine, the wrong sort, and a mixer, a good one but still not the right sort; and we made our own tile machines.' Instead of the original Winget machine that Owen Aisher had been operating for a year or more, Marley now had six tile machines, and a complement of eight men. One man could make up to 1,200 tiles a day and the output averaged some 20–25,000 tiles a week or the equivalent of over a million tiles a year. By 1926 that factory was already too small and a new one was built in the middle of the field though it was still primitive. 'Don't forget there was no water and no electricity. We had to develop our own power by diesel engines. Also get our own water from across the field through a pipe and pump it up into the factory roof into a tank and we could just about get enough during the night time to last all the next day.'

The early tiles were hand made and although production methods were continually being improved, it was 1930 before the first mechanised tile line was developed. Bill Borgia, who joined Marley in 1928, remembered the early Winget machine. 'The tile maker had a big bench. There was a hole to drop his tile pallet in [each tile was formed on a metal pallet]; there was a foot lever underneath to lift the pallet up. On his bench he had a load of pug, in other words sand-cement mix, and he would just get a scoopful of it in his trowel, drop it in, trowel it well in, get it as hard as he could, drop some sand facing on it to give it the colour, press his pedal, up came the tiles on his pallet [there were two tiles per pallet] and he'd stick these into a portable rack. When the rack was full, it was pushed into a drying tunnel. The next morning, the trolleys

Early staff photograph

were pushed out to the other side of the main shed and there were a lot of young boys who took the tiles off the pallets and stacked them in little holders.'

The need for supply and fix

The decision to gear up production to what, in terms of the local Kent market, were substantial volumes can only be described as an act of faith. The weekly output was the equivalent of about four standard small houses. 'Very quickly we discovered we had to sell them'; how the family went out to sell them is an object lesson in determination and enthusiasm but from those early experiences stemmed the marketing philosophy which dominated the Marley organisation for half a century. The direct sale of the product to the end user via an in-house contracting organisation, or "supply and fix" as it became popularly known, without recourse to the independent merchant, was undoubtedly Marley's pre-war strength. Without supply and fix, it is unlikely that the little known, and even less loved, concrete roofing tile would ever have been established as a serious product. We will argue in later chapters that the overriding success achieved through supply and fix led later to rigidities within the organisation; failure to react to changes in the structure of the roofing tile market in the 1970s and a reluctance to consider alternative approaches in overseas markets. However, at this point in the story, the Aishers were about to launch a marketing revolution – whether they knew it or not.

Sir Owen Aisher, salesman

Sir Owen describes the early selling efforts: 'I remember taking two tiles on the back of my old police bicycle, wrapped in brown paper, into Ashford to find somebody who needed tiles. Anyway, the builder said he didn't know who was going to put the tiles on (everybody was short of labour) and I said we would send somebody to put them on if necessary providing you pay. And as we had some spare labour who had been putting these tiles on our own houses, off they went on a motorbike, one on the back, and laid these tiles and that was the beginning of supply and fixing. At the same time the Aishers were also trying the traditional builders merchants: 'they said they didn't think much of the tiles but if anybody wanted them they might try and sell them and anyhow, what was the price? When we told them 75 shillings a thousand they said 'Oh no – that's no good, you will never sell them at that price'. Obviously, they were treating them as something that had to be pretty cheap, so we wrote them off and had to get on and do it ourselves.' Throughout his career, Sir Owen maintained that the merchant was no more than a provider of goods which already had an existing market: if you wanted to sell a new product, you had to go out and sell it yourself, preferably without troubling the merchant. 'The merchants wanted to treat us as they treated the rest of the building materials industry, by bargaining. Because we were local, we could only do local business and we did it personally with builders who didn't need merchants because they had been used to buying from the local clay works. Because we had labour from building houses, we could offer the fixing service.'

Using their own labour may have been forced on the Aishers, but they took to it with enthusiasm. There were also other advantages for a "new" product. The early tiles were apt to be a bit "green", i.e. not fully cured, and therefore had to be handled differently from clay tiles; the tilers could not sit on them very easily and therefore had to work away from them on the roof instead of over them, so Marley having its own men proved an advantage. Ernest Smith who, as a 15-year-old, tiled the York exhibition pavilion for Marley in 1924, and later became a director of the tilers Hardgraves, remembers those first tiles as 'very soft but waterproof'. To begin with, Marley used the men from its building business to do the tiling but this soon proved insufficient. 'When there weren't enough we got some more men locally, put them on motorbikes, until in the end Chapman, the man with the steam wagons from Ashford, was delivering the tiles and our men were following it up and laying them for the customers.' Before long, Sir Owen had to look further afield for his labour force, an experience which clearly left memories: 'our own men were busy so we got what you might call a proper tiler from London, called Bert Hills, who was rather a drunken sort of chap but in fact many of these tilers were a bit like that. He got extra labour from somewhere, went across the other side of London from where he lived and did the job.'

Gradually Marley pushed out into the surrounding areas, including Canterbury and Maidstone. Very quickly, Marley received its first large order

Marley tiles being fixed

– for 57 local authority houses at Tolworth. 'The architect needed tiles which he couldn't get and he wanted them to be plain and English looking and he came and had a look at ours and he thought they looked pretty good. He didn't know as much as we knew and we didn't know as much as we thought but anyway they were full body coloured and we got the job and we put them on.'

Marley tiles — the right colour and the right profile

Colouring and design marked out the Marley tile from most of the other concrete roof tile manufacturers of the time. While still in the police force, Sir Owen had discovered a German called Baumgarten, trading under the name of Wilde, in a basement in Victoria, importing machinery. 'I went to see him and discovered you could put a bit of sand on the surface; I asked why he did that and he said, well, some people like it. It really wasn't what we call sandfaced but it was the beginning of it. When we started to make these tiles, I was there and probably made some of the first, and mixed sand and colour together and put it on the surface — and how marvellous it looked. Of course, we didn't realise the sand would come off and wouldn't be so good after a while but we did make the tiles full body colour.' The competitors tended to make plain concrete tiles, trowelling the surface without any sandface: 'I think we can honestly say, if not the first, we were really the true pioneers of making what we called a handmade sandfaced Kentish tile.' Looking back, Redhill (Redland) directors admitted to their own early problems with tile colouring: 'We had a great deal of trouble colouring our tiles. We could put cement and sand together and could make a tile which was weatherproof. But that was all. When we tried to colour the tile we found the colour lasted a few months and came off.'[13]

The clay tile was naturally self-coloured, arising from the iron oxide which occurs naturally in the clay, but the natural colour of the concrete tile was grey. Incorporating colour throughout the concrete tile may have been effective at the beginning but it was not a long term economic solution. Sir Owen sought an effective means of applying the colour to the surface only of the tile and his success at so doing was an important contribution to gaining the acceptance of the concrete tile within the building trade. Early methods of surface colouring consisted in applying a slurry of cement, pigment and water. It was durable but suffered from a number of defects including a fading of the colour and efflorescence. Every variation was tried — dry mix, more cement, less cement, more colour, but to no avail. Sir Owen's breakthrough was based on his observation of the durability of the reddish stains which form on stone beneath unprotected ironwork; this is due to the precipitation of iron compounds in the pores of the stone. Sir Owen found that this effect could be reproduced by dipping the tiles into a solution of sulphate of iron.[14]

---

13 *Unpublished reminiscences of A F F Young, Chairman of Redland, 1970.*
14 *When a concrete tile is dipped into a dilute solution of sulphate of iron there is a slight change of colour caused by insoluble iron compound precipitating on the surface. On exposure to the air the iron compound oxidises to a reddish brown film giving the tile its clay-like colour. The film was also found to be capable of binding pigment on to the surface of the concrete and, as a by-product, the chemical process also dissolved any bloom which had formed during the curing of the concrete, thereby eliminating efflorescence. These discoveries led to the development of the dipping process for finishing tiles. In short, the tile is formed and coated with a slurry colour*

The dipping process became standard practice for a number of years but the pigment bonding was still not perfect and colour loss could still occur over time. The final improvement in colouring to take place before the Second World War was the use of coloured facing sand. When raised to high temperatures, most sands become reddish in colour, due to the formation of oxide of iron from the sand impurities. By selecting sands with a high iron content a strong brownish red could be produced. After the War, these sands were replaced by mineral granules.

The other attraction of the Marley tile was simply that it was made the same size as the traditional plain clay tile (10½ by 6½): the early concrete tiles had been diamond shaped, which looked odd on traditional English houses. Redhill, potentially the most serious local competitor at that time, made interlocking tiles which again looked different from the traditional clay tile; Marley did not make an interlocking tile until 1935 (the Ludlow) by which time the concrete market was sufficiently well established to support a diversity of product range.

Incorporation and expansion

By the end of 1925, the cowshed which had housed the first tile machines had outlived its usefulness. Joinery, which was by then only of minor interest, was stopped and the joinery works was dismantled, put down the other end of the field and made into a much bigger tile factory. Within a year this too was unable to cope on its own and an additional tile works was built in the middle of a field at Harrietsham (now within the extrusions factory). In 1925, the Aishers made 747,000 tiles; Marley Tile was on its way – and with a whole family behind it.

Sir Owen was, by eight years, the eldest of six children; following him were two brothers, Richard Harry (born 1908) and Jack Edward (1910) and then three sisters, Ena, May and Jane. With the exception of Jane, all the children worked in the business, Richard and Jack playing significant roles in the history of Marley. Richard, or Dick as he was generally known, ran the sales side of the group until his untimely death in December 1960. Jack became responsible for production in the late 1930s, after the war switching to administration and finance; he succeeded Sir Owen as Chairman of Marley in October 1982.

cont.
coat; facing sand is dropped on to the tile; and the tile is cured. On removal from the pallet the tile is dipped in a solution of sulphate of iron containing red pigment in suspension and after a couple of hours the colour of the tile is developed.

1920s production line

When Dick joined towards the end of 1924, at the age of 16, it was actually into the joinery business where one of his first jobs was to make the wooden trolleys used to take the tiles into the curing tunnels. Jack Aisher can remember the exact day he started work – Monday 5th April 1926, just short of his 16th birthday. 'I was just an office boy to start with. I was brought in because we needed somebody else to do office work. My sister Ena was in there as a part-time operator. I had to do all sorts of jobs; I had to go over to, well it can't be called the works because it was the old cowshed, and do whatever I was told. Go up and see that the men were there first thing in the morning; that was half past six. Then come back and Owen would make out a job sheet and I had to put it in the job book – those sort of things.' Jack remembers that by the time he started at Marley, Dick had just about graduated from the works. 'Owen was chasing around on his motorbike trying to sell tiles and then Dick was put out on to the road. There was no motor car

Jack Aisher   *Dick Aisher*

for brother Dick – he went by bus. Owen did the London area and Dick was given the country area, so he had to go to places like Ashford, Ramsgate, Faversham, places like that. He was a salesman and remained doing that all the time.'

The business was now ready to move into a more formal stage. The old partnership (for which there is no surviving documentation) was incorporated as Marley Tile Limited on 20th July 1926. The Board consisted of Arthur Blackman as Chairman, Owen Aisher and Lancelot Blackman, Arthur Blackman's only son. The consideration for the Company's purchase of the tile business was £4,500 and the £1 shares were allotted one third to Owen Aisher and two thirds to Arthur Blackman and his two children:

Owen Aisher	1,500
Arthur Blackman	900
Lancelot A Blackman	900
Isobel A Blackman	1,200
	4,500

It was now evident that substantial sums had been advanced by Arthur Blackman. On incorporation, part of his loan account had been converted into £12,800 of a 5% Mortgage Debenture, all of which remained in his name, while the first balance sheet in January 1927 showed a further loan account amounting to £7,807; of this £2,763 related to unpaid accumulated interest suggesting that the partnership had yet to bring him any return. It appears to be at this point that the Blackman interest increased from the original 50% to two-thirds, in consideration of his taking up the debentures.

On the formation of the Harrietsham company, Sir Owen entered into a ten year service agreement; this provided that the Company would procure the transfer to him of a maximum of 10% of the shares over that ten year period. It was understood that these shares would come from Owen Aisher senior and Arthur Blackman, pro rata to their existing holdings. These shares were never formally transferred but the entitlement became relevant at the time of the flotation.

The accounts for 1926 (actually the year to January 1927) conveniently show the trading results for the two halves. The modest first half profit was insufficient to cover directors' salaries and interest payments, producing a net loss of £421. Higher sales in the second half put the company in the black for the first time and the year finished with a token loss of £118 on sales of just under £20,000. From then on Harrietsham expanded at breakneck speed.

Calendar	Tile output (000)	Sales (£000)
1925	747	
1926	2,115	19.8
1927	3,332	36.0
1928	4,232	45.3
1929	6,411	54.9
1930	10,467	64.5
1931	15,627	108.7

Source: Letter to Snell & Swaffield (stockbrokers) 30th May 1933

Profit figures have not survived for individual factories in the period above but we do know that Harrietsham made pre-tax profits of almost £5,000 in calendar 1930 and two or three years later was probably averaging between £10–15,000. What is clear is that no sooner were the first profits beginning to emerge than plans were made to build two completely new factories. By that time the tiles were being delivered by steam wagon and 35 miles was about as far as they could go from Harrietsham – out and back in a day. Hence, factories to the north of London at Leighton Buzzard and to the west at Storrington in Sussex.

Leighton Buzzard

Not surprisingly, capital was again the major constraint and the ownership of the two new factories, especially Storrington, moved even further away from the Aisher family. The Leighton Buzzard factory brought in an ex-steel man called Charles Edward Daniel. His father had been a steel founder in Leeds and prior to the First World War had started up the Medway Steel Works, running it with his two sons. Medway Steel traded with Marley in its early days, supplying steel pallets for the Harrietsham works. Between 1924 and 1926, UK steel production halved, Medway Steel went into liquidation, and 48-year-old Charles Daniel, among others, was looking for employment. By that time he had become friendly with Owen Aisher and the proposition duly emerged: if Daniel could raise the money, he could run the proposed new factory at Leighton Buzzard.

The initial capital for Leighton Buzzard was £7,800; 1,300 shares were issued at £2 each and the balance of £5,200 was financed through debentures. Daniel's daughter can remember him going round his friends to raise the money: 'in the evening he'd come back and say, well I've got £50 from so and so and £100 from someone else; a great boost was £1,000 from Owen Browne, who was the Mayor of Rochester and the other one who put £1,000 in was Mrs Hammond who was the wife of the Vicar of St Mary's Stroud, later Dean of Lichfield.'

Marley Tile Company (Leighton Buzzard) was incorporated on January 18th 1927 and on April 15th Marley Tile Company signed an agreement with (Leighton Buzzard) for the sale of tile making plant to produce a total weekly output of the Marley tile at a rate of 40,000 tiles of 11 by 7 inches, the right to advertise and sell as 'The Marley Tile', and the secret process and formula and all patent rights and instruction to employees. The tiles could only be sold within a 40-mile radius of the factory. Everything was at arm's length. The consideration paid to Marley Tile, i.e. Harrietsham, was £3,000 in cash and 650 £1 shares in Leighton Buzzard; that gave Harrietsham 50% of the original Leighton Buzzard share capital. Although the minutes contain references to changes in the share capital, complete lists of shareholders do not survive. By the time the three companies were amalgamated in 1934, Harrietsham owned 2,450 (63%) of the 3,900 shares; other shareholders included the Daniel family with almost 16%, Arthur Blackman, Walter Hoar (the Company Secretary), Owen Browne, Ethel Hammond and a number of other individuals.

The initial layout was done by Sir Owen: 'I worked it out on a piece of paper which I think I've still got, and with £6,000 we went to Leighton Buzzard, bought seven acres of land, built the factory, put in some machines, put in a diesel engine and a mixer and started making tiles.' Output began at 40,000 tiles a week but before the year was out, capacity was raised to 100,000 a week or 5 million tiles a year.

Storrington

Storrington was developed almost simultaneously with Leighton Buzzard but the financial arrangements proved much more contentious; ultimately the precedent set by Storrington was to lead to the split between Arthur Blackman and the Aisher family. Marley Tile (Storrington) was incorporated on June 2nd 1927 with a capital of 10,000 ordinary £1 shares. Harrietsham owned none of these, merely receiving a royalty (15% of profits); the only Aisher equity was 100 shares held by "young Owen". The rest of the shares were held by Arthur Blackman and his friends. Thus, Arthur and Lancelot Blackman held 6,280; Sydney Menneer, Blackman's solicitor, 1,540; the Pritchard family 1,540; and Arthur Collard 540.

The directorships were not the same in the three companies. The directors at Leighton Buzzard were Arthur Blackman and Charles Daniel. Although Sir Owen attended the occasional board meeting there was no formal Aisher representation until December 1929 when Owen Aisher Senior was voted on. In contrast, Storrington, which was almost completely controlled by Arthur Blackman and his friends, had Owen A Aisher (Junior) accompanying Blackman as its first directors. This arrangement continued until 1932 when strains between the two men led to Sir Owen resigning and E J Dicker, first a salesman and later manager of the company, replacing him. These two continued as the sole directors until the amalgamation.

Despite the differing shareholding interests, particularly for Storrington which was little more than a licencee of Harrietsham, there seems to have been a genuine attempt to run the three factories as a cohesive group. Arthur Blackman made an interesting reference to this in his speech at the AGM of Leighton Buzzard at the National Liberal Club in December 1930. He first outlined the rapid progress made by the Company: 'The works were originally put up to produce 50,000 tiles per week and now the output was 5 times as much. He also looked to the future and was hoping to be turning out half a million tiles per week before the Summer of 1931.'

After some new product information 'Mr Blackman also pointed out how the three works helped each other out with deliveries and all worked happily together. With regard to the radius of deliveries from Leighton Buzzard works, this was fixed at about 40 miles but this has been far exceeded and it might at some future date be altered. At the moment, we were delivering in the west to Gloucester which is 85 miles, in the east to Cambridge which is 60 miles, in the north to Warwick, Stratford-on-Avon which is also 60 miles.' Someone has obviously had a closer look at that statement for the minute book has been altered: the 40-mile radius loses its 'about' and becomes 'according to the agreement' while 'might at some future date be altered' is hardened to 'it is clearly understood that the excess area is gratuitous and may be withdrawn at any time'. Co-operation was all to the good but it was not without its sensibilities!

Marley's Storrington factory

The Board minutes a few months later restate the same principles but also show that there was give as well as take; referring to Isleworth, which was within Leighton Buzzard's 40-mile radius 'this should, for the time being, be handed over to Storrington owing to their shortage of orders'. It could be rectified at any time when demanded by Leighton Buzzard. Later on, in 1934, we find a number of references in the Storrington minutes to discussions with both Harrietsham and Leighton Buzzard on boundary problems.

There is also some evidence of willingness to spread the manufacturing load. The December 1931 minutes of Harrietsham record that 'It was arranged that in view of the extraordinary stocks of tiles at Leighton Buzzard, Harrietsham and Storrington should push the sales a little more than normally even at a lower figure. The tiles required would be supplied by Leighton Buzzard at 50/- per thousand.'

The Blackman involvement

While Arthur Blackman was not involved in the day-to-day running of the business he was very closely involved in managerial control and in making a wide range of operational decisions. For instance, the Leighton Buzzard minutes of 28th March 1928 record Mr Blackman obtaining a reduction of 6s per ton in the price of cement and that he personally would be seeing the Cement Marketing Company before the end of the month. He clearly kept close contact with the cement industry for the Harrietsham Company Secretary was obliged to remind the Board (in August 1933) that 'he had no contract notes in his possession in respect of the new cement contract recently fixed by Mr Blackman. Mr Blackman said they were in his possession and would send them on'.

It was not just the major issues. We have him at Leighton Buzzard in 1929 asking for the price of a salesman's car to be submitted to him so that he 'would endeavour to better it'. Or in May 1929 when it was decided to erect additional tunnels: 'Mr Blackman would order the necessary trolleys and pallets'. Weekly reports would be sent by the Company Secretaries to Blackman at his home address. These showed the weekly order intake, manufacture and deliveries. They were regularly accompanied by detailed letters while Blackman was also capable of conducting his criticisms by post. Examples from Storrington in June and July 1929 are reproduced in Appendix B to give a flavour of the correspondence.

The outside shareholders in Leighton Buzzard could also make their voices heard. At the 1930 AGM to which we have already referred, the 'floor' expressed its concern that Mr Daniel was receiving his just desserts. 'Mr Winch asked what salary Mr Daniel was paid, for he considered that the persons who had done the hard work should be paid accordingly... The Chairman replied that it was out of order to discuss salaries at this meeting but he was quite prepared for the matter to be proceeded with if it was the wish of the meeting.'

'Mr Browne said he put his money into the concern to help Mr Daniel, he would like to know what Mr Daniel was getting out of it'. At that point Mr Blackman and Mr Daniel left the meeting 'and afterwards Mr Daniel told the meeting that he was quite satisfied with Mr Blackman's proposals'.

The ladies then took over, clearly less satisfied than the Chairman. 'Mrs Hammond said she would like some satisfaction that Mr Daniel would get all that he was entitled to; the Chairman assured her this would be so.' Finally, Mr Daniel's wife stood up to ask 'whether the money that she had put into the concern would be taken into consideration when Mr Daniel's remuneration was gone into, the Chairman assured her it would not, pointing out that whatever money Mrs Daniel had put in was quite apart from Mr Daniel's affairs' – sentiments truly worthy of the venue.

The re-financing of Marley

The late 1920s and early 1930s saw the arrival of Marley, its concrete roofing tiles and its roofing contracting, as a significant force in the building industry.

The reasons have already been touched on in the text so far; no single reason in itself provides a sufficient explanation. There was opportunity: the shortage in supply of the traditional roofing product, particularly from the slate industry with its structural weakness dating back to before the First World War, created the space for a substitute product. There was luck: the chain of circumstances which led Owen Aisher senior to buy his own hand tile machine only for his son to find that he needed to sell the product to other builders to survive. Even the good fortune to be based in the South East which clearly lacked an indigenous slate industry and had little in the way of large clay manufacturers, thereby giving Marley a natural advantage in transport costs. But above all, as in so many pioneering ventures, you have to point to the man, Sir Owen Aisher: his seemingly limitless energy; determination to let nothing or nobody deflect him; and above all, his vision. More than anything else, the success of Marley was based on Sir Owen's realisation that, although the merchant might not want to buy his concrete tiles, nor even the builder, if you could offer the builder a completed roof at an all-in cost, then the tile sales would follow automatically.

During this period, tile output increased dramatically for not only had the new factories been opened, but the individual units were themselves being continually expanded and modernised. Output figures for the three factories on a consistent basis prior to the flotation of Marley have survived from the Prospectus correspondence and are shown in the table below:

Marley tile output (millions)

Year	1925	1926	1927	1928	1929	1930	1931	1932	1933
Harrietsham	0.7	2.1	3.3	4.2	6.4	10.5	15.6	21.4	27.8
Leighton Buzzard			1.4	3.0	6.7	11.3	16.6	17.8	27.6
Storrington			0.5	3.0	3.3	8.5	10.0	12.5	17.8
Erith									4.9*
Total	0.7	2.1	5.2	10.2	16.4	30.3	45.2	51.7	78.1

Note: Nearest financial period in appropriate calendar year
*3 months

The three Marley factories were, by the standards of the time, also beginning to earn good profits, the flotation prospectus shows:

Combined pre-tax profits (£000)

Year to October	1929	1930	1931	1932	1933	1934
	13.5	18.3	36.8	43.1	64.6	89.0

With the three original factories running flat out, Sir Owen was ready for the next phase of expansion. His 1932 notes on the possibilities in Essex provide a glimpse of the long term planning that went into the Marley business:

> It seems difficult to fix upon a site for many reasons. The sand pits are usually not likely to last long and our object has been to get sand cheaply and at a place that would last at least 21 years; so far only two pits fulfil these requirements – Bowyers at Chadwell Heath, and Corry's at Stanford le Hope. Bowyers is in the heart of things. He wants 5/- per yard and £50 per acre per annum. Corry wants 5/6 but would take less.
>
> If we went further from London, we may get a site more suitable but we should not gain our point, which is to get cheaper haulage.

Eventually Marley settled on Aveley. A letter from Alfred Savill in April 1933 throws light on the terms available:

> … we have now heard from our clients, Thames Land Co. Ltd. and they state that they would be prepared to lease land at Aveley… for the use as a ballast pit and factory for making cement tiles on the following terms:-

1. **Surface Rent**	£2 per acre per annum for the ballast pit. £20 per acre per annum for land used as a factory site.
2. **Royalty**	Sand 1/- per ton for all sand used for the factory or sold. Gravel 3d. per cu.yd. for all gravel. Minimum royalty £300 per annum, corresponding to a minimum quantity of 6000 tons of sand per annum.
3. **Length of Lease**	The Company suggest a lease of 14 years with option of renewal for 7 year periods.

Not surprisingly, there was some negotiation: 'We agree the minimum royalty due to you… but we do not agree the rentals suggested by you. We think it would be fair to have a free period for the establishment of our works, and we suggest six months.'

About the same time, Marley had also identified sites at Riverhead near Sevenoaks (later to become the Group Head Office) and Burton in the Midlands; a rented factory was found at Erith (on the Thames near Dartford) in 1933 which Sir Owen's younger brother, Jack, went down to run. However, Arthur Blackman was not as enthusiastic as the Aishers about further expansion. It cannot have been a matter of principle; the Storrington minutes of 30th September 1933 record Blackman stressing the urgency of getting another sand pit half way to London for a possible new works. However, enthusiasm is relative. By 1931 he was already 63; his only son was seriously ill; and Blackman was unwilling to commit further capital to the business. In turn, Sir Owen was adamant that he would not agree to expanding Marley unless the Aisher family could enjoy half of the additional profits.

Conflict with Blackman

The opposition of interest between the Aisher family and Arthur Blackman clearly reached a head in the early 1930s. Occasionally, formal reference to the growing tensions between the two men creep into the minute books. The Harrietsham minutes of September 29th 1933: 'At the Board meeting a request was made to Owen to meet Mr Wall for the purpose of considering the whole of the Wagon question, with a view to presenting a Report to enable the Board to decide what is our best course, and Owen refused to act on these lines or to meet Wall upon the matter.' Three months later they were even in dispute over personal expenses, the Secretary being instructed by the Chairman 'to pay only those expenses to Owen for which he produced vouchers'. At the next Board meeting Owen Aisher Senior had to mediate between the two – and this in Christmas week.

By the early 1930s, Sir Owen's strong personality meant he was the dominant force in the business. His father, though still occupied with Harrietsham, had little to do with the other factories; indeed, he moved from Harrietsham to Bournemouth shortly before the Second World War. Jack Aisher summed up his elder brother: 'Owen really followed in the mould of my Mother. My Mother was a very positive, very determined character, and Owen inherited his determination, bloody-mindedness if you like, from her.' And as for Arthur Blackman, 30 years Sir Owen's senior, successful political figure and businessman, he confided in Fred Hardy many years later 'the only man that ever wore me out was Owen Aisher'. Matters finally came to a head when Sir Owen refused to implement the planned factory expansion programme, within the existing financial structure. There was some element of withdrawal from the Marley business. The Kent and Sussex Brick Company was formed as a separate Aisher family business, though it was never particularly profitable and was sold after the war.

How long the pressure had been developing can only be conjecture but it is unlikely that Sir Owen was ever totally relaxed about the Aisher holding in Harrietsham being only a third, much less the virtually total absence of a holding in Storrington; what had been a financial necessity to start the roof tile business became a source of increasing frustration. 'At Storrington, Blackman wanted to keep the whole of it for himself and his friends and only pay a royalty to Marley at Harrietsham. We could hardly stop him because he had been putting up some of the money but we didn't like it. I got a very small share and £75 a year for looking after it.'

Jack Aisher, though very much the younger brother then, remembers the sense of conflict growing. 'I became conscious of it about 1929/30, more particularly two or three years before we became a public company. It was brought about by Owen's desire to expand, very enthusiastically. Blackman, yes, but with no great enthusiasm and really wanting a bigger slice of the cake because he was going to put money in. Owen's thoughts were, "that's all very fine, but you can't do it without me." It became clear to me, as a young chap of twenty, twenty-one, that Owen by then was a very vigorous young man of thirty. He was running the show. I am quite clear that in spite of what anybody else has done in Marley, my brother Dick, myself, Fred Hardy; Owen created Marley... and without him I have no hesitation in saying it wouldn't have happened.'

Sir Owen actively examined the alternatives open to him; when interviewed by the author he still had the pencilled notes where he sketched out his 'suggested methods' of developing the Marley business:

1) Merger of the three companies, building of further works by means of bank overdraft and raising debentures at the end of the programme. *Points* This would mean perhaps some complications with the present shareholders and necessitate rearrangements of share capital which would not be easy and would of course mean that shareholders in Leighton Buzzard and Storrington would share in proceeds.

2) A holding company which would share the control of the three companies existing. This could be arranged with Storrington and L B shareholders more easily than the above... we should have ample security for the funds necessary to extend and any profits accruing would come to those concerned viz Blackman and us. Difficulty would be Blackman's idea of his share and control also the fact that it does mortgage our properties for at least a year while developing and if we then issue permanent debentures of course permanently. But I think that with say a first issue at the end of the year of debs and then two years, further shares could be issued on the basis of profits. This ties things up for at least three years, puts no money in pocket immediately and leaves us for three years holding the baby which may or may not grow. Much may happen in three years.

3) A series of smaller companies based on the lines of L B and S. This would mean (unless otherwise arranged) that B would get 2–1 which could not be agreed to. Subject to an amicable arrangement with B and the above being possible 15% of profits could come to Harrietsham with a percentage of the profits based on the dividend paid to the directors viz B and us. The above would bring no immediate money but should prove satisfactory. The 15% or as agreed should be secured by shares and interest in the concern because at Storrington at the end of the agreement we have nothing whereas we have the equity at L B which has and is growing. Subject to B's agreeing, I think the above could be arranged.

4) Failing B agreeing, we could let Dick and Jack put up works on their own. This could be arranged and B must be told this if necessary.

Marley for sale

Despite their natural desire to obtain control of what they regarded as 'their company', there seemed then no possibility of the Aisher family buying out Blackman. The impasse between Arthur Blackman and Sir Owen continued until eventually (probably during 1932) it was agreed that the Marley companies should be sold and that Blackman should be charged with finding a buyer. To what extent Blackman's acquiescence was also influenced by his own personal and family needs remains unknown, but the overriding motive behind the agreement was undoubtedly a recognition that the business could not be taken forward under its existing shareholder structure.

In any event, Blackman made his decision and the process of unlocking the controlling shareholder began. It was a process which took over two years to complete and was probably the most convoluted episode in Marley's history. It spawned at least two legal actions; numerous intermediaries; an international tobacco company; a Canadian financier; and vendors who did not always have an identity of interest. Most of those involved are no longer alive and, in any case, the background to the flotation has never been regarded as an appropriate subject for discussion by the Aisher family. Of the documentary evidence, we have the minute books of the Marley companies and of Dean Finance (the issuing house), and the Prospectus and supporting documentation; perhaps of most help in understanding some of the behind the scenes negotiations is the correspondence contained in *The Sir James Dunn Papers* held by the National Archives of Canada (more of Sir James later). Not all the pieces in the jigsaw puzzle are available but the events appear to unfold as follows.

Early in 1933, Blackman sought out one of his friends from the National Liberal Club, a Mr Abrams — 'a man who was apparently used to acting on commission as a sort of general agent by persons interested in financial schemes. It appears that Abrams was instructed by Blackman to find what was virtually a purchaser for the whole of the undertakings of the three Marley Tile Companies, the approximate value of which was then stated by Blackman to be about £400,000.'[15] The first serious response appears to have been from Charterhouse. Strangely, it is the Leighton Buzzard minutes of March 30th 1933 which provides the record: 'Mr Abrams joined in and some discussion took place regarding the possibility of a new Company, and Mr Blackman arranged to see Mr Harvey after lunch with a view of keeping open the negotiations with the Charterhouse people.' The following month there was a meeting at Hastings between Mr Blackman and Mr Aisher senior. A letter was read from Mr Blackman to Captain Nutcombe Hume, the founder and managing director of Charterhouse Investment Trust[16] offering the sale of the

---

15 Sir James Dunn Papers, *volume 377*; E B Ridsdel *v.* Marley Tile, *instructions to Counsel.*

16 *For background see Laurie Dennett,* The Charterhouse Group 1925–1979, *London, 1979.*

Company at £450,000. 'It was agreed that if we cannot get the £450,000 we should hesitate before refusing the figure of £400,000.' These figures were repeated at further meetings between the two men over the succeeding weeks; thus, on May 5th, 'Mr Blackman expects to meet Captain Hume during the week and the decision previously arrived at with regard to price will be adhered to.' After that, no further references can be found in the Marley records and it is not known why the deal fell through.

The next documented Abrams introduction was to Ernest Ridsdel (1881–1939); Ridsdel had his own small issuing house. E B Ridsdel of Salisbury House, London Wall and looked to be a professional company director, City and plantation companies featuring high on the list. Abrams contacted Ridsdel in January 1934 and by February 19th Ridsdel was in a position to write to Owen Aisher Senior to the effect that 'we are prepared to promote a Company to acquire the [Marley] undertakings.'[17] The capital was to be £500,000 of which £275,000 was to be issued to new subscribers for cash and £225,000 (45% of the total) in fully paid-up shares to the existing shareholders; the Aisher family shareholdings would, therefore, have been more than halved as a percentage of the new Company. Meetings took place between the two parties, in particular one on 22nd February as a result of which Ridsdel believed he had an oral acceptance of his offer to buy. When the proposed deal eventually fell through, Abrams sued (unsuccessfully) for his commission; subsequently, Ridsdel too sought damages for breach of an agreement to purchase the Marley undertakings but it was not until after the public flotation that the case was eventually settled out of court with a payment of £1,000 to Ridsdel.

The different interests of Blackman and the Aishers was clearly behind the failure to reach an agreement: 'Whilst... it appears that Mr Blackman was prepared to agree to the terms offered by the Plaintiffs, subject to the agreement of others who were interested, it is clear that Mr Aisher Senior did not agree, and at an interview early in March which Mr Aisher Junior had with Mr Ridsdel, he made it clear that he was an interested party and he would certainly not agree to the terms.'[18]

Enter Jimmy Dunn

By this time, Sir Owen was close to a number of the leading housebuilders, particularly Leo Meyer of Ideal Building, Frank (later Lord) Taylor of Taylor Woodrow, and Godfrey (later Sir) Mitchell of Wimpey. Indeed, in the late 1930s, the four men formed a partnership to build houses in the USA. At the time Blackman was seeking a buyer for Marley, Leo Meyer was preparing the

---

17   Sir James Dunn Papers, *volume 377; correspondence.*
18   *Ibid;* Ridsdel *v.* Marley.

flotation of his Ideal Building Corporation (effected in May 1934) with the involvement of Jimmy Dunn, a Canadian entrepreneur and Dean Finance, a subsidiary of British American Tobacco. Knowing of Sir Owen's unease over the Abrams proposals, Leo Meyer introduced Jimmy Dunn to Sir Owen and the Marley float was on the way. (As a reward for this introduction, Dean Finance authorised the issue of 150,000 options to Leo Meyer to run for a year from the flotation, though it does not look as though the option was exercised.[19]) Dunn and Dean Finance also floated Taylor Woodrow Estates in February 1935.

Jimmy Dunn was a larger than life character, to put it mildly. James Hamet Dunn was born in 1874 in New Brunswick, Canada, the son of a boat builder and a childhood friend of Max Aitken (later Lord Beaverbrook) and Richard Bennett (later Prime Minister of Canada). He became involved in legal work for railway promoters and in 1901 married the daughter of a wealthy timber merchant, buying a seat on the Montreal Stock Exchange the following year. He rapidly became an active promoter of new companies first in Canada and later London, where he founded the merchant banking firm of Dunn, Fischer in 1905. 'All Dunn's underwriting was done on the basis of closely controlled syndicates. The syndicates coordinated their selling of shares, carefully feeding the market so as never to overextend the supply of a company's shares in the market. To entice small, independent buyers to take up these stocks, Dunn made use of "paid puffing" or planted articles in the press.'[20] After the First War Jimmy Dunn promoted a series of electrical and fibre trusts in London (including British Celanese) 'using stock "pyramiding" techniques' and in the early 1930s there were further industrial issues including Ideal Building and Taylor Woodrow. A particular success of Jimmy Dunn, along with Sir Hugo Cunliffe-Owen (Chairman of British American Tobacco) and Lord Trent was in bringing control of Boots back to England from the USA in 1933.

Jimmy Dunn's scheme offered one clear advantage to the Aisher family, and to Owen in particular: it left them firmly in managerial control and with the prospect of an enlarged and, in effect, controlling shareholding. It scarcely needs documentary evidence to surmise that the lack of such opportunity in the various Abrams' proposals lay behind the Aishers' unwillingness to lend them their support. In contrast to the negotiations with the Abrams' clients, the negotiations with Jimmy Dunn where handled by Sir Owen, who had the former's complete confidence:

19 *Dean Finance minutes, 28th January 1935.*
20 *David Jeremy and Christine Shaw (eds),* Dictionary of Business Biography, *Duncan McDowall.*

Sir James Dunn: detail, Salvador Dali (attributed) (1904–89) Sunrise: Sir James Dunn, 1958 oil on canvas 96.8 × 72.1 cm (38 1/8 × 28 3/8 in.) Gift of the Sir James Dunn Foundation. The Beaverbrook Art Gallery, Fredericton, N.B., Canada.

21st February 1934

Dear Mr Aisher,

I am leaving the Marley Tile business in your hands and Mr Macnaghtens [Dean Finance] and I count on you to see that nobody else gets away with it. You can send me all the cables you like on the Olympic and I will be on deck to deal with the business.

Yours sincerely,

(signed) J H Dunn

Owen A Aisher Esq.,
Faygate,
Lenham, Kent.[21]

---

21 Sir James Dunn Papers; *correspondence.*

Although later there were meetings between Blackman and Dunn, it appears that the original proposals from the Dunn/Dean Finance consortium to Arthur Blackman were actually put through a stockbroker, L P Hose of Messrs Snell & Swaffield. The Dunn/Dean Finance initial offer for Marley was actually made as the Ridsdel negotiations were collapsing; in view of the timing and the use of yet another intermediary, it is not clear whether Arthur Blackman knew that the Aisher family were interested parties as purchasers as well as vendors.

As a footnote, Sir Owen had later to write to Snell & Swaffield: 'I understand that you have made an arrangement with Mr A Blackman under which he agreed to pay you a commission of 2½% in the event of you introducing a purchaser of Marley Tile Co. but that Mr Blackman is not endeavouring to repudiate his agreement. If Mr Blackman persists in his refusal to pay you the set commission, I on behalf of myself and my father agree that in consideration of your having introduced the Tobacco Securities Trust Ltd., as a proposed purchaser of the said business, if a sale results, we will pay you a commission as below, namely, £1,000 on the completion of sale and a further £1,500 if and when a public issue is made.' Blackman's reluctance to pay commission may have stemmed from an uncertainty as to who was acting for whom.

During March and April 1934 broad agreement was secured between all the principals on the terms and conditions of the purchase of the Marley companies by Dean Finance; but behind that was a separate understanding between Sir James Dunn and Sir Owen to increase subsequently the Aisher percentage shareholding. This had been first expressed in a letter from Dunn to Sir Owen on 14th February 1934:

Dear Mr Aisher,

re MARLEY TILE BUSINESS

With reference to conversations we have had about the purchase of this business or rather the interest of Mr Blackman in it I confirm my verbal statement to you that if we succeed in buying the whole business or Mr Blackman's interest in it... we will at cost sell you such an amount of that interest as will with the 30% of your father and the 10% of yourself give you a 51% interest. I also confirm that we desire you to have control of the business and we expect you to devote your time to its operation and development... We will of course reserve the right to put one or two Directors on your Board.

Yours sincerely,

(signed) J H Dunn[22]

Although the sense of the letter is that the Aishers were being offered 51% of the totality of the Marley business, the shareholdings quoted clearly relate solely to the Harrietsham Company; Jimmy Dunn's working papers prepared three days later for the purchase of the whole of Marley for a suggested £375,000 were clearly based on the assumption that the Aisher family already had an attributable 40% of the whole group. As we will see later, the Aisher percentage ownership was increased but never to the extent once hoped.

The proposal that emerged was for Dean Finance to provide the cash to buy out Arthur Blackman and any other of the non-Aisher shareholders who would sell and to consolidate the three separate entities into one holding company; that holding company could then be floated on the Stock Exchange. In between the buyout and the float there would then be a rearrangement of shareholdings to give the Aisher family its increased shareholding.

A number of meetings were held during March, again with a threat of legal action to enforce a purported oral agreement to sell, this time by Dean Finance against Blackman. However, by April 1934, Blackman's solicitors finally wrote to The Hon F F Macnaghten, Chairman of Dean Finance, to clarify the details of the sale. In that letter, Mr Blackman agreed to sell all his shares and those of his family 'subject to their consent which we understand is likely to be a formal matter' and to do all he can to obtain the consent of all the other shareholders; Mr Aisher undertook the same obligations. Service contracts and salaries were confirmed and the positions of other directors and the three Company Secretaries were secured. Finally Mr Blackman covenanted that he would not, for five years 'be concerned in any way whatsoever with the making of tiles from cement and sand'.

On May 17th 1934, the Board meeting of Dean Finance approved the purchase of the majority of the shares in the three Marley companies. Significantly, the next Board meeting a fortnight later elaborated on the Marley shares: '50% thereof were purchased and are held for the account of Sir James Dunn Bt'. All through the transaction, including the eventual offer for sale, Sir James Dunn was in equal partnership with Dean Finance, albeit in the best entrepreneurial spirit – using Dean Finance's own money; this was presumably the return for bringing Dean the issue. There was also a side effect in that Marley never technically became a subsidiary of the tobacco company. A letter from Hugo Cunliffe-Owen of Dean Finance to Jimmy Dunn dated 5th July 1934 spelled out the terms of the transaction:

Dear Jimmy,

The Marley Tile Co Ltd
The Marley Tile Co Ltd (Storrington)
The Marley Tile Co Ltd (Leighton Buzzard)

Our arrangement with regard to the shares in the above companies is that my
company shall pay for all the shares which you may acquire in any of the above
companies and that Dean Finance Co Ltd holds 50% of such shares for its own
account and 50% of such shares in trust for you, subject to you paying the company
50% of the cost price of the shares... together with 4% interest from the date of the
purchase to the date of repayment. In the event of any profit accruing to my company
by reason of Mr Blackman having transferred to it any debentures, or loans made by
him to any of the companies, you are entitled to 50% of the profit, in other words we
are on a 50:50 basis in the deal.

A further footnote on Jimmy Dunn's career puts his Marley sponsorship in context. By far the biggest of the fortunes Jimmy Dunn made (he left an estate of C$70 million in 1956) was made out of the Canadian Algoma Steel Corporation. He had been buying into Algoma for years and by 1934 he held 20% of the equity but the Company had become insolvent. 'The crisis that faced James Dunn in 1934 can therefore be simply stated: he was one-fifth owner in the equity of Algoma – an obsolescent and bankrupt concern. His fortune was invested in the company. The struggle for reorganisation was, for him, a momentous issue.'[23] Dunn was now aged 60 and working furiously to save his position. Yet through all this he was negotiating as a principal on the Marley flotation. In December 1934 he formed a new Algoma Steel Corporation to acquire the assets of the bankrupt business at a time when the final Marley documentation must have been in preparation for the issue the following month.

Under a verbal agreement of 6th July 1934, Dean Finance and Jimmy Dunn bought out the shareholdings of Arthur Blackman, his family and associates for £290,000 in cash. For that they acquired 60% of Harrietsham (after providing for the transfer of the "shadow" shares due to Sir Owen), 73% of Leighton Buzzard and virtually the whole of Storrington. Specific values are not available for each company but working backwards from the relative values later put on the three companies, it looks as if the whole of Marley was being valued at £400,000.

23 *Lord Beaverbrook,* Courage: The Story of Sir James Dunn.

It is interesting to see how the individual companies fared in this first stage of the reorganisation. Marley Tile Company (Harrietsham) was simple: the Blackman family sold their 3,000 out of 4,500 shares leaving Owen Aisher senior still holding the other 1,500 (Sir Owen's shadow shares still make no formal appearance). The Leighton Buzzard shareholdings had varied over its seven year life but by 1934 there were 3,900 shares in issue of which 2,450 (62.8%) were owned by Harrietsham. These were sold to Dean Finance for cash along with around 400 shares owned by Charles Daniel's friends – Owen Browne being the largest with 100 shares. However, the Daniel family themselves retained their holdings along with some of the other original subscribers and also Walter Hoar and Walter Corbett, the two senior men at Leighton Buzzard. At Storrington, 14,700 of the 15,000 shares were sold: 9,655 from the Blackman family, 810 from the Collards, 2,310 from the Menneers and 1,925 from the Pritchards. Of the remaining 300, 200 were in the hands of the Aishers.

Amalgamation

The next stage was to effect the amalgamation of Harrietsham, Leighton Buzzard and Storrington; for this, Marley (Holdings) was incorporated on August 1st 1934. A E Aldridge, a BAT accountant was the first Chairman with the Owen Aishers, father and son, as co-directors. By now Dean Finance and Jimmy Dunn controlled all three companies, the only other significant recorded shareholders being Owen Aisher senior's one third of Harrietsham and the Daniels and friends' 27% of Leighton Buzzard. Marley (Holdings) then made a share exchange offer to each of the three companies, issuing £300,000 of new preference capital and £500,000 of ordinary shares to a nominal value of £800,000 – twice the price the Group was valued at for the buyout of Arthur Blackman. A key element in the exercise was the use of preference shares as part of the consideration; these could be realised on or after the flotation and effectively recouped three-quarters of the original consideration. It provides an early example of the use of fixed interest gearing to extract additional value on the change in ownership of a business. The shareholdings in the amalgamated Marley business now stood as below:

| | Number of shares; | |
	Preference £1	Ordinary 5/-
Dean Finance and Sir James Hamet Dunn, such shares being equally divisible between them	230,377	1,533,302
Owen Aisher	45,851	305,211
John Benjamin Hewitt	225	1,500
Ethel Anne Hammond	900	6,000
Amy Charlotte Hoar	7,600	
Westminster Bank	114	760
Edgar James Dicker	213	1,420
Edgar Walter Hoar	4,566	30,440
Walter Thomas Corbett	2,694	17,960
Mary Winifred Harris Daniel	10,383	69,220
Susan Daniel	684	4,560
Charles Edward Daniel	2,853	19,020
Total	300,000	1,996,993
*Issued for cash on 2–10–34		3,007
		2,000,000

*Directors' subscription shares
Source: The Marley Tile (Holding) Company Prospectus, 23rd January 1985

At this point, the recorded Aisher holding in the Group was only 305,211 shares plus 2,000 directors subscription shares, giving the family 15.4% of the total. They then had to move towards the original family objective, agreed with Dunn, of increasing their holding. On August 1st, the family bought a package of 53,968 preference shares and 360,249 ordinary shares for £74,484 from Dean's holding; 50,000 of the ordinary shares were sold on the flotation. The net addition of 310,249 shares doubled the family shareholding to 31%; allowing for the sale of the preference shares and the 50,000 ordinary shares, this appears to have been achieved at a cost of under £5,000.

	Owen Aisher	Owen Aisher Jnr	Total
Directors' shares	1,000	1,000	2,000
For Harrietsham	305,211		305,211
Purchased	115,423	244,826	360,249
Sold on issue	(25,000)	(25,000)	(50,000)
Leaves	396,634	220,826	617,460

The public issue took place at the end of January 1935. The issued capital comprised 300,000 £1 preference shares and 2,000,000 ordinary 5/- shares; of these, 250,000 preference shares were offered at 21/- each and 750,000 ordinary shares at 5/6 each: Marley was now valued at £865,000. Of the preference shares offered to the public, 171,888 came from Dean and 78,112 from the Aishers; the ordinary shares were sold as to 700,000 by Dean and 50,000 by the Aishers. This left Dean Finance and Jimmy Dunn together holding 468,053 of the ordinary shares, or 23.4% and the Aishers with 617,460 or 30.9%.

Despite those figures derived from the prospectus, Sir Owen Aisher was adamant that the family holding rose to around 42 or 43% on the flotation. There are no records or other memories to substantiate this. However, an undated shareholders list deposited with the Stock Exchange prior to the flotation, which tallies with the Prospectus on all the minor names, has a different split between Dean Finance and the Aishers. Owen Aisher senior, Sir Owen and Bert Aldridge (known to be acting as a nominee for someone) were shown as holding 42.9% of the ordinary shares between them. Was this what Sir Owen sought but was never able to achieve? Or did this represent the beneficial shareholdings which were subsequently hidden under the Dean Finance holdings? After the flotation, the shareholders' register shows that Dean Finance transferred a further 219,848 shares to one William Underwood, a member of the Stock Exchange. A 10% shareholder that no-one has heard of suggests another nominee. If this holding was as a new nominee for the Aisher family, then the Aisher holding in total would have been 837,308 shares or 41.9% of the Company.

On the first day of dealings the shares opened at their issue price of 5s-6d, where it was held (with a little support) for the next month. After that it began to drift, falling below 5s by the end of March.

The relationship between Marley and its sponsors did not end immediately after the flotation. Despite further share transfers following the issue, Dean Finance retained a significant shareholding for some years and Marley continued to use BAT's legal, insurance and transfer departments. Sir James Dunn also kept an active watching brief – the *Sir James Dunn Papers* contain two years of further Marley correspondence concerning the running of the business, profits, breakage problems, machinery purchases, etc. Indeed, Jack Aisher remembers meeting him for the first time after the flotation when he came down to see Erith at seven o'clock one morning: 'I showed him round the plant and he asked a lot of very pertinent questions and that was that.'

To end the chapter, a final exchange of letters between Sir James Dunn and Dean Finance:

8th December 1936

Dear Mr Aldridge,

I have your letter of the 2nd instant in which you say that when I pay you £653.11.1 I will then be free of all liability in respect of the contract guaranteeing the Marley Tile which forms the greater part of the amount shown in the books against me. Before paying this amount I would like to know what else you have on your books against me. Since doing this excellent business there has been first one claim and then another and I would like to know that when I pay the one now under consideration that it completes the matter.

Yours sincerely.

(signed) J H Dunn[24]

And after an exchange of reassurances:

15th December 1936

Dear Sir James,

I thank you for your letter of the 14th instant, enclosing cheque in settlement of all accounts between us up to date.

The Marley Tile business continues to do well, as you say, and it looks very hopeful for next year.

·Yours sincerely,

(signed) A E Aldridge[25]

---

24 Sir James Dunn Papers; *correspondence*.
25 *Ibid.*

Appendix A: The early history of the concrete roof tile

According to Charles Dobson, the first concrete roofing tiles were made in the 1840s at Staudach, a tiny agricultural village in Southern Bavaria. 'The tile was invented and pioneered by a young man named Adolph Kroher, who was at the time no way connected with the building industry.' Charles Dobson visited the Kroher house in the late 1950s and learned from Adolph Kroher's grandson and great-granddaughter what he called 'The Staudach Story'.

Kroher was born in 1825, and one summer in the 1840s he spent his holiday at a guest house in Grassau a few kilometres from Staudach; there he met a forester named Pauli, and the manager of the local salt works, Graf. These two men were supplementing their regular incomes by making a stucco from a local mineral deposit, which they burned in a primitive fashion and mixed with sharp sand from the local river. Kroher became interested in this activity to the extent that he decided to see if there was a possibility of using this mineral deposit, which proved to be a quick-setting natural cement. Adolph Kroher sent samples of the deposit to Vienna for testing, the results were satisfactory, and he was able to establish the manufacture of the cement on a commercial scale, incorporating it as the Staudacher-Cementfabrik in 1858.

Evidence that this works produced the first concrete tiles comes much later when, in 1907, the German Association of Manufacturers of Concrete Products set up a committee to report on the concrete roofing tile in Germany. The *Guben Report* said that 'the views regarding the year in which the concrete roofing tile was first made have been, until recently, widely divergent, but it is

Adolph Kroher

clear that the diamond-pattern tile is appreciably older than the interlocking tile. The first roof tiles to be made of cement were prepared in 1844 in the Kroher Cement Factory at Staudach in Bavaria.' This view was corroborated by other professional bodies and, in 1919, Adolph Kroher's grandson (Eugen) wrote an article for the German *Clay Industry Journal* in which he claimed that cement tiles where first made by his grandfather in the 1840s in Staudach. The tiles were made from the quick-setting local Staudacher cement 'as a house industry for workers who were unemployed during the winter'. Charles Dobson argues that Eugen Kroher's statements are supported by his own extensive travels around northern Europe: 'I have visited most, if not all, of the areas in which concrete tiles have been made, and nowhere have I found tiles so old as those to be seen in and around Staudach.'

In his article, Eugen Kroher mentions early experimentation with different shapes. Adolph Kroher finally decided that the diamond pattern of the local slates was also the best shape for concrete: it was easily carried up the roof, easily laid by semi-skilled men, and was less fragile than any of the types made with rolls or other features. However, the replication of this diamond pattern in England was one reason for the poor acceptance of the product by the housebuilder.

Transport limitations made it difficult for Adolph Kroher to sell his tiles over long distances; instead, he helped promote the spread of concrete roof tile production in Germany as a means of increasing the sales of his cement. 'He sold his cement to anybody who wanted to make tiles, and with it the moulds or presses and printed instructions for making the tiles. His scheme resulted in a more widespread use of Staudach cement and Kroher tiles, but it had the long term disadvantage that the manufacture of tiles was done by amateurs who did not understand the importance of a correct mixing of the cement and aggregate.'

The Kroher family stopped making concrete products in 1929, and the cement works passed into other hands. Eugen Kroher blamed the German currency inflation but also told Charles Dobson that the manufacture of concrete tiles 'had already become unprofitable because of the formidable competition of the clay tile'.

Dobson's travels took him across northern Europe where he successfully identified other concrete roof tile factories active in the late nineteenth century. Notable was the Dane Jorgensen who patented a concrete roof tile design in Schleswig-Holstein in 1882, building his first factory at Wedel the following year and a second at Quickborn in 1895; this later passed into the hands of the Rademacher family who were still producing concrete tiles there at the time of Dobson's visit. Also notable was the Huser pre-cast concrete works; the firm had been established around 1850 and in 1878 Hartwig Huser took out a patent for a diamond-pattern concrete tile.

Sufficient has been said to show that by the late nineteenth century, concrete roof tile technology was reasonably widely available and a range of patents had been deposited. Yet clay and asbestos-cement remained the dominant medium for roofing tiles. In the conclusion to his book, Charles Dobson explains why the concrete tile 'never established itself in the land of its origin'. He suggested that 'until comparatively recent times the manufacture of the concrete roofing tile has been carried on in small works, each of which has necessarily served a very restricted area. Adolph Kroher probably worked further afield than most of his successors in the industry. Many of these small works made very few tiles. The inescapable truth is that in many places the concrete tile has been produced by inexperienced men... The clay tile has always been a serious competitor of the concrete tile, and its competition has been all the more serious because the problem of colouring has never, until quite recently, been seriously considered in Germany'.[26]

Appendix B: Blackman Marley correspondence

The first example illustrates the operational detail that Arthur Blackman expected to receive, but this letter was also chosen for the light it sheds on the motoring hazards of sixty years ago.

A. Blackman, Esq.,   *12th June 1929*
Stonehenge,
Laton Road,
HASTINGS

Dear Sir,

    We beg to enclose statements and returns for week ending June 6th.

New Benches. *As you arranged, when last here, the three new Benches have been installed and three of our men have started making on them. Two of these men, will, however, be replaced by two tilemakers whom Harrietsham are sending down to us next week.*

Sand Pit. *The work on the left hand bank is proceeding as per your instructions.*

Road Charges. *Cheque for £160 was paid to the Thakenham R D C on Monday last.*

26 Dobson, p 20

Attwood's Agreement. *We note no further action is to be taken in this matter until you have spoken to Owen about it.*

Claim. *No doubt you will remember when you were last here, mention was made of the fact that one of our drivers had been fined for dangerous driving. At the time of this occurrence he ran over, and killed a dog, which was really the cause of the Summons being issued. We have now received a letter from a firm of Solicitors at Horsham (as per copy enclosed), and on Owen's instructions we have claimed on our Insurance Company, leaving them to deal with the matter.*

On Tuesday last, while on the way to Bognor in Mr Williams' car to see one of our customers regarding his Account, Mr Williams knocked a middle aged lady off her bicycle. The accident was absolutely unavoidable as the lady lost control of her machine and ran right into the car. Fortunately when the Doctor arrived he reported she was suffering from slight bruising and shock only, and so far, we have heard nothing further. We have made a preliminary claim on the Insurance Company.

Outstanding Accounts. *A number of these have been paid and a full report will be sent you at the end of this week.*

Yours faithfully,

A month later we have Arthur Blackman doing his own calculations on the returns and finding that all is not to his liking.

BLACKMAN, PAVIE & LADDEN, LTD.,

43, King's Road,
ST. LEONARDS.

17th July, 1929

Mr. Kelly,
The Marley Tile Co. Ltd.,
Storrington,
Near Pulborough.

Dear Kelly,

Your monthly budget, in which you give the total outstandings and the total accounts owing by us, which, together with the stock of tiles and bank balance practically shows a balance sheet of the whole concern, is rather a good idea, but in comparing the list at the end of May with that of the end of June, there seems to be some discrepancy.

At the end of May you book debts are		£3886
Balance of stock of tiles 812,000, which		
roughly speaking we will call £5 per 1000		£4060
Bank balance		300
		8246
You owed a balance of		800
	Balance	£7446
whereas your statement at the end of June		
shows Book debts		£4220
Balance of stock of tiles, 642,000 @ £5		3210
Bank balance		350
		£7780
You owed		1216
		£6564

from which it will be seen that instead of having made a profit as shown on your weekly sheets, there is a loss of £882. How do you account for this?

Furthermore, how was Leighton Buzzard's account for £178.1.2. omitted, as per your letter of the 11th? Do you not treat both Leighton Buzzard and Harrietsham as ordinary customers in so far as book-keeping is concerned?

Regarding the question of your stock of tiles, you still show them in stock, but I imagine a great portion of these are not fit to send out until they are re-dipped. I assume also that you are taking steps to have this done at once, because they will never be in greater demand than now, and whilst I should like you to oblige either Harrietsham or Leighton Buzzard in so far as you can do so, yet you must make perfectly sure that you retain sufficient of the right class for your own requirements.

Regarding the accounts, some of them are not quite so close as they should be, and you should nurse them along and use just such pressure as is necessary to prevent the list mentioned in yours of the 8th.

As regards accounts owing for Leighton Buzzard and Harrietsham, there is no need for you to ask them for money at any time unless you are needing it in the business to pay your way.

The moment you are short of sufficient labour to keep all your machinery going, please let me know, together with the cause of the shortage.

Yours faithfully,

for A. BLACKMAN
S.R.G.

Finally, we have Mr Kelly's somewhat plaintive reply as he explains how the figures really tie in, accompanied by the usual daily happenings at the roof tile factory.

THE MARLEY TILE CO. (Storrington) LTD.

STORRINGTON.

23rd July, 1929.

A. Blackman, Esq.,
'Stonehenge',
Laton Road,
HASTINGS.

Dear Sir,

We beg to enclose herewith statement and return for week-ending July 11th.

Replying to your letter of the 17th inst., I have spent a good deal of time in going into the figures and endeavouring to find out how the discrepancy of £882 arises.

The amount owed by us at May 31st as per the list sent you was £800, but this list does not show the total owing at May 31st, but only the amount due at May 31st.

With regard to the figures for June, the Book Debts of £4220 do not include amounts to be charged for tiles delivered to jobs in June, which jobs we were not able to charge up to June 31st either because the jobs were not finished or because the measurements had not been checked. Furthermore, two items were paid in June which it seems to me should be taken into account. They were:-

Repairs to Chantry Lane	*£160*
Attwood's Car	*140*
	£300

Therefore, to get a truer idea of the position the figures should read as follows:-

At May 31st.	Book Debts.	£3886
	Stock 812,000 tiles @ £5 per 1000.	4060
	Bank Balance.	300
		8246
	We owed.	1100
		7146

At June 31st.	Book Debts.	£4220
	Jobs (tiles d/d in June)	750 *Approx*
	Stock 642,000 @ £5 per 1000.	3210
	Bank Balance.	350
		£8530
	We owed.	1216
		£7314

and this latter figure of £7314 does not include the two items amounting to £300 paid out in June.

Leighton Buzzard's account for £178.1.2. was omitted in error and should have been noticed by me before sending you the list.

We treat both Leighton Buzzard and Harrietsham as ordinary customers in so far as book-keeping is concerned, but with regard to asking them for money, I do not, as a rule do this until it is absolutely essential, although at the end of June when writing Leighton Buzzard for money I worded the letter a little more strongly as Owen stated that if I did not, in all probability we should not get a cheque from them.

As to the tiles which have to be re-dipped, we are at the moment in a much better position for labour than we have been for the past six weeks or so, and a number of men are now engaged on dipping up these tiles. We have today had to take two of our best makers off and put them on work in the yard, as their arms were breaking out badly, but we have been able to fill their places with outside workers.

Harrietsham have just written me asking for a cheque for £198.15.10. for Formation Expenses and I understand from Corbett that you have agreed this should be paid for now. I am therefore sending Harrietsham a cheque for this amount tonight.

Re Salesmen for Southampton District. About the beginning of June, following Owen's instructions, we inserted an advertisement in the local Southampton and Portsmouth papers, and also in 'The Builder'. I enclose a summary of the applications we have had for this position which I had already sent to Owen. On bringing the matter to his notice when he was last here a fortnight ago he said he thought the matter had better remain in abeyance for the present.

Yours faithfully,
MARLEY TILE CO. LTD.

E. Kelly.

Part 2

Expansion once again: Marley goes national

As soon as Dean Finance had bought out Blackman's interests in the three Marley Tile companies, Sir Owen was immediately ready to activate his expansion strategy. Marley Tile (Aveley), Marley Tile (Burton) and Marley Tile (Riverhead) were formed as £500 companies in the September and October of 1934; the land was leased and the factories began to go up; all this while the Prospectus was being drawn up. Riverhead came into production in February 1935 and Aveley and Burton followed in June.

As if doubling the number of factories within a year was not enough, in September 1935 Marley was negotiating with Hall & Co. to buy the latter's Minster Tiles business. A month later, Marley leased land at Poole and the eighth factory came into production at the end of 1937. Burton had firmly established Marley in the Midlands and the Company was now ready to strengthen its base in the North. Planning permission was obtained at Woodford near Manchester in 1938 and in the following year land was acquired at Bishopbriggs near Glasgow. War was then close; the Manchester proposal was abandoned but a limited operation was just begun at Glasgow as war began.

Thus, by the end of the 1930s, Marley had eight concrete roof tile factories; Harrietsham was being run down in favour of Riverhead, while Glasgow was on the drawing board. In order of development these were:

Year opened

1924/25	Harrietsham	(assets transferred to Riverhead in 1938)
1927	Leighton Buzzard	(closed in 1986)
1927	Storrington	(closed in 1970)
1933	Erith	(temporary factory closed in 1936)
1935	Aveley	(closed in 1970)
1935	Burton	
1935	Riverhead	(closed in 1989)
1935 (purchased)	Bedfont	(closed in 1949)
1937	Poole	(closed in 1990)

Unfortunately, complete records of factory output after Marley became public have not survived; in particular there are no records of Burton. However, we do have enough information to see that the pace did not slacken. At the beginning of 1935 the capacity of the three original factories, plus Erith, had reached 2.25 million tiles a week or 117 million a year. The addition of Riverhead, Aveley and Burton and the closure of Erith were expected to raise capacity by two thirds, from 2.25 million to 3.75 million a week or a short 200 million a year. With the help of the Bedfont acquisition, Marley looks to have achieved a manufacturing output of around 195 million tiles in 1937. The small Bournemouth factory added a little the following year but by then Harrietsham was being run down and housing demand was levelling out.[1]

	Tile output (millions)	
	1937	**1938**
Harrietsham	14	4
Leighton Buzzard	55	52
Storrington	21	22
Aveley	22	24
Riverhead	39	37
Burton (estimated)	35	35
Bedfont	9	9
Poole	–	7
Total	195	190

It would be difficult to imagine a more favourable environment for Marley: the housebuilding market enjoyed a long period of sustained growth; the slate

1 *These figures are consistent with the 200 million tiles quoted by Marion Bowley in* Innovations in Building Materials, *1960, p265, from information supplied by the Company.*

industry was in decline, and the traditional clay tile manufacturers seemed unable to exploit what should have been their natural preserve. The 1920s housing boom, which had first created the shortage of roofing tiles, peaked in 1927 with UK completions of 258,000 – an achievement that today's housebuilding industry would welcome. It was, however, based on rapid growth in the subsidised housing programme, primarily local authorities but also in the private sector where certain types of building qualified for assistance. This element of the housing programme reduced sharply in 1928 following a cut in Government subsidies taking the industry down to its 'low' of 208,000. However, these quieter years masked the start of an unprecedented boom in private speculative housing. Having averaged between 60–70,000 a year through the 1920s, the speculative market literally took off, rising every year to a peak of 292,000 in 1934 – a figure never since exceeded. Total housing completions reached 345,000 and, with local authority housing once again increasing, that 1934 total was exceeded each year until 1939.

Official figures were published for concrete roofing tiles for the first time in 1935 and then again in 1938; only after the war were they published on an annual basis.

	Production of roofing (000 squares)	
	1935	**1938**
Clay tiles	1,226	1,512
Concrete tiles	639	960
Roofing slates	710	661
Total	2,575	3,133

Source: Annual Abstract of Statistics

Thus, by 1935, concrete had achieved around 25% of the pitched roof market, a striking achievement from what must have been a very low percentage ten years earlier. A fortunate footnote to the statistics of squares produced for 1935 tells us that the equivalent number of concrete tiles was 320 million. We have already indicated that Marley's output is not known exactly, with 1935 being a particular problem as it was in the middle of its factory building programme. On the basis that Riverhead came into production in February, with Aveley and Burton following in June, Marley's total production would have been 150 to 160 million tiles, equivalent to half the concrete tile market or a market share of 12–13% of the whole pitched roof business. The full impact of Marley's increased production, and of its competitors', could be seen when the next figures were produced in 1938. Concrete industry production had increased by a half to take over 30% of the roofing market. Assuming that the number of tiles per square was unchanged, the concrete industry had a production of 480 million in 1938; Marley's production looked to be a touch under 200 million or a market share of 42%. Other producers had clearly jumped on to the bandwagon and we will see later the impact this had on prices and Marley's profitability.

From hand to machine: technical change in the tile factory

We described in an earlier chapter Marley's first Winget hand machines. Since then, the product has changed little. The expert will obviously point to improvements in strength, durability, colour fastness and fittings, but show a layman a concrete tiled roof and only the ageing process and the house that it is on will tell him whether it was laid in the 'twenties, 'forties or 'sixties. What has changed almost beyond recognition is the manufacturing process. Marley had little outside help it could draw on in the early years. There were manufacturers of tile machines but they existed only to supply the small local

Charlie Randall

tile companies; they were not expecting the concrete tile to become the dominant roofing medium. Although they worked with companies like Lintott, Marley had no option but to commit itself to the search for new production techniques.

While Sir Owen led the search for better and better manufacturing efficiency, one man is mentioned above all others for Marley's early engineering development – Charlie Randall. Charlie Randall left school aged 11 ('I always regret how little formal education I had') following which he worked as an agricultural and then a building labourer before finishing up at the Dickley farm adjoining the Aisher land. Sir Owen remembers his arrival: 'We relied on a chap called Charlie Randall who, with his brother John, came to us with scythes over their shoulders, asking to cut hay in the fields, who couldn't read and write properly.' And from a contemporary 'In the early days, we had a very good foreman at Storrington named Charlie Randall, he could hardly read or write, but you give him a machine to muck about with and he would scribble some bits on the back of an envelope, pass it over to someone like Lintott and they'd get on.'

Charlie Randall was not the only one to come from the agricultural community. Sir Owen also remembers two blacksmiths, Reg Armstrong and Doug Butcher who 'came from the marsh looking for a better job; they were practical blacksmiths and engineers and so little by little, until we got electricity, they were doing the whole job developing things. I remember drawing with a piece of chalk on the concrete floor at Storrington with Charlie Randall, the arch which we put in the machine which enabled us to make a cross cambered tile. Charlie said he could do it, and I left it to him and in the next week he had nearly done it.' That Charlie Randall was held in high regard is confirmed by the 1938 salary sheets at Riverhead: read and write or not, he was paid £12 per week which compared with £8 for Fred Hardy, then in charge of administration and £10 for Dick Aisher.

By 1929 or 1930 Marley started a primitive form of mechanised tile-making. The first machine was at Harrietsham 'which we kept altering', followed quickly by one at Storrington. Sir Owen had bought it from his old friend Mr Baumgarten, whom he had first met in 1924. Baumgarten had imported the machine from Ringstedt in Denmark. 'It didn't really work, so we cannibalised it, more than once, and eventually got it working. I remember originally we thought 10 tiles a minute – well we found it wouldn't go properly at less than 20. We got it up to 30 and for many years we made our machines work at the rate of 40 a minute.' The works did not have electric power and the machines were driven by belts, powered by a diesel motor. Leighton Buzzard was the first to have electric power, about 1932, and that then drove the line shaft.

Bill Borgia remembered the first automated machine to come in at Storrington around 1930 as 'a very primitive affair. You put a pallet in at one end and a pusher came along and pushed it underneath the hopper which was full of pug. The pug was then extruded underneath a plate so that the tile was formed and moulded on the pallet; you still took it off the end of the machine by hand and put it on one of the trolleys. To the extent that you hadn't got the trowelling to do and the sand facing, then it was automatic.'

Having imported that first machine from Baumgarten and effectively rebuilt it, not just to get it to operate at its design speed but at well beyond its original specification, Marley carried on developing and improving their machines. However, the manufacture of the machines was contracted out. 'Lintott used to make a lot of bits for us and in fact were pretty well producing tile machines for us, almost complete ones.' In practice, Lintott (a Horsham firm) appears to have provided the engineering capacity for Marley's design: 'we were able to buy the machines practically ready made but very quickly the progress was such that we hardly got a new machine before we were altering it, making it go better or faster.'

Reference to the standard works on roofing published during the 1930s are more instructive for what they omit than what they actually say about the manufacturing techniques of the concrete tile industry. For all Charles Dobson's exposure to the Aisher family, his *Roof Tiling* (1931)[2] does not even have a single mention of the concrete tile; neither did Alfred Searle's 1930 *Modern Tilemaking*.[3] By the mid-1930s, what seemed an almost reluctant mention of the concrete product was beginning to appear. Thus, the 14th edition of Edward Dobson and Alfred Searle's *Bricks and Tiles* (1936)[4] has a whole chapter on the manufacture of concrete roofing tiles – all 350 words of it! Bennett and Pinion's *Roof Slating and Tiling* (1935)[5] also manages a couple of pages on the manufacture of the concrete interloper. The closing paragraph of the first chapter, which must have been written about the time Marley was going public, and five years after the company claimed to have become the country's largest roof tile manufacturer, shows more clearly than anything how the Aishers had to force their way into a sceptical and traditional industry. 'The concrete tile is another curious hybrid, the outcome of our mechanical age. Its imitations of the plain tile is almost perfect when new, and seen from a distance none but the expert can detect the difference. We mention its advantages and disadvantages in Chapter 6, but again only time, with its effect of weathering, can effectively show how significant or insignificant this tile is to become in the future of roofing.'

Bennett and Pinion describe the 'Winget' hand machine, to which we have already referred, and a slightly more sophisticated 'Vickers' machine

2   *Charles Dobson*, Roof Tiling, *London, 1931.*
3   *Alfred Searle*, Modern Tilemaking, *1930.*
4   *Edward Dobson and Alfred Searle*, Bricks and Tiles, *London, 1936.*
5   *Frank Bennett and Alfred Pinion*, Roof Slating and Tiling, *London, 1935.*

where the colouring appears to have been applied semi-automatically but the manufacturing process was still largely by hand. A year later, Dobson and Searle acknowledged that:

> The manufacture of concrete roofing tiles has recently assumed the dimensions of a large industry and has created very serious competition with clay tiles, particularly with plain tiles. Their manufacturing description has recognised the arrival of the first automatic machine.
>
> The 'paste' is fed through a hopper into the tile-machine in which the paste is compressed on to oil-sprayed iron pallets or moulds which are fed into the machine in a continuous stream except in hand-operated machines where each tile is made separately. The mass of paste on the pallet next passes under a roller which compresses and shapes it, the mass being further consolidated by being passed under one or more knives which seal the pores in the back of the tile. When the surface is to be coloured, the tiles next pass under one or more boxes containing mixtures of colour with dry cement and then under a water spray.
>
> Just before the tiles leave the machine the nail-holes are punched in them. The tiles are then separated automatically and are removed by hand from the conveyor, placed on a suitable car and pulled into the 'curing chamber' where they remain in a moist atmosphere until sufficiently 'cured'. Some firms consider 24 hours in the curing chamber is sufficient and complete the curing in the open air, aided by spraying the tiles daily with water for a week or more, and afterwards at longer intervals for at least a month.[6]

The only exception to this public disregard for the concrete tile was what appears to have been a relatively obscure book by Baumgarten (the same) and Childe in 1936: *Manufacture of Concrete Roofing Tiles*,[7] and published by Concrete Publications. Author and publisher clearly had a point to make. There is detailed description of the whole manufacturing process though it is difficult to tell whether it represents the industry as it actually was, or the equipment that Mr Baumgarten would have liked to sell.

The machines installed in Marley's second generation of factories in 1935 must have been as modern as anything and, with a combination of Marley memories and Baumgarten's book, we can see what standards were being achieved a decade after Owen Aisher bought his first Winget hand machine. Speeds were notably faster. On the early hand machines at Harrietsham, one man could make about 1,000 to 1,200 tiles a day. The new machines would handle plain tile pallets at 36 a minute; the pallets produced two tiles each giving 4,320 an hour; 173,000 on a standard 40 hour week; and around 8.6 million a year. Thus, a three-machine shop (e.g. Aveley) would have a theoretical capacity of a little over 25 million plain tiles a year. Leighton

6   *Ibid.*
7   *R H Baumgarten and H L Childe*, Manufacture of Concrete Roofing Tiles, *London, 1936.*

Buzzard, the largest works, had 8 tile machines running by the late 1930s. Sir Owen emphasised the halfway stage that Marley had reached: 'Riverhead was more modern although, let's face it, these new factories were still not quite mechanised but semi-handmade. The only factory that was partly mechanised was Scotland, and that was a great failure as a mechanised factory but we learned so much from it.'

Archie Orme described the tile machines as he remembered them in 1935: 'We had Erich pan mixers up in the roof. There were skips loaded outside and they went up a runway and tipped into a mixer; the mix came down chutes to the tile machines. Normally one mixer would deal with three machines.' The standard mix, according to Marley's advertising literature, was made with one part 'Rapid Hardening English Cement' and 2½ parts of high grade silica sand; it also included the colouring for the body of the tile. Once the pallets were on the tile machine, they passed in a continuous stream under the hopper which spread the 'body' of the concrete over the top of the pallet. There followed a roller and steel blade which compacted the concrete and screeded it to the required thickness; a colour box which sieved the coloured sand facing on to the tile (a Marley patent); a knife which cut the strip of concrete longitudinally, and another which cut it transversely leaving two plain tiles on each pallet. The fittings and ridges were, of course, still being made on the hand machines.

Once the tiles had been cut and formed they were lifted from the machine by hand and placed on racks which were pushed into curing tunnels where they remained for 24 hours or until the tiles were strong enough to be taken from the pallets. As soon as the new factories were operational. Marley began to improve the machines. 'The machine improved rapidly. Instead of putting the pallets in one at a time you had a box and you put a whole pile in.' However, the next major steps forward were to be automatic racking of the tiles for curing and mechanical handling using conveyor belts, but these had to wait until after the war.

The tile type referred to above was the plain tile, made in standard sizes of 10½ × 6½ in. and 11 × 7 in., marketed by Marley as their Broseley, after the generic name of the clay tiles coming out of the potteries. That stung the clay Broseley manufacturers to advertise that they alone could use that name. The plain tile remained Marley's staple product until the mid-1930s when the larger 15 × 9 in. interlocking tiles were introduced. The first interlocking tiles, called Ludlow, were made at Burton in 1935.

Factory building

The early factory building was primitive, reflecting the limited resources of the business, not only financial but also a management team that was having to learn as it grew. There was no such thing as an outside contractor or clerk of works. The organisation was provided by Sir Owen and helped, at Leighton Buzzard, by Charles Daniel. Everything that could be done by Marley itself was done; the blocks for building the factory, for example, would be made on site out of Marley's own sand. More imaginative use of available materials could sometimes be seen. Fred Hardy, later to become Deputy Chairman, remembers rebuilding at Storrington and knocking down the original tunnels: 'I said to Charlie [Randall], "you told me you built these tunnels – what did you use for reinforcement!" He said, "We'd got no money, so we used old bedsteads or anything to reinforce it." I suppose we were on a shoestring. That's how they built the business: it was all go and hard work.'

Bill Borgia remembered Storrington when he arrived in 1929: 'Our office was a little lean-to shed on the side of the wagon shed. One small office with a concrete floor and a Valor oil stove. After about a year we put another bit on the other end and had two small offices and two Valor stoves. No running water, no toilets – the toilets were buckets. If you wanted to wash your hands you went over to the water butt, there wasn't anything else. No finesse.

'They built a small office down the bottom end of the factory, after I'd been there about a year or so – where we had got running water and a toilet.' The factory conditions were no better: 'Horrible! We just had one large shed, no heating of course, no extractor fans, or anything. Beyond the shed, there was a building with a flat roof, only about as high as this room, made into four long tunnels and in that we had a quantity of coke braziers. The tiles were pushed into these tunnels as they were made. In the evening the braziers were fired up as high as they could, the doors were shut and then they were left to cure through the night. Of course when you opened these tunnels in the morning the coke fumes practically asphyxiated you.

'At that time the men were nearly all on piece work. They used to start at seven in the morning and once they made what they thought was their sufficiency they'd go home but it was usually not before five or half past. I forget what the rate was, I think about nine bob a thousand. A good tile maker on a good day could earn up to £5 to £5.10s a week. That was a good wage. The labour rate was 11d an hour. We used to pay a penny over. And your ordinary labourer normally worked a fifty hour week. If he did any overtime which was very scarce it was time and a quarter. But the conditions were really appalling.'

The sheer speed of Marley's expansion during the 1930s imposed its own strains on the organisation. As far as possible, the factories were still built by Marley people but more professional assistance was also available, and now Jack Aisher was involved with the construction supervision. 'The next one of course was [Riverhead]. There again, Owen engineered the thought of how it was going to be done. We had an architect called Leslie Apps who came from Maidstone; Leslie got out the plans and got whatever approval was necessary and I supervised it. Did we go to a contractor like Wimpey or Costain? No, we didn't.'

Archie Orme remembers the early days at Burton: 'Burton in those days was full of old fashioned businesses, breweries... the other firms had been there so long and they were very conservative, and I think Marley came with new ideas because coming almost into the Potteries and making concrete roofing tiles took a bit of swallowing.' The key figure to start with was the carpenter, who did the setting out. 'Albert Hood of Burton, he was the works carpenter that stayed on... and retired with the Company, having come there when it was a field to set it out.' Three factories were being built almost simultaneously and each had its carpenter, but where possible Jack Aisher supervised the construction; the craftsmen and labourers were recruited directly and the bricks were still being made on the site.

Fred Hardy, later to become Deputy Chairman, joined Marley at Burton as it was being built. He had previously been keeping the books for a small firm but 'I could see that things were pretty bad in those times and I thought the building industry was worth getting into... they put an advert in for staff at Burton. The factory was in the process of being built so I went to Barclays Bank for the interview. Julius William Borgia interviewed me. I said have you got a job in your Accounts Department? and he looked a bit peculiar. I hadn't realised that he had not got such a thing as an Accounts Department, they were just setting people on; it was a mess really. He said you can have a job as a cashier, £3.10s a week, if you don't turn out all right you get the sack.'

Fred Hardy rose rapidly through the organisation and when Jack Aisher left the Company for active service in the Army he effectively took control of all production, was appointed to the Board of Marley Tile in August 1942 and

Fred Hardy

to the Holding Company in 1962. He was a man of strong personality and outspoken views. He was probably the only senior executive to stand up to the Aisher family and acted as a counterweight to some of the more speculative of the family ideas. His description of what he found at Burton maintains his succinct style. 'When I got there I soon found that nobody really knew what they were up to, not on the administration side at any rate. They hadn't got a set of account books or anything. Then, when we moved into the Burton office... they just put a partition across the end of the factory and it was an open space. I arrived on the Monday morning... and we had not even got any chairs or desks.'

Conditions slowly improved during the 1930s but then they had ample opportunity to do so. A particular problem in the factories was dermatitis, frequently mentioned in the minutes and the accounts. Fred Hardy: 'When I joined everybody got dermatitis, it was just from the filth. The men were using crude oil to wash off the grime. Also cement dust was getting in the crooks of their arms and their fingers. The crude oil took out the body's natural oils. These chaps then discovered that if they got a certificate for dermatitis they could get compensation. This was soon remedied by barrier creams in the morning and showers in the evening and gradually the production process was made cleaner.

The BAT influence

Once BAT became involved, in 1934, the administration became a little more formalised. On the flotation, BAT had two of the four directors − Percy Millard, recently retired from China, and Bert Aldridge, the Chairman of Dean Finance; Sir Owen and his father were the family representatives. Percy Millard was appointed Chairman of The Marley Tile (Holding) Company. Sir Owen recalled Sir Hugo Cunliffe-Owen, the Chairman of BAT saying to him 'Owen, you're too young; you can't be Chairman and anyway you're busy'. In the summer of 1935 Charles Daniel was appointed to the Board followed by BAT's A C Hartley a year later. Marley had been formed through the legal department of BAT who provided John Stoker as the Marley Company Secretary. BAT became the Marley registrars and their legal and insurance departments continued to provide services for Marley.

One of the first things Percy Millard did was to bring in a BAT accountant, Reg Crossman, who had been a travelling auditor for BAT around the world. He toured the branches putting in an accounting system based on BAT principles. According to Fred Hardy 'it was a really first class system, there's no doubt about that, and it embodied everything, from the costing of the tiles to the whole set of books of accounts'.

With the grouping of the three semi-independent factories into a public

John Stoker   Percy Millard

company, followed almost immediately by the construction of three more factories, there was also a need for a Production Manager. Although the position was soon filled by Jack Aisher, he was by no means the immediate choice. Edgar Dicker had been a director of Marley Tile (Storrington) prior to the amalgamation and was still running the factory on a day-to-day basis. Jack Aisher describes what appears to have been a half-hearted and none too successful appointment: 'He wasn't really appointed as such. You weren't told. You were just told to go and look after those places. Anyway he didn't do it well enough... in a very short while it was obvious that he didn't fit in.' The Storrington minutes of 12th June 1936 record Dicker's resignation as director; it was accepted with the conventional 'regret' but nevertheless 'to take effect forthwith'. A gratuity of £137.10s was forthcoming.

Next, Ted Hoar was considered for the position. Hoar had been Company Secretary of Marley Tile (Leighton Buzzard) on its formation, becoming its General Manager in 1929 on Owen Aisher's recommendation. He was remembered for a remarkable ability to add up columns of pounds, shillings and pence in his head but that didn't help him survive as a production manager. 'He didn't succeed; he became ill.' Jack Aisher describes how, at the age of 25, he was eventually chosen: 'Owen, and Percy Millard and Charles Daniel were looking around, we'd got to have somebody and Owen said "Well

Jack's being doing this in Erith, why not let him have a go" ' and that's how I got the job. I virtually became the Production Manager; that I did right through until the war.'

Jack Aisher had cut his teeth on Erith, a factory which was leased from Vickers Armstrong in 1931 as a means of avoiding undue capital expenditure. The housing market in South London was booming and Harrietsham was too far away to service it effectively. 'At the age of 21, I was instructed to take a machine and go to Erith, install it and start making tiles, which is what I did.'

Sales – the Marley philosophy

An earlier chapter described how Marley's supply and fix policy had been born of necessity. The merchants' reluctance to stock new products led to the direct sale policy but Marley did not stop at selling direct to the customer; the tilers' unfamiliarity with the concrete product also created the need for Marley to do its own fixing. The concrete tile, which was cured, had a lower initial strength than the clay tile which had been kiln fired. Sir Owen remembered the early sales from Harrietsham: 'Our tiles had to be laid differently to clay tiles. You couldn't sit on them very easily, they were tender, especially when they were new, green as it were, so you had to work away from them on the roof instead of over them. This meant that whenever we went to London and you wanted a tiler up there we had to show him how to do the job. But we succeeded in doing that, until today – everybody does it like that.'

As was mentioned earlier, Sir Owen's younger brother Dick was primarily involved on the selling side. Dick had Kent, south of Harrietsham to work, travelling by train and bus until Sir Owen passed over his first car and bought a new one. The first salesman the Aishers employed was a man called Collard; 'he found his own car and we paid him £2.10s per week and $1^{1}/_{4}\%$ commission and £3.10s per week to run his car. And that remained the system until the War came and also after the War,' recalled Sir Owen.

The supply and fix system revolved around the salesman; not only did he have to secure the job but he also organised the tiler and collected the money from the customer. The salesman measured the job and produced a cost card which was then sent to the factory for the estimate. Once he received the estimate, the salesman was not allowed to post it to the builder – he had to take it personally. This seems to have been due less to courtesy than suspicion; 'if you sent it he could show it to somebody else and all sorts of things'. When the builder said he was ready, the salesman would send in the order to the factory which held the estimate; that was taken from the file and sent to the delivery department which would deliver it on the day or the day before. It was the salesman's job to arrange for the tiler to put them on. When the tiler finished the salesman issued him with a note which the tiler then sent to Marley for payment.

Each salesman had a geographical area chosen on the basis that there were a thousand houses a year built in it and he had to get 40% of them. 'If he did, he would earn himself something like £8 or £9 a week, which was good money in those days.' Thus, central to Marley's success in developing supply and fix was not simply the salesman's ability to win new business but to estimate correctly and organise the job. Sir Owen had a ready source of such men; 'We found the best fellows were those who had been to sea and could navigate and work out figures properly. At this time shipping was in the doldrums and we could take on salesmen who had got a Master's ticket and had been at sea all the time. They thought it marvellous to come back and earn £7 a week, and so by the time the War came we had about 150 chaps among our salesmen who had in fact Masters' tickets.'

By 1932 Marley had become easily the largest roofing contractor in the country. Sir Owen was in no doubt that this was the basis for Marley's competitive success. 'When we started there were as many as 80 competitors. They nearly all failed because they couldn't supply and fix the tiles. They failed because they were selling to merchants and had to sell cheaply. They got a hit and miss order book. The result was they could never really be efficient in manufacture because they were never running flat out, whereas we were running flat out all the time. When Sir Owen was asked why other manufacturers had not copied Marley's supply and fix, the answer was simple: 'Because it was bloody hard!'

Perhaps a more realistic explanation of Marley's marketing success is not that they were the only proponents of supply and fix, but that they practised the policy more exclusively, with greater commitment and more efficiency than any other manufacturer. If the merchants were hostile to Marley's concrete roof tiles, then they were going to be antipathetic to other manufacturers' tiles as well. This inevitably drew some of Marley's competitors into forms of direct marketing to the ultimate customer, the builder. Colonel Young of Redland, reminisced in similar vein to Sir Owen about the early marketing of the concrete tile: 'Our customers were the builders. We supplied direct to them. They bought our products because they were cheaper than clay tiles... Builders' merchants throughout the country would not look at our tiles; they, they... were all tied up with the slate and clay manufacturers and scorned the concrete tile. We found it necessary to do something we didn't like doing – that is to fix tiles as well as sell them.'[8]

In the South, Marley had little competition from independent roofing

8 *Unpublished interview with A F F Young, 1970.*

Early Marley delivery vans

contractors. Before the First World War the builder put his own tiles on the roof; there were no roofing contractors to speak of. Neither was there much need for the builders' merchant: 'the builder on his bicycle or horse and trap was as close to the local tile yard as he was to any builders' merchant, who was a foreign chap as a rule to him, importing timber or bringing goods for a distance that were not made locally.' Sir Owen went on to describe the system he found in the mid-1920s: 'The builder ordered the tiles from a merchant and they were sent to him by rail and delivered by horse and cart. They were disorganised. They were put on the job before the builder started the house; and they got damaged. Then, the builder having bought them, along came a fellow with a cloth cap and he said "how much?" and after two or three chaps had come along the builder would beat them down. We said to these chaps we would give you five shillings a square which they said was not enough but they all did in the end; we said we will employ you all full time, we'll keep you busy. And they very quickly found that being busy working for Marley at five shillings a square was the finest job they had ever had – and very happy to travel outside their towns.'

Marley's aggressive policy inevitably led to resentment from established roofing contractors. Sir Owen had little sympathy: 'When the roofing contractors used to complain that we were too cheap and they couldn't buy tiles and compete with us, and we had them down and showed them the books, and they said, "well we can't do them for 12%". I said then you'd better find out how and do it like us.' However, when Marley opened up in the Midlands, at Burton, and more particularly in Scotland, they had to face up to more substantial independent roofing contractors. A particular advantage that Marley had was its ability to move its labour around freely between jobs, whereas antiquated Union rules limited the existing roofing contractors. 'When we went to the Midlands, they had never seen anything like this [our tilers]. If you were in Birmingham you couldn't really do a job in Coventry, because under the rules, which were very carefully worded, the man had to report to his yard before he went to work. The fellow in Leeds couldn't do a job in Sheffield unless he had a yard in Sheffield. We could do a job in Sheffield this morning and Leeds this afternoon if they wanted. Our fellows came on a motorbike, like cowboys, but they came and did the job, and they did it better than anybody else.'

Sir Owen quickly built up close relationships with the housebuilders, some of whom he eventually partnered. Lord Taylor, founder of Taylor Woodrow, came down to London in 1929 continuing to favour the Staffordshire clay tiles they had used in the North. 'Owen and his father came to say "why don't we use the Marley concrete tiles?" We said that concrete tiles break easily and that we wouldn't want his concrete tiles. Well, he said "We guarantee them, a long time, almost for life. Why not let us do a pair of houses for you". And they did and they were good, and the service was good and from then on we used nothing but Marley tiles, from 1931. They had it so well organised that when you wanted the tiles they were there waiting and the men came and put the roof on very quickly, very efficiently, very good workmanship.'

Marley's pre-eminence

There can be no doubt that Sir Owen had found a unique formula. He produced in volume, sold aggressively into one of Britain's most conservative industries and, as we saw earlier in the chapter, succeeded in increasing Marley's tile output from 30 million in 1930 to approaching 200 million before war broke out. It is less clear that Marley achieved the full financial returns that the Aishers' pioneering deserved. Under the contemporary Companies Acts there was no requirement for public companies to produce consolidated accounts and the surviving records do not provide a complete picture of Marley's financial performance. After the flotation, the new subsidiaries contributed additional profit flow but the older works at Harrietsham and Storrington were finding it harder to sustain their previous profitability. The peak year transpired to be 1937 but even with the benefit of substantially enhanced production capacity and a buoyant housing market, Marley's profits cannot have risen to much in excess of £100,000. The company's strategy was to run its manufacturing plants at full capacity and if that meant being aggressive on price, then so be it. Of course, not only had Marley's own capacity been doubled but there was a host of other manufacturers all seeking to capitalise on a product with high rate of growth and low capital cost of entry.

Marley's best known, and probably largest competitor, was The Redhill

Tile Company (now better known as Redland), formed in 1919 as one of several offshoots of The Concrete Tile Syndicate Limited. By the outbreak of war, Redhill had four concrete tile factories (at Redhill, Surrey; Syston, Leicestershire; Henshall, Yorkshire; and Belfast) but the company was barely into profit – the highest profit it made during the 1930s was £7,767.2s.1d in 1935.

The battle with Redhill Tile was particularly fierce, leading to suggestions that Marley tried to force Redhill out of business; even today, relationships between the two companies are reminiscent of the impact that the Wars of the Roses had on County cricket. But Redhill was only one of many competitors. The ready supply of the necessary technology helped: after Marley had developed its own tile making machinery, the engineering company Pegsons brought out a machine which it sold widely – to such names as Moorhouse, Anchor, Cam, Dri-roof, Ivor, Crendon and others. Competition inevitably intensified and although Marley again achieved record tile volumes in 1938, the Chairman reported that severe competition in many areas had forced Marley 'considerably to reduce their prices in order to maintain sales'. Indeed, having increased the dividend from 7½% to 8½% in 1937, the directors felt obliged to cut it to 6%; the next accounts were not drawn up until after the declaration of War and there were to be no further dividends for the duration.

The War

With the onset of the Second World War, new housebuilding came to an almost complete stop, roofing tile production ceased, and men were dispersed throughout the armed forces. Many of the men went back into the Navy from where Marley had originally recruited them. Jack Aisher served in the Army and, among the more interesting postings, Marley personnel provided the harbourmasters for both Gibraltar and Reykjavik. Some of the factories were requisitioned: Leighton Buzzard was taken over by the RAF; Harrietsham by the War Office for storage (Marley never found out what for) and Bedfont was used by Vickers Armstrong for armaments manufacture. The outlook was immediately perceived to be bleak. At the Holdings Board meeting on September 12th the directors decided 'with reluctance' that there could be no contribution to salaries of employees called up owing to 'the gradual cessation of our trading and the very grave doubt as to whether or not we will be able to collect amounts now due from customers'.

The factories that were left to Marley were all shut down and the remaining staff concentrated on collecting monies that were outstanding. The October Board meeting discussed customers' inability to pay and Sir Owen recommended that Marley 'negotiate with such customers for the purchase of any of their suitable properties'. In practice, this meant Marley doing deals with small builders and taking completed but unsold houses in payment. Sir Owen: 'Brother Dick and I went round and if they could not pay us and had a house half finished we took it. We took what we could get. We finished building the houses and we rented them; we had about two or three hundred.' After the war the other houses were finished and they and the rented houses gradually sold at a profit.

It did not take Marley long to start finding war work, first on a small scale with such products as concrete huts, shelters and concrete mats for hard standing for lorries and tanks. The first reference to war work is in the Marley Tile minutes of October 10th 1939, recording an agreement between Marley Tile and the British Concrete Corporation relating to the supply of Government air raid shelters. These were largely built for Wates who installed them for local councils. Next to follow were agricultural buildings and then anti-tank blocks. Fred Hardy remembers the invasion scare: 'The army wanted road blocks to stop the tanks. We were rung up and asked could we make them in 36 hours – they couldn't give us the timber licence for the moulds. We got some old packing cases for support and cut them to shape like a circular drum. We also had a sisal kraft paper (a bituminous waterproof paper) which we used to line the "moulds" to stop the cement leaking out. We spread sand on the floor of the concrete casting yard. We used Cement Fondu which achieved maximum strength after 24 hours. It was all arranged on the telephone – no contract and no price. When they were made the army came out on our lorries and we rolled them off from Essex to the Coast. It was our first rush job. We made them at Aveley and Sevenoaks and it lasted about 4 weeks. We also made mats to go on the front of tanks. They were used when going up beaches and they could be dropped in front of the tracks.'

Marley's leadership in the manufacture of concrete roof tiles provided it with considerable expertise in cast concrete manufacture, though of a very specialised kind. There had also been limited experience in block making. The technology of cold forming concrete in moulds was not complicated and Marley had made its own blocks when building the tile factories. Trianco block making equipment was purchased for the Riverhead factory at the end of 1939 and for Aveley two months later. Perhaps of greatest importance, Marley had become a member of the National Association of Cast Concrete Product Manufacturers in 1936. The members used to meet and parcel out the available Government work around the country. The amount of work received depended not just on the companies' technical competence but also their ability to find sufficient labour.

The Board minutes during 1940 contain frequent references to negotiations to obtain additional concrete technology and know-how. Indeed, during 1941 Marley made a number of patent applications for its own concrete products: the 'Marley Snug' Indoor Shelter, hollow block designs, and reinforced girders. These last two were patented jointly with a man called Steinhard. Steinhard had been a big builder in Vienna before the War and Sir Owen had met him there on one of his visits. At some point, Steinhard fled Austria and early in the war, Sir Owen gave him a job at Marley where he first patented a clay beam, pre-tensioned with steel. The beams fitted together to make a floor and a concrete screed was then laid over them to make a monolithic structure; however, sales were difficult to achieve and the product was soon abandoned. Steinhard was clearly more successful when he turned to concrete for by the time the concrete girders were patented in September 1941 he was trading as Steinhard & Co.

Further benefits accrued to Marley when Sir Owen visited the USA in May 1940 as part of a Government mission to study pre-stressed concrete technology and practice. Sir Owen's diaries provide a detailed record of a month's travels across the USA starting in New York with his old friend Jimmy Dunn and progressing through a range of block making companies. An important early contact was with the Besser Company, the leading manufacturer of block making machinery: 'Besser very nice man, a quiet thinker. Then to his house. New type block. Must get particulars.' A week later, Sir Owen was talking terms: 'Spoke about Royalty, 25 cents per square yard. Seemed keen. Wants $2,500 deposit with order.' Although Sir Owen got as far as talking to Jimmy Dunn about finance, there is no evidence that any deal was done though, after the war, Marley's Irish associate did buy a Besser block making machine – the first one to be imported to Europe. Other entries which will be of significance later in the story included a visit to the roofing tile manufacturer Ludowici-Celadon, and Sir Owen's first observation of the asphalt floor tile.

Not all the imaginative ideas worked. Sir Owen: 'In the first year of the War, Iorys Hughes [a yachting friend and consulting civil engineer] and I – he was the chap who built the tunnel under Hyde Park and the bridges on the M1 – we thought of building concrete ships. We travelled the country looking at all the old places where they had been built in World War One. It was the frozen winter of 1939/40, when the icicles hung off the trees; there was no coal, no food, it was terrible. Norman Wates knew Iorys and he got into it and they built a prototype up at Vickers, Barrow-in-Furness, and we made some pieces for it. When we went up and saw it there, well, they were building submarines... and they did not want our concrete thing, so we pulled it down and nothing really became of it.'

On more conventional lines, Marley continued to widen its product range and invest in new equipment, albeit modestly. During 1941, for instance, new beam equipment was installed at Riverhead and by the end of the year Marley was able to refer to its structural floor department. Acquisitions were also being sought. In the spring of 1942 Marley was inspecting the various works of Norcon with a view to its acquisition, though the proposal came to nothing. However, in September, Marley made what was to prove its most significant investment to date, Surrey Concrete.

Surrey Concrete was based in Guildford and was also doing work for the Cast Concrete Association. It was owned by Ernie Gates (of Cow & Gates) who professed little understanding or interest in the business. Fred Hardy remembers Ernie Gates saying 'if you take it off my hands you can have it for nothing. We took all the stock and raw materials at valuation, transferred some contracts from the Federation and took on more labour.' John Stoker, then Company Secretary, remembers it being a cheap purchase: 'We bought that for paying off their creditors. The accountants that were running the show didn't seem very interested in whoever was owning it; we got it for a song.' The site was only two-thirds of an acre, rented from the Loseley Estate (of ice cream and yoghurt fame) but Marley subsequently bought the freehold and substantial adjoining land. Guildford then became the base for the future Marley Concrete.

The Mulberry Harbour

As Marley developed its concrete capacity the projects became larger but the Company still worked closely with Wates. Thus, Marley made panels for concrete barges on the Thames and then a floating dock. All the component parts were made at the Poole factory which had to be extended to cope. The units were assembled by Wates on the Beaulieu River on a site where, by one of those strange ironies, Owen Aisher Junior now has his house. Finally, Marley worked on one of the war's largest construction projects – the 'Mulberry Harbour', used in the Normandy landings.

Without doubt, work on the Mulberry Harbour was Marley's largest wartime contract as it was for so many other building firms. Winston Churchill described the scale of the Mulberry project. 'The whole project involved the construction in Britain of great masses of special equipment, amounting in the aggregate to over a million tons of steel and concrete. This work, undertaken with the highest priority, would impinge heavily on our already hard-pressed engineering and ship-repairing industries... The whole project was majestic. On the beaches themselves would be the great piers, with their seaward ends afloat and sheltered. At these piers coasters and landing-craft would be able to discharge at all states of the tide. To protect them against the wanton winds and waves breakwaters would be spread in a great arc to seaward, enclosing a large area of sheltered water.'[9] Although the principle of a floating harbour had long been agreed, there was no shortage of ideas for its design and

---

9 *Winston Churchill,* The Second World War, *vol v, 1951.*

Mulberry harbour

construction. A final decision was not taken until the Quebec conference of Chiefs of Staff in August 1943 when the Americans conceded responsibility for the artificial harbours to the British.

Two harbours were built, one for the British troops, and the other for the Americans although the latter was severely damaged by freak storms shortly after D-Day. The main breakwater comprised blockships, old merchant vessels which were taken out and sunk on the spot, and concrete caissons which were built in Britain and towed across the Channel. The largest task facing the construction industry was to build the caissons (code-named 'Phoenix') which would be sunk to form part of the breakwater. 'The caissons varied in size from 60 to 200 feet in length and 25 to 60 feet in height'.[10] A team of 24 contractors led by Sir Robert McAlpine built over one million tons of these structures in only 26 weeks.

Within the protection of the breakwaters came the floating piers and roadways over which all the invasion support passed; these were code-named 'whales'. The individual bridge spans consisted of two 80-foot girders and a 10-foot wide roadway, weighing about 30 tons. There were 10 miles of these roadways and the bridge spans were connected to each other by flexible joints and supported on floats – pontoons of reinforced concrete code-named

10 *Guy Hartcup*, The Challenge of War: Scientific and Engineering Contribution to World War Two, *1970.*

beetles, which is where Marley comes in. In total, the Mulberry project called for 470 reinforced concrete beetles. The contracting firm responsible for the construction of the roadways appears to have been Wates and once again we find Marley working as a sub-contractor. Wates made most of the concrete beetles with Marley making the vibrated pre-cast concrete panels as designed by Messrs Mouchel & Partners.[11]

Fred Hardy stressed that, to Marley, the Mulberry Harbour was a top priority job. 'It was very quick and rushed. We had to make our own moulds and we set up our own mould making shop; they were all made out of timber because you couldn't get steel, well you couldn't get timber very easily. We made all the sections in pre-cast concrete and they were delivered down to the various sites and the contractors on the site would assemble them all in jigs and pour the concrete ribs into them to mould them all together as one unit. It had to be very high grade concrete: it had to pass a test of 5000 lb per square inch compressive strength for buffeting in the sea and protect the reinforcement from the corrosive action of the seawater.'

One of the more interesting moves that Marley made during this period was the purchase of Wellinlith which, as a manufacturer of wood wool slabs, did not immediately fit into the drive for cast concrete expertise. The business had been founded in August 1938 by two German Jewish refugees, brothers Herbert and Max Stern (with financial backing from other family members), and one Alfred Helmut Carl Kantorowicz. The wood wool product was a panel which had a core of shredded timber, treated with chemicals and coated with asbestos cement. Until acquired by Marley, all its output was distributed by Gliksten, the timber merchant, and used for partitioning and other lightweight construction. The company was never profitable; it was rift by dissension between the directors and within the family. They were clearly looking for buyers as a way out of their problems and their first contact with Marley was through Claude Hartley, one of the BAT directors. He first saw Wellinlith at the end of 1939 and the Holdings Board meeting of 2nd January 1940 agreed that O A Aisher should see the owners 'without delay to initiate negotiations for the acquisition of the business'.

The negotiations continued off and on through the early months of 1940 and Wellinlith was acquired in the April. Once within the Marley fold the relationships were no less tempestuous; there were soon disputes over service agreements and legal action was eventually taken against Max Stern in the closing stages of the War. In the meantime, the Welwyn factory was requisitioned by the Government and the plant moved to Storrington.

---

11 *Excellent further reading on the construction of the Mulberry Harbours is provided by articles written shortly after the war by two of the leading participants: Major W J Hodge, 'The Mulberry Invasion Harbours', The Structural Engineer, March 1946; and Sir George B White, 'The Mulberry Harbours', The Central, December 1946.*

Kantorowicz had left immediately after the acquisition and the link with Herbert Stern was ended after the war. At the end of 1945 Max Stern actually offered to buy Wellinlith back on what the minutes politely described as 'terms, judged to be inadequate'. The product was renamed Marlith and was manufactured until 1982. How that fitted into Marley's wartime production we will see later.

Side by side with the call on the building industry to support the war effort, where airfield construction and the invasion support stand out, was the mundane, but equally important, task of repairing bomb damage. It is self-evident that the main demand on Marley was for roofing. Surprisingly, Marley had no need to make tiles during the war; the Company had found itself with sufficient stock when demand collapsed at the onset of the war. Fred Hardy: 'We had a lot of the old sales managers that we retained; if they were over calling up age we kept them and they did all the bomb damage repairs. Their jobs were to get the tiling labour and use the materials that we could supply to repair the bomb damage.' One silver lining in the clouds of war was the demand for camouflage tiles. 'All we used to do was to mix the different coloured tiles together and dip them in a green solution to make them motley green; the more patchy it was the better they liked it and the more patchy it was the better we liked it because we could mix the different coloured tiles that we had, and get rid of them.'

Probably of more importance than domestic repairs was the need to keep Britain's factories in production and here Marley found an active use for its new wood wool slabs. 'We used to lay these 2-in. slabs in between T-beams (made at Burton) onto these factories; they were about three feet across and we would screed over the top and then felt over that and you had got a waterproof roof. It was lightweight, insulated and stopped condensation and if you didn't render the underneath it acted as an acoustic slab at the same time.'

The Wellinlith panels were to find another use in the closing stages of the war as part of the ubiquitous 'prefab'. A private company called Uni-Seco had the contract from the Government to produce the prefabs but, as Fred Hardy found 'they could not get anyone to make for them in sufficient quantities. They hadn't got the machines and were getting into trouble with the wrong material.' Marley offered to make all Uni-Seco wanted, provided they could get the timber, cement and asbestos (all licensed). 'At the peak we got up to 125 bungalows a week, and we were making the roof, the external panels and the internal partitions. We worked on a cost plus basis re-negotiated each six months with Marley getting half any savings if the price was lowered. We charged £62.10s all in at the end. They were all Government contracts and went on for two or three years.' This appears to have been the only Government contract which had any degree of pricing flexibility. All the other war work was cost investigated. Fred Hardy did much of the negotiating: 'All jobs, irrespective, were cost investigated. We were allowed 5% profit on turnover and no allowance was given for interest even if we had to borrow to finance it.' Even then, it does not look as if the money came in quickly: it was the 1946 accounts before the Company could take credit for the final £52,000 profit on its wartime contracts – a figure larger than any the annual profit earned in any of the war years.

Part 3
After the war: recovery and expansion

Roofing

In 1945, Percy Millard resigned as Chairman and from the Board owing to ill health. At 45, Sir Owen could no longer be regarded as too young and was appointed Chairman, then no more than a formal recognition of the role he had been fulfilling since the formation of the Public Company. His determination to develop new markets continued to be the driving force at Marley, behind which the provision of finance generally took second place – and sometimes a poor second at that. The post-war reconstruction of the roofing tile factories and the entry into the floor tile market were being undertaken at a time when Marley was still paying off its wartime arrears of preference dividends; with high rates of corporate taxation, retained profits were modest and the expansion of the business relied on support from the group's bankers – almost £400,000 at the year end of October 1948. The Chairman's statement the following July warned that, despite the bank's support 'the Company's activities have been hampered by lack of Working Capital.' However, the Aishers were not prepared to be limited and even their houses were mortgaged to secure sufficient funds to support the new flooring activities.

Restarting the roofing factories

Despite the entry of new firms into the market, the pre-war building boom had still finished with Marley as the dominant manufacturer of concrete roofing tiles, accounting for over 40% of the total market. The immediate post-war requirement was to claim the old roof tile factories back from their war footing as soon as possible and resume the physical expansion programme. The market, of course, also needed rebuilding. A housing industry which had averaged 350,000 completions a year in the five years before the war had all but vanished: resources, both financial and physical, were scarce and it was the local authorities who were used to rebuild; constrained by an elaborate system of materials and building licences, the private sector confined itself to little more than repairing the extensive war damage. Housing completions were no more than 55,000 in 1946, the first full year of peace, equally divided between the public and private sectors. From then, the housing market was unquestionably driven by the public sector – by the time the industry had reached its temporary peak of 228,000 in 1948, 84% of dwellings were completed by the local authorities. Theirs was the market that seemed ready made for Marley, offering large contracts which could be serviced by the in-house contracting force, and sensitive to competitive pricing.

Housing completions (000)

	Public	Private	Total
1946	25	30	55
1947	99	41	140
1948	195	33	228
1949	171	26	198
1950	171	27	198

Source: Department of the Environment

The resumption of normal working in the roofing tile factories was not immediate. Demand was not there at pre-war levels and production and tiling labour had to be integrated back into the business. Beneficial though the continuation of the wartime Uni-Seco contract was, it had the disadvantage that it competed for Marley labour. The Marley Tile Company minutes of April 1946 state that labour was still being switched from the Uni-Seco contract and plans were outlined 'to put Harrietsham, Leighton Buzzard and Bedfont factories into production at the soonest possible date'. Marley had only regained its Leighton Buzzard factory from the Air Force in February. In May, the Board was discussing Jack Aisher's report on the minimum rehabilitation requirements of the existing factories 'bearing in mind that the estimated amount of monies available for these schemes, including new factories, will not exceed £100,000'.

The war had prevented Glasgow coming fully on stream and that became an immediate priority. Archie Orme remembers Glasgow as a difficult factory: 'if you sent an Englishman up there it never seemed to work. We had a lot of bother there until we found a good Scottish manager. I said I would interview the applicants at the Delamere works. There was a rail strike and when I got there, there were three telegrams saying "Can't come" but Bob Summers came down by taxi and we gave him the job. He'd got the will to win; from then on Glasgow never looked back.'

Concrete products: a wartime legacy

The requirements of a war economy had forced Marley into a wide range of concrete products, other than its traditional roofing tile, and although its particular product lines were no longer required after 1945, the new concrete technology which had been amassed during the war years remained with Marley. The restoration of concrete tile production remained the priority but Surrey Concrete continued producing its agricultural buildings, supplying them for industrial use as well. Indeed, Marley itself became a customer with its new Delamere factory. In 1946, Marley introduced a new range of products designed to serve the farmer, including silos, cattle troughs and even mangers; Marley was prepared to look in all directions for the right products.

In July 1947, Marley recruited Bill Courtney, another executive with a naval background, having been an officer in the Royal Marines. Bill Courtney was eventually to rise through Marley to become Deputy Chairman. 'I was in the Royal Marines, Commandos, as a young officer and at that time Marley were looking to regenerate the business after the war. I think Sir Owen particularly, because of his sailing connections, felt they were the right sort of type to take the business forward. At that time they had a retired colonel who was selecting chaps and I was offered a job very quickly – in July 1947. I was based at Poole as a sales representative on about £6.10s a week and £4.15s a week car allowance because the company in those days did not provide motor cars. I was sent to Exmouth to be trained for one week only, even though I had not been in the building materials and construction industry before. I reported to a senior Marley rep, who based his office at the Conservative Club by the billiard table where there was a telephone; because roof tiles were short and petrol was also short he tended to take the orders in the Conservative Club which was very comfortable and convenient – saved petrol and saved his time rushing about the hills of Devon. So I had a week's training with "Mac", mostly playing snooker and billiards. Thereafter, I was made the roof tile representative in Dorset, part of Wiltshire and a little bit of Devon. It wasn't

Bill Courtney

long before *Yeoman I*, which was a very nice ketch, appeared in Poole Harbour and I had a 'phone call from Harry Hale who was my boss and the brother-in-law of Sir Owen saying would I crew in *Yeoman I*. We raced in *Yeoman I* on a number of occasions. Then after about a year, during which I had married, I had a call to say would I go to Guildford to be the Sales Manager of a company called Surrey Concrete.'

When Courtney arrived at Guildford, he found a small operation employing around 10 people. Gradually, the loss making products were phased out and newer ones added, often using the expertise that Marley had gained from its wartime concrete structures. One of their main contracts was Ministry of Works huts, made to a standard size – 24 ft. span concrete frame buildings – and they could be developed into other markets. Fred Hardy negotiated a contract with the GPO for pre-cast concrete roof structures, to go into their new telephone exchanges, timber still being rationed then. Bill Courtney: 'These were little buildings that you still see around the countryside, brick walls, the roof is made Marley concrete trusses.' Useful though that work was, the breakthrough was the adaptation of the concrete structures to produce prefabricated garages. This catered simply for the growing private car ownership in the days before integral garages became a feature of new house construction, and the garages were sold both to members of the public directly and to builders. Although the local authorities were the main customers, a prefabricated garage was acceptable in all walks of life in those early days. *Marley News* of January 1958 has a photograph of Field Marshall Viscount

Montgomery and his Marley garage

Montgomery of Alamein standing proudly by his new Marley garage at his home in Alton.

Modelled on the successful roofing strategy, Marley garages inevitably became a supply and fix operation. Bill Courtney: 'We found builders took so long, understandably because they were not familiar, whereas our chaps could come and put up a Marley double garage weighing 8 tons and tile the roof and go away with your tip in their hand after 2 days. A builder would still be struggling after a week. The contract labour were full-time employees, guaranteed time and a quarter. This really stemmed from the teaching of Sir Owen. When I arrived as a new boy one was always taught that builders' merchants weren't really the sort of people that we should deal with, we could go direct to the customer as soon as possible.'

Roofing expansion – the third wave

Further expansion was already in train before the war in addition to Glasgow; extensive surveys of sand had been undertaken around the Bridgend area in 1938 and in the same year planning permission had also been granted for a factory at Woodford in Cheshire, to the south of Manchester. Woodford had been left in abeyance as war threatened and it was never taken any further; indeed, no one even seems able to remember it now. Instead, Marley went a few miles to the west to Delamere near Chester. It was another instance of the Aishers' determination to let nothing stand in their way that three further factory sites had been secured during the war. In July 1943 Marley bought the plant of the Delamere Gravel & Sand Company; the agreement to buy 150 acres of farmland at Beenham in Berkshire was reached in April 1944 although it was not actually purchased until the summer of 1946; and in February 1943, negotiations began on the purchase of a six acre site at Clay Hill, Bristol, but although the land was bought in June 1944, it was never used as it was considered that Bridgend and Beenham could cover the area effectively.

Delamere was the first new plant to start in December 1947. Its existence was due to a man named Rex Foster who used to work for the Liverpool Artificial Stone Company. Sir Owen had met him through the then Cast Concrete Products Association and given him a job during the war to capitalise on his knowledge of concrete products. Foster knew H M Devereux who had a site in Delamere and wanted to sell it; there was little more there than an old sand plant, an old shed and a weighbridge, and a lease from the Crown Commissioners. Bridgend, in Glamorgan, was the next plant to be brought into production, in March 1950, and a second line was installed in 1952. However, it never grew beyond that in size. The idea then was to have strategic plants to minimise the substantial haulage costs but, as the big automatic plants came in during the 1960s, reducing production costs, and the motorway network developed, haulage became less important.

Dick Aisher had always wanted to have a plant in the North East. Marley had been selling tiles into the Newcastle area from its Glasgow and Burton plants but was facing local competition. In September 1951 they bought the lease on a sand pit at Newlands (near Ebchester in Northumberland). It had been owned by the Ayton brothers who were in debt to the bank; one of them left but Willie stayed on as foreman. There were immediate problems as Marley was unable to secure planning permission for a factory. However, it was still licensed as a sand pit so the area intended to take the foundations was systematically cleared of sand and sold. When the building licence was finally obtained it took only five months and £30,000 capital to have the factory operational. Production started in March 1953 and within months additional plant needed to be ordered.

With Delamere, Bridgend and Ebchester successively under construction, Beenham was kept on hold. The site had been found by Ben Rees during the war; it was owned by a brewer named Strange who had the misfortune to be run down and killed by a bus while out shopping. (Ben Rees himself had been recruited by Claude Hartley when they found themselves sitting next to each other on a each during a pre-war holiday.) Construction eventually began in September 1953 and roof tiles came off the line in July 1954.

Within ten years of the war ending, Marley's third round of factory building had been completed and additional machine lines had also been added to existing factories. Capacity had reached around 650 million plain tile equivalent compared with around 200 million before the war.

The new factories were still built with an eye to the cost saving which had characterised pre-war construction. As before the war, the first factories were built using direct labour. However, instead of the previous steel framed construction, Marley switched to concrete, a natural development of Surrey Concrete's expertise. Jack Aisher: 'We had created a small contract business within Marley Concrete, as it became. They went and put the frame up and then we hired a local builder to come and do the infilling.' The component parts were probably not too dissimilar to the agricultural buildings that Marley had developed.

Marley roof tile factories and their capacities, 1954

		Year Opened	Plain	Ludlow/ Anglia	Large Tiles	Total P.T.E.*
Pre-war	Leighton Buzzard	1927	12.0	–	7.0	54
plants	Storrington	1927	12.0	7.0	–	36
	Aveley	1935	12.0	7.0	–	36
	Riverhead	1935	12.0	7.0	7.0	78
	Burton	1935	12.0	14.0	7.0	102
	Poole	1937	12.0	–	7.0	54
Post-war	Glasgow	1945	12.0	7.0	–	36
Plants	Delamere	1947	12.0	7.0	–	36
	Bridgend	1950	12.0	–	7.0	54
	Ebchester	1953	12.0	–	7.0	54
	Beenham	1954	–	–	7.0	42
	Total		120.0	49.0	49.0	582

Capacity millions

*Note: *Plain tile equivalent; all figures based on single shifts running at speeds of 48 tiles per minutes.*

As well as new capacity coming in, Marley was also taking old production out. Some of that was Marley's own. Harrietsham, where it all started, was on the way out as a roof tile works before the war and Bedfont, which was only a rented factory and unmodernised, closed as a production unit in the spring of 1949. Marley had been making pre-cast concrete unit (e.g. shelters) on the Bedfont site before it was requisitioned by Vickers and after the war continued making concrete units. By then, the site was not economic for mechanised roof tile production; unfortunately, the contract with the freeholder was drawn up to provide him with a share of roof tile profits. 'So to make it legal we produced handmade tiles and fittings but it didn't make any money so we handed it back', recalled Fred Hardy.

Most of the closures were of competitors' factories that Marley had deliberately bought for that purpose. An obvious benefit was to remove locally aggressive competition but Marley was also concerned that some of the smaller companies were producing a low quality product that reflected on all concrete tiles. Thus, Shurdcrete (Shurdington near Cheltenham) was bought in 1950 for around £4,500; the roof tile line closed but the site was developed as a factory for the concrete products company. Buckland Tile Company of Reigate was in a similar condition and was taken out in 1952; Marley tried to get permission to use it for concrete products but without success.

The Macmillan boom

Ironically, the year of Beenham's opening, 1954, proved a post-war peak in the housebuilding industry; the Conservative Government had delivered the famous 300,000 houses a year – and more. At the opening of Parliament on October 31st 1950, Winston Churchill gave notice of his Party's intention to move a vote of censure on the Labour Government for its housing record, maintaining that it was possible to build houses at a rate of 300,000 a year. Ernest Marples moved the amendment and the Conservatives' housing target became a key issue in the coming election campaign. In October 1951, Churchill formed a Conservative administration with Harold Macmillan as Housing Minister. In a speech to the House of Commons on November 13th, Macmillan reaffirmed Churchill's statement in the Manifesto that housing would have a priority second only to defence and that the target remained 300,000 houses a year. A dismantling of the range of wartime controls on planning and building materials, including the licensing of timber and steel, and coming after ten years of only minimal private housebuilding, provided the requisite conditions for a boom.

The Macmillan boom: housing starts and completions (000)

Year	Starts		Completions	
	Public	**Private**	**Public**	**Private**
1950	184	20	171	27
1951	192	27	172	23
1952	242	52	206	34
1953	265	83	256	63
1954	223	107	257	91

Source: Department of the Environment

By 1954, total housing completions of 348,000 were back up to the record levels achieved in the late 1930s and were not to be matched again for a full ten years. Indeed, the temporary excess of production capacity that Beenham created gave rise to some discussion on the possibility of closing Leighton Buzzard. The year 1954 therefore offers a useful vantage point to assess how far Marley and its competitors had succeeded in displacing the traditional roofing products.

GB roof tile production (000 squares)

	1938	1946	1947	1948	1949	1950	1951	1952	1953	1954 (estimated)
Concrete tiles	960	341	637	824	818	837	955	1,256	1,825	2,049
Clay tiles	1,512	518	788	842	753	697	641	718	806	818
Roofing slates	661	276	252	328	311	300	280	278	262	250
	3,133	1,135	1,677	1,994	1,882	1,834	1,876	2,252	2,893	3,117
Concrete, as %	30.6	30.0	38.0	41.3	43.5	45.6	50.9	55.8	63.1	65.7
c.f. GB housing completions										
(000 units)	359	138	186	246	198	198	195	240	319	348

Source: Department of the Environment

Once the concrete producers had retrieved their factories from the wartime uses, they were able to respond rapidly to the demands of the housing market. The clay producers seemed slower. Of course, they had longer making times but it has also been suggested that they were keen on preserving their clay reserves.

The concrete tile manufacturers overtook the traditional clay companies in 1949 and by 1951 accounted for over half the pitched roof market (as defined by totalling concrete, clay and slate). Within that, Marley was increasing its share of concrete. In August 1948 the Holding Company accounts reported that 'by additional and improved mechanical means of production and... new factories, we have been able to increase our productive capacity considerably above our pre-war output.' As can be seen from the table above, that was not true for the concrete industry as a whole and Marley must have been increasing its market share.

Detailed production statistics for Marley during this period are no longer available but in May 1951, the Holding Company accounts were claiming over 25% of the new roofing market which would have been equivalent to around half the market for concrete roofing tiles or some 250 million plain tile equivalent. The next clue is in Board minutes which gave September 1953 output as in excess of 50 million plain tile equivalent or an annualised rate of

600 million. This would have included Ebchester but was prior to Beenham. The actual figure for the full year would presumably have been less than this annualised rate but it still implies a share of some 50–55% of the concrete tile market.

Technical consolidation

Technical and marketing changes during this dash for growth were marginal. Indeed, why should they have changed? Resources after the war were limited; Marley had developed a formula which earned it the dominant position in the roofing industry; the priority was to create the new capacity fast enough to sustain that domination. The tile machines themselves changed little for perhaps 15 to 20 years after the war. There was always pressure to make heavier duty machines to reduce breakages and downtime. Machine speeds, which had been around 36 pallets (two plain tiles) a minute were still at that level at the start of the 1950s slowly rising to 48 and then 52. The most important change within the factories was the successful development of conveyorisation.

Bill Borgia remembers the first conveyor going in at Glasgow just before the war: 'Glasgow just about got its wheels turning before September 3rd when it immediately stopped – they didn't really have time to run it long enough to test the system'. In fact, it never did work and was eventually removed. The plant had gone beyond the first stages of conveyorisation and attempted to anticipate the automatic racking that was not introduced until the 1960s. Fred Hardy: 'We ordered it from an engineering firm which guaranteed that they would make it work and the contract said if it didn't they would take it back. The conveyor system picked pallets off the machine and took them overhead to feed into racks to go into the tunnel. The tunnels were even made into separate little cubicles. But it never worked; the engineers took it back.'

Instead of the ambitious Glasgow plant, a more limited but nevertheless extensive programme of conveyorisation was implemented; this confined itself to linking the tile making machines with the curing tunnels but no further. Archie Orme: 'In 1946 all the foreman fitters were brought in from the works to build all the conveyors under old Charlie Randall. That was the first part of conveyorisation – all the machines were conveyorised from the machine to the tunnel. Instead of the takers off working at the end of the [tile] machine, they would work in the tunnels.' Conveyorisation from the curing tunnels and automatic racking did not come for another 15 years.

The typical Marley concrete tile plant in the mid-1950s could therefore be described as semi-automatic. Summarised simply, the tile line was laid out in the form of a loop with the tiles leaving the tile machine on a conveyor to the curing tunnel. The tiles were placed manually in racks and the next day the dry tiles were removed from the racks and placed back onto the conveyor. The tiles could then be separated from the pallet, thus leaving the pallet on the conveyor to be automatically fed back into the tile machine extruder. The tile extruder, which was a continuous process was of a "press plate" type. The alternative technology was the "roller and slipper" which was then used by Redland and all the smaller tile manufacturers; it was adopted by Marley in the mid-1960s.

Marley had developed its press plate system in the 1930s – described by Trevor Aisher as 'a belt and braces system. There was a simple roller which rolled the concrete on to the pallet and then it was extruded or squeezed through under a solid plate. The idea was that you created so much pressure under that plate, 90 tons per square inch, that you produced a very dense piece of concrete.' In effect this was an automatic version of the old single press system. The roller and slipper system operated on different principles. The tile machine had a very small roller which pulled the concrete mix down on to the pallet. The shaped slipper forms the upper profile of the tile, the lower profile being formed by the pallet. 'The theory was that because you were pre-forming the material the wear on the plant was less whereas with our system all the pressure took place under the plate so the wear was greater. The difference was that we could make our plates out of case hardened steel which was very cheap; [the roller and slipper plates] were special steel and cost three or four times as much.' Trevor Aisher argued that both systems worked equally well at the machine speeds then ruling but under the higher speeds that were later possible, the slipper and roller process gave a better control over the extrusion process and the shaping of the tile profile.

After the tiles had been extruded, they passed through the slurry box and then the granulator (to apply the surface colouring) on to a two-wire conveyor belt, supported on little wheels. On either side of the conveyor were fixed racks to hold the green tiles, 4 rows deep and 22 rows high. The racks were encased in 22-foot long tunnels made of Uni-Seco insulating panels and under each rack was a purpose built curing coil, like a large radiator. The tiles were taken off the conveyor manually by teams of three men; when the rack was full a curtain was pulled down, the heating turned on and the tiles left to cure. The curing time was 24 hours but if a night shift was operating, then half that. The racking stations extended down the conveyor line and around the bend with the teams of men leapfrogging each other. After curing, the tiles were manually removed from the racks and placed back on the conveyor from where they went into the de-palleter which, as the name suggests, parted the tile from the pallet; the empty pallets then completed their circuit on the conveyor back to the tile extruder. The tiles were then unloaded manually by another team of three men and stacked on a barrow. This was towed into the outside curing yard by little diesel tugs where yet another three man team would manually unload and stack them.

Although the manufacturing was fully automatic, the subsequent curing and handling was labour intensive in the extreme. As the business developed, Marley generally had each tile line dedicated to one profile. So most of the factories, even the small ones, would have three lines with larger ones like Burton and Delamere having four making anything between 36 and 52 tiles a minute. 'We were therefore totally dependent on a large labour force which at the time was a very effective way of making concrete tiles; efficiencies never went below 90% because we were relying on men not machines – it was a simple process but very efficient.'[1]

New profiles

The technology may have changed after the war but the marketing followed the same pre-war principles. Marley resumed its supply and fix selling policy which, before the war, had accounted for all but a few per cent of its output. The Company was still actively having to promote the concrete tile as the preferred roofing product and an essential part of that strategy had always been the capacity to deliver the complete roof to the builder. Marley still saw no reason to place the company's future in the hands of the more traditionally oriented roofing contractors or merchants.

The range of tiles offered was beginning to widen. So far, the description of Marley's activities has implied that the concrete tile was a standard product. The concrete tile was, of course, introduced as a substitute for the clay tile; concrete was sold on the basis of cost and reliability, not alternative designs. Thus, for most of its life, the concrete tile has been designed to look as much like its clay precursor as possible. The clay tile was made in widely different profiles, and to begin with the concrete product did no more than replicate the traditional product. Clay tiles were originally designed in three main patterns – the small plain tile; the pantile (originally single lap but then interlocking) and the Double Roman (flat with a roll in the middle and at the two sides; in laying, the side roll laps over the side roll of the adjoining tile) – and these determined the subsequent profiles adopted by the concrete tile manufacturers.

The plain tile relies for its waterproofing on extensive vertical overlapping; they are never laid with less than two thicknesses of tile at any point in the roof. By its nature, the plain tile comes in only one style. All other tiles are lapped tiles with different systems of lapping and wide variety of style. Single lap tiles are laid mainly in one thickness thereby reducing the cost and weight of the roof. Like plain tiles, single lap tiles have a top and bottom overlap but much shallower; they also have a narrow overlap at the side. There is also a side lock or other device at the side to prevent water penetration. The pantile is the traditional form of single lap tile in Europe and the tile from which

1   *Trevor Aisher interview.*

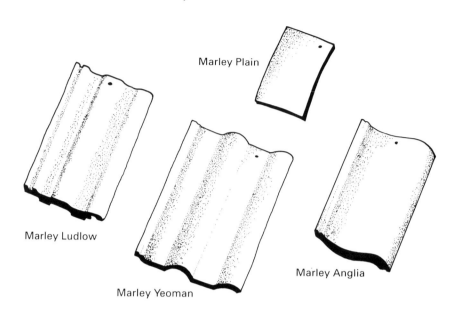

Marley Plain

Marley Ludlow

Marley Yeoman

Marley Anglia

Early Marley roof tiles

most modern single lap tiles develop. It is about twice the size of the plain tile and covers three times as much surface when laid; the pantile's profile is best described as a very flattened 'S' shape. Finally there are what are generally described as interlocking tiles, which are designed to give the maximum degree of weather resistance.

Marley Tile had modelled its first tile on the traditional plain tile and confined itself to that one profile for a decade; its concrete tile was based on the traditional 10½ × 6½ inch clay tile with an 11 × 7 inch as an extra. The early colours were variations of red but gradually extended and in time appeared in Cotswold Grey, Light Grey, Purple Grey and Dapple Green, either straight or cross cambered. In contrast to Marley's concentration on the plain tile, Redland chose to introduce the interlocking design but it was not until 1935 that Marley produced an interlocking tile, the 15 × 9 inch Ludlow, at its new Burton works. With the success of the Ludlow, the range was soon widened and by the time war came, Marley was offering a 16¼ × 13¾ Roman tile; a Bold Roll Old English Pantile (15 × 10¾); a Mendip "very bold roll" (16⅞ × 13½); and a Cubana Tile (17 × 8½).

After the initial post-war reconstruction period, the emphasis swung further towards the interlocking tile. One of Marley's most successful tiles, based on a double roman tile made by hand before the war, was the interlocking Yeoman (named after Sir Owen's yacht). It was introduced at Bishopbriggs in June 1952 and then manufactured at Leighton Buzzard in

October. At 16½ × 13¼ inches, it was 60% larger than the Anglia and Ludlow single lap tiles; it had particular production advantages as it could be made on the same line as the plain tile where two 6½ inch width tiles could be neatly replaced by one Yeoman. The Yeoman name assumed a prominence in yachting circles as Sir Owen also used the name for a succession of his yachts, until in 1983 the ruling body finally realised that one of its members was racing under a trade name. Something had to give: the Yeoman tile was renamed Double Roman, the generic name for that style of profile; the Yeoman yachts sailed on. Before the Yeoman was marketed, Marley had introduced the Anglia pantile at Storrington and that too proved to be one of the Company's long standing profiles. The main lines therefore became the Plain, Ludlow, Yeoman and Anglia, although Marley also offered the Roman, Mendip, Old English Pantiles and Cubana Spanish Pattern that had been available before the war.

The profits flow

The financial benefits to Marley in this period were considerable and it reaped the benefits of its market dominance. The figures below do not relate solely to the concrete roof tile business but also include the contracting activities of the flooring business. The high contracting element within Marley Tile always produced margins on turnover lower than would be expected from a pure manufacturing operation but, by the end of the period, Marley Tile was earning a return of around 50% on its fixed assets and was close to achieving a pre-tax profit of £1 million – a far cry from its pre-war struggle to sustain £100,000.

Marley Tile accounts (£000)

	1945	1946	1947	1948	1949	1950	1951	1952	1953	1954
Fixed assets	190	235	453	491	510	549	650	1,311	1,626	1,863
Sales	N/A	N/A	1,601	2,230	2,530	3,368	4,184	5,711	7,614	8,773
Pre-tax profits	38	89*	86	155	181	201	186	346	851	935
Profit margins, %			5.4	7.0	7.2	6.0	4.4	6.1	11.2	10.7

includes £52,000 final settlement of wartime contracts

It was at the end of this period of rapid growth for Marley, that Redland began to emerge as a serious competitor. Barely profitable before the war, Redhill Tile had merged with two other small concrete tile companies at the end of 1945: Timsbury Tile with works near Southampton, Bristol and Farnham; and Moorhouse Brick Tile & Concrete Products which possessed extensive sand deposits at Westerham. The Company's name was changed at that stage to Redland. The acquisition of a further works at Stockton-on-Tees followed in 1948 and, like Marley, Redland also modernised its productive capacity. By 1954/55, Redland Tile's profits before tax had reached £164,000 out of a group total of £271,000, still substantially smaller than Marley, but soundly based and already possessing tile interests in Germany and South Africa. During 1955, the Redland business was 'reversed' into the Bursledon Brick Company to give Redland a Stock Exchange quotation, and the base for a substantial acquisition programme.

The Little Man – Marley becomes a flooring company

Marley's post-war entry into the flooring market typified the Aisher approach to business. It combined an insight into the future of the housing market; the opportunistic recognition of, and capitalisation on, what was being achieved in other countries; and a determination to succeed unchecked by any initial lack of expertise. The decision to make asphalt, and then plastic, floor tiles had consequences far beyond the narrow confines of that particular product: it provided the base for Marley's rapid international expansion; and it took the Company into extrusions, particularly the rainwater goods market, and into plastics for the motor industry. Ultimately it was to prove a market with limited long term potential as rising standards drew the consumer into more luxurious floorings and left the plastic flooring industry with damaging overcapacity. A generation later, this European overcapacity left Marley facing one of its toughest challenges – but first we must pay tribute to the success story that plastic flooring initially became.

An introductory comment on the asphalt tile is appropriate before we take the story further. Asphalt itself is a compound made by mixing 10–12% of bitumen with limestone; the mix is dough-like when hot and is widely used for road surfacing, roofing and dampcoursing. The asphalt floor tile was developed in the USA by rolling asphalt into a sheet and cutting it into tiles. To give the product some flexing strength a low grade fibre was added and there was also an inorganic filler for bulk. The product was coal black. However, by using a naturally occurring binder from Utah called Gilsonite, brown, dark red and muddy green colours could be made. As the demand for brighter colours increased, the bitumen was replaced by coumarone (a lightly-coloured thermoplastic resin) still using Gilsonite for the darker colours. Machinery similar to that used in the rubber industry was employed.

Prior to the introduction of the asphalt, or thermoplastic tile as it was also known, the resilient flooring market had been dominated by linoleum and the cheaper printed felt-base flooring of which Congoleum was the best known name. The felt base flooring comprised a bituminised paper felt on which was spread paint; another decorative paint layer was printed on top and a protective finish then applied. This latter product was inexpensive but as the protective finish was thin it was only used where the traffic was light or at the poorer end of the market. By the time thermoplastic flooring was being introduced after the war the standard for resilient flooring was undoubtedly linoleum and, it remained so until the early 1960s, especially in the retail market when its greater widths and colour range were finally overtaken by vinyl sheet flooring. Linoleum, which is based on linseed oil, was developed in Britain in the 1860s largely through the work of Frederick Walton who built his first factory in Staines. Trade in the new product was initially slow 'and it was not until Walton opened a linoleum shop in London to display his goods that things began to look up'[2] – an interesting forerunner of Marley's marketi method! In 1877, Michael Nairn & Company built its first linoleum factory to become the dominant UK producer in the industry and eventually, though belatedly, a direct competitor of Marley.

Marley had had some involvement with floor tiles before the war, though not asphalt. Hans Berger had made marble patterned terrazzo tiles in Czechoslovakia where Sir Owen had first met him in 1934. Berger came to the UK in 1938 and Sir Owen offered him a job at £400 a year letting him live at one of the cottages at Faygate (Sir Owen's home).[3] By that time, Marley had stopped making roof tiles at Harrietsham and Hans Berger set about getting presses and sieves to make his tiles. The mix was marble dust, cement and sand with the patterns formed by the stainless steel mould. It came to nothing but it did provide a valuable planning precedent after the war.

Another early flirtation with flooring is indicated by the Marley Holdings Board minutes of January 2nd 1940 when 'Mr O A Aisher reported on his further investigations into the product "Flexoleum" and submitted samples and after a general discussion thereon it was agreed that we were interested in this product and that we should arrange for its manufacture for a trial period of three months during which time Mr Bond, the present proprietor, should be engaged by us for this purpose at a weekly wage of £8–0–0. Subject to the trial proving successful a Company should be formed at a later date to exploit this product in which Mr Bond should be given a share interest of from 10–15%.' Nothing else was ever recorded of Mr Bond or his product.

Lessons from America

Five months after that Board minute, Sir Owen was in the USA on behalf of the Government to see what the Americans were doing in pre-stressed concrete.

2   *Augustus Muir*, Nairns of Kirkcaldy: A Short History 1847–1956, *Cambridge, 1956.*
3   *Marley Tile (Holding) Company minutes, 1938.*

Again before the war, Sir Owen had been building houses in the New York area; this was in a private capacity and in partnership with Leo Meyer (Ideal Building), Godfrey Mitchell (Wimpey) and Taylor Woodrow. It was there that he had first seen the asphalt tile though with no immediate effect. On his 1940 visit to the houses the partnership was building he again saw the floor tiles but this time the response was more positive: 'I saw them in a porch on a house we built. I said to Les Turner "what is that?" "Oh, that is a new thing over here. We don't use quarries, we use these." So I said have you got any samples? I took them back and as the War progressed I could see that there was going to be no wood and they were building houses with concrete floors.'[4]

Sir Owen recognised not only the simple fact that people would need something to put on those concrete floors, but also that the post-war rebuilding of Britain would need high-rise housing – just as many dwelling units as the pre-war estate building but far fewer roofs. Sir Owen: 'Roofing had its limits... and if you follow the thing logically, we got into floors because, let's be clear, we had enough sense and knowledge to know that to rebuild London you had to go up. That was tried out before the war, so we knew immediately that we wouldn't be selling roof tiles to them.' Sir Owen's foresight had to be tempered by short term practicalities. Fred Hardy well remembers Sir Owen's return from America and his own reaction: 'He came back and he said to me, "there's going to be a shortage of timber after the war and these Americans, Johns-Manville, are making an asphalt floor tile." We were too busy looking after the war and trying to keep our heads above water, so I never paid any attention.'

The idea would not go away, however, and in March 1945, as hostilities were drawing to a close, Sir Owen returned to the USA. The introduction to his diary states flooring as one of the three reasons for the visit. 'I wanted to investigate the manufacture of asphalt floor tiles. Samples of these have been at Riverhead since my last visit in 1940 but owing to the War, it was felt that we could do nothing in regard to the matter. I thought in 1940, however, that it was a business we should know more about and, if possible, manufacture the tiles ourselves.' The extracts which follow give a clear idea of Sir Owen's approach.

'Before leaving for America, I contacted Messrs Johns-Manville who are large manufacturers with an office in this country. I saw these people several times and visited their main factory at Manville, New Jersey [there follows a description of the plant with measurements]. I contacted various other manufacturers whilst I was in America and am in communication with a firm called Flintkote who have representatives in this country. I am continuing my negotiations with them.

---

4 *Sir Owen Aisher interview.*

'Messrs Johns-Manville generally have a policy whereby they are prepared to take an interest in projects in countries abroad on the basis that they put no money into the concern but they be given an interest of, say, 20% or 25% of the ordinary stock and a royalty on the turnover. The figure of 25% of the ordinary stock and 5% of the selling price was named to me – I said I thought we would agree to the principle but that we were not likely to agree the amount and further, were they prepared to consider no stock interest but a straight royalty? They said that they would be prepared to do so and are sending full particulars and data through their London Office to me and I will let you know more of this in due course. Substantially, however, the money required to erect a plant, including the building and machinery and some money for the purpose of stocks would be £100,000.

'Messrs Johns-Manville manufacture an excellent product, no better maybe than some others in the United States, but we should consider very carefully whether it would be worth our while to pay a royalty and have the benefit of their experience and knowledge for a number of years, as from what I saw I believe that with intense application and effort we could find out how to make the tiles for ourselves. We should certainly be able to get someone in America who would give us some information and perhaps eventually we could find a man willing to assist us. On the other hand, it is a comparatively new business, i.e. about 10 years old and the established firms would undoubtedly have the best people. The machinery used is a combination of that used in the rubber industry and linoleum industry.

'The product ready for sale is not dear; it varies between 7 to 15 cents per square foot according to colours and the business is growing at a rapid rate.

'I saw one of the big linoleum manufacturers in America, Messrs Sloane Blaybon; I had a long talk with their President, whom I had met socially. He said they had commenced manufacture as they felt that in time the asphalt floor business was going to affect the linoleum business very considerably. The Armstrong Cork Company are also large linoleum manufacturers in America and they are also producing asphalt floor tiles.

'From what I saw, I think this is a business we should and must get into as soon as possible – we should be the first in this country to do so as it has enormous possibilities and scope and it will certainly be a business which will go on for many, many years and it does not depend entirely for a market on new houses being built. I will report in some detail in regard to this when I receive the Johns-Manville information and again later when I hear from Flintkote, but from now on I think we should be very active in regard to this matter. Samples will be available at Riverhead, together with literature.'[5]

It is clear that Johns-Manville expected to agree some form of licence

---

5 *Sir Owen Aisher Diaries, 1945.*

arrangement and had given Sir Owen access to the factory on that basis. Equally, one can only presume that they thought that showing an Englishman around the factory a couple of times was hardly sufficient to allow him to go back across the Atlantic and start up in a completely new industry. Little did they know Sir Owen. 'Our friends in France, Eternit, did take out a licence with Johns-Manville, but we never did. They were always friendly about it; but I went and saw it but never did [take out a licence].'[6] In fact Johns-Manville seemed surprisingly relaxed about it, later becoming partners with Marley in more than one overseas venture.

Can we make it work?

Following his stay in the USA, Sir Owen visited the Building Research Centre at Garston where he had long discussions with two of their Scientific Officers, Fitzmaurice and Brady, and the more he talked to them, the more he began to think Marley could go it alone with the right technical support. Eventually Sir Owen went to see C J Mole, then the Director of The Directorate of Works at the Ministry of Works, and said simply 'we need somebody'; as a result Laurence Brady joined Marley becoming Technical Director in June 1945.

The Aisher family was committed to enter this new flooring market but this was one of the rare occasions when the BAT directors took a different view. It was a view which led to the family becoming directly interested in the flooring business and to some recriminations later when Marley eventually bought in the shares it did not own. Fred Hardy recalls the Board Meeting when Sir Owen announced that Marley was going into floorings: 'At first everybody said that it was a good idea but then the non-family directors asked about finance and said that Marley ought to concentrate on the business it knows. The outside directors said that they didn't think that we could finance it. Owen said "We are going to do it – or we will do it as a family." Sir Owen said that Jack would resign from Marley and be the full-time manager of the floorings business.' Jack Aisher remembers even now 'We felt very strongly, I felt very strongly, there was a future for this, and the Board didn't.' But the BAT directors also found the idea of a family split unappealing and in the end a compromise was reached in that the family agreed to raise the finance, but Marley Tile and the family would share the equity. Jack Aisher: 'Owen mortgaged Faygate; I mortgaged my house; Dick mortgaged his. We sank everything we had into it and it looked as if we were going to lose everything. We lost it all in the first year and put more in – borrowed up to the hilt.' Jack Aisher had to go to Lloyds Bank to secure further funds for the family's investment. Other directors had also invested money and when The Marley

---

6   *Sir Owen Aisher interview.*

Floor Tile Company was formed as a corporate entity in July 1948 the original shareholdings were divided as follows:

Marley Floor Tile Company	% owned
The Marley Tile Company	51.3
O A Aisher	14.2
R H Aisher	14.0
J E Aisher	14.0
L Brady	2.6
F G Hardy	.6
J W S Stoker	1.5

Source: Marley Floor Tile minutes, July 1948

Although the visits to the American flooring manufacturers had given Sir Owen the outline of the production process, and Brady the technical support, the hard work was only just beginning. Sir Owen asked Fred Hardy what he knew about Banbury mixers. 'I said that's a mixer for mixing rubber in the tyre industry... there's this old school pal of mine, J J Smith, who was in the Greengate & Irwell Rubber Company. When Pirelli came to Burton on Trent, they made tyres and J J Smith worked there. I used to go down to Pirelli's factory; he was an engineer who put in Banbury mixers and calenders for making tyres.' Fred Hardy took Sir Owen up to J J Smith at his factory to see the process. The trip had one memorable feature – we went round and they were processing this rubber and they'd got camel dung in it and the place stank to high heaven. When we were waiting on Manchester station, I said the smell of this camel dung in this rubber is all in our suits. So we got in the train, it was crowded; we got in the carriage and everybody got up and walked out. We were left on our own. I said that's one way.'[7] (A more mundane, but probably more accurate explanation of the smell was plasticisers!) It was after that site visit that Sir Owen decided to go back to the Building Research Station and acquire Brady.

The essential capital equipment required were the mixer, to produce the formulation, and the calender, to roll it out, more of which later. At that time there was a three year delivery on the Banbury mixer but J J Smith, who was now playing an important advisory role, directed Marley to Francis Shaw, who made the Shaw Intermixer; the calenders were ordered from Joseph Robinson. J J Smith offered to order the equipment and install it for Marley; the mixers were ordered and Marley now needed premises to put them in. The Leighton Buzzard plant had been handed back by the RAF – 'we then had this clapped out old roof tile factory, and we were going to put in this equipment.'

7   *Fred Hardy interview.*

F L Brady

While the mixers were on order, Laurence Brady was experimenting to try to get the formulations right.[8] 'J J Smith very kindly allowed Brady to do some formulations and go and put them in his Intermixer. The first one we put in, we could not get the... stuff out, it just stuck there like glue and would not discharge, so it was in poor old Smith's Intermixer for three days.'

The formulation of the mix was vital not just for the smooth operation of the plant but for the composition and performance of the floor tile. There were substantial changes in the mix over time and the modern product bears little chemical resemblance to those early tiles. There were four main elements to the mix: the binder, the fibre, the filler and the pigment. The binder is, as the name indicates, the product that binds the rest of the mix together. In America, Johns-Manville had been using Gilsonite, as did Armstrong Cork and Dunlop Semtex, Marley's two UK competitors. Marley actually imported 200 tons of Gilsonite but soon wanted a domestic substitute. Brady quickly found "low temperature pitch" (LTP) being made by Coalite. Before the war there had been a big trade in spreading asphalt as a flooring medium. This was an important business for Coalite who could make a lighter coloured pitch and provided a good cheap flooring.

Peter Amsden, who joined the flooring business in 1946, remembers the early struggles to obtain the LTP from Coalite. 'They couldn't understand who this upstart firm of Marley was and why we insisted on having all this tonnage of LTP. They were selling the LTP to a firm who weren't making floor tiles but

8 *Ibid.*

went along and boiled up the mix on the site and spread it all over your floor. They said to themselves, "we've got a good market selling our pitch to these people and why should we sell it to Marley who we don't know anything about"; every time the tipper came in with a load of LTP they insisted that the driver be given a cheque. In the end Mr Owen came down with Mr Hardy and they brought down the Chairman of Coalite. They took him round the plant and showed him how clever we were and from that moment on there was no trouble. We had all the LTP; he decided that we would completely knock those other people out, which we did, and we were the people to sell the LTP to.' Len Griffiths, chief chemist for Dunlop's flooring company at the time remembers Marley's acquisition of the LTP supplies as a very successful move; 'we felt crushed'.

The next product was the fibre and in the case of the early floor tiles this was asbestos; Marley used a specification known as 7RMJ to start with, from Canada: 'We used to put in 43% which was a colossal percentage'. It was expensive to put that much in, and the more asbestos the mix contained, the more binder it needed – which was also expensive. This did not leave a lot of room for the third product, the filler, which in this case was limestone powder. Finally there was a pigment for colouring.

To return to Marley's first production attempts, there must have been an element of high farce. Fred Hardy: 'after we had got the equipment installed and we put the mixes in, they acted just the reverse to what the rubber did – instead of discharging off this front bowl it was taking the plastic out of the back bowl – we'd got the mills… about face. Smithy had to change them all round.' That was not the end of it; rubber sticks and plastic does not so the mix kept falling off the calenders. It was a pioneering plastics plant put in by people who understood rubber.

Peter Amsden remembers the plant being assembled in 1947. 'Immediately after the August Bank Holiday I moved to Leighton. One K4 Intermix, two sheeting mills and four calenders had been installed. All that was needed was to connect electricity, steam and water to these two production lines and dig the drains. Although these machines were installed, the factory was still being used for roof tile manufacture and the sheeting mills and calenders were islands around which German prisoners of war were working very hard (for cigarettes) to make roof tiles. These roof tile activities gradually grew less as the new roof tile factory at the end of the yard came into production.

'The time then came when production could begin. Mr Hardy took over and Mr Randall installed the conveyors between the Intermixers, sheeting mill and calenders. The floor tile carpet was calendered down to its finished thickness and then cropped into strips. These strips were fed into four punch presses each of which punched one tile at a time. The cropper was operated by a man who had to be very strong since it was worked by a foot pedal. Before going to the punch presses the strips were fed round a cooling drum but this was cumbersome and time consuming and soon discarded in favour of a longer production line which gave the strips a chance to be cooled by fans.

'There was immediately a big demand for the floor tiles which Mr Owen had foreseen when he ordered the machines for two production lines and not just one. Within a space of ten months, production increased from one shift on one line to five shifts on two lines and continued like this until 1955 when the much more efficient third line started punching eight tiles at a time instead of one. To give you some idea of the early days at Leighton Buzzard, going from one shift to five shifts in ten months, one of the problems was finding foremen. We had 400 displaced persons, who used to get up from the camp next door and work for us; we employed far too many men because we were not automated. One day a little man appeared. He was a Yugoslav, he had very little English at all and he said "I want work". Before he left the door, I'd made him a foreman; he learnt English in the space of a very few weeks and he became my general foreman. He was one of the people I took to Germany to help put right the factory there.' Paul Nemet retired in 1987 after 40 years with Marley.

David and the two Goliaths

Marley probably came into production in the early spring of 1948, only a few months after Dunlop but several months ahead of Armstrong. That is possibly one of the most remarkable achievements in Marley's history. Put Marley's efforts in context: still no more than a small company, trying to recover from the dislocation of the war, and without any previous experience of the flooring, rubber or chemical markets, Marley was competing head on with two very much larger companies each of which had specific experience of the flooring and rubber industries.

Dunlop was, of course, the leading UK producer of tyres and therefore experienced in rubber technology. Prior to the war, Dunlop had a cement/latex flooring product which was spread in a liquid form, like a cold mastic. In 1938, Dunlop formed a joint company with Limmer & Trinidad Lake Asphalt Company called Semtex (*cement/latex*). The idea was that Limmer would use their men to spread the Dunlop product. However, towards the end of the war, Dunlop bought out Limmer & Trinidad and Semtex became a wholly owned subsidiary. Len Griffiths, who was the Semtex chief chemist, was in the USA at the end of the war and remembers receiving instructions from Dunlop to look for a new flooring product; he visited many of the same factories as Sir Owen and, like Marley, Semtex developed their product without the benefit of any technical agreements with US producers.

Armstrong Cork, as it was then called, was formed in Pittsburgh in 1860 as a cork cutting business and from this moved into other cork products including the cork floor tile in 1904. Armstrong was also a supplier of cork dust which was used in the production of linoleum. At the turn of the century the company 'became concerned that the growing National Prohibition movement might eventually threaten the cork stopper business if alcoholic beverages became illegal'.[9] In 1907, Armstrong decided to diversify and built a linoleum plant of its own at Lancaster, Pennsylvania. A decade after the asphalt tile had first been produced in America, Armstrong entered that market in 1931 with its own asphalt tile. The new flooring tile rapidly became one of the strengths of Armstrong's building materials division and in 1937 a new factory was built in California. This, then, was the second competitor that Marley faced after the war when Armstrong decided to establish itself in the UK market. Assisted by Government grants, Armstrong built a factory at Team Valley in the North East; it was opened in 1948 by Harold Wilson, then President of the Board of Trade.

Three manufacturers were now producing the new flooring tile; that they could all be kept occupied owed much to the restoration of a public sector building programme, but they were also peculiarly helped by the change in methods of building construction. Before the war, standard house construction was based on timber flooring but with '... timber in very short supply a new method for constructing the ground floor of houses was developed. This involved filling an excavated brick or concrete lined shell with hardcore, which was then covered with concrete with a thin screed of sand/cement. However nobody could expect families to live in houses with exposed concrete floors, and therefore a new form of hard wearing flooring was essential.'[10] The available products were the cheap felt-based flooring or linoleum, but the new construction techniques posed problems for the latter.

A newly laid concrete raft floor contains both water and alkali (from the cement); linoleum is very susceptible to alkali and therefore the linoleum should not be laid until the subfloor is well and truly dried out. In contrast, Marley's tiles had the property of being able to transmit water through the tiles. Denis Moss, who joined Marley's central research office in 1956 and eventually became Technical Manager of Marley Floors describes the practical effect. 'If you have water going into the back of a flooring, it has to expand; if it expands it curls because the bottom is getting bigger quicker than the top is. Linoleum suffered from alkali attack which would eventually cause breakdown of the flooring and excessive moisture in a newly laid subfloor would bring about such alkaline conditions. Floor tiles containing asbestos proved to be very tolerant of excessive moisture in the subfloor, one unproven theory being that the fibre transmitted moisture very quickly through the body of the tile,

9 *William A Mehler Jr*, Let The Buyer Have Faith: The Story of Armstrong, *Lancaster PA, USA, 1987.*

10 *Anon, 'The Marley Tile Company'*, Plastics Today, *no 29.*

Owen A A Aisher

overcoming the conditions which causes edges to curl. Another advantage was that the tiles were laid using a moisture resistant bitumen adhesive which maintained adhesion in conditions where other adhesives would have failed. There were specifications concerning the maximum moisture content of the screed allowed before the tiles should be laid but builders wanted to get the floors installed as soon as possible, and they found they could take chances with our tiles and lay under moisture conditions which no other flooring covering available would accept.'

Creating the market

An early participant at Marley Floors was Sir Owen's eldest son, Owen A A Aisher, known to another generation as 'Mr Owen Junior' or 'Young Owen'. After six years' wartime service in the Royal Navy, Owen Aisher joined Marley as a management trainee, one of a small group who were given operational postings to familiarise themselves with the business. Owen was sent first to roofing tiles but was soon transferred to Leighton Buzzard where he worked closely with Peter Amsden in establishing the new tile plant – living on site in a converted RAF hut in the old roof tile stacking yard! In April 1948, 'young Owen' became closely involved in the next stage of development: 'Once we got the bugs out of making the thermoplastic floor tiles, obviously people realised that it's all very well to make them but you have to sell them and to know how they are laid and fixed. Father was having discussions with Frank Taylor and before I could think twice about anything he said "we've booked your passage on the *Queen Mary*. You're going across to New York; I've fixed you up with a floor tile layer and you'll be there for a month to learn how to lay floor tiles and you'll come back and tell everybody how to do it." So I came back and had to explain to all the various people how these tiles could best be laid. We had to write a book about it; tell all the area managers, the representatives and train gangs of floor tilers.' Lord Taylor remembers that month: 'he became an expert at laying these tiles... and then he came back... he was the one who taught all the men to lay them.'

The supply and fix concept that Marley had so successfully used to develop the market for concrete roof tiles lent itself naturally to the floor tile market. As in the roofing industry, the flooring market lacked a contracting labour force that had any familiarity with the new product, let alone any disposition to innovate. Many of the early floor tilers were brought in from the joinery trade; they were used to squaring a floor and setting out straight lines. Marley already had the sales force and the systems in place within Marley Tile, the roof tile company, and rather than establish a parallel organisation within the Marley Floor Tile Company, the latter sold its production to the former. Thus Marley Tile (roofing) had within it a contracting division with an organisational structure which serviced roof tiles and floor tiles (with other products to follow later), and salesmen who were able (after some persuasion) to sell both products. Only when it came to the fixing and laying did the personnel diverge.

Richard Aisher (Junior) argued that not only did the existing roof tile organisation lend itself to a similar supply and fix operation in flooring but that without the infrastructure provided by the established roofing business, Marley would have had difficulty in financing the marketing of the new flooring product. 'The reason it worked was the supply and fix organisation because we had this system of area managers and sales managers covering the country supply and fixing roof tiles; it wasn't very different to organise supply and fix for floor tiles in houses. At that time the market for floor tiles was fundamentally housing. The market for the roof tiles was fundamentally housing. You were therefore selling to exactly the same customer, you were fixing the things on the same site, therefore there was very little difference for the representative in organising both, but the real point was that the floor tiles on their own could never have covered the overheads of that organisation.'

As well as convincing the customer of the merits of the new tile, Marley also had to sell the concept to its own representatives – all roofing men. John Dewar was a sales manager in the Midlands at that time and remembers his first experience with the new product. 'There was a lot of hard work done in the selling division to get the products sold. The first time I ever saw an asphalt tile was when Dick Aisher came to Burton with some little pieces in a box. He said we're going to sell floor tiles... we passed them round; we didn't try to break them but they broke. He said you might be laughing at them and think they're no good but in about ten years time you'll all be having them in your kitchen and you're going out to sell them at 15 shillings a square yard. And we did Council property — miles of it.'

Whereas Marley stood out from the rest of the roofing industry with its supply and fix concept, in the new asphalt floor tile market the two major competitors had a marketing approach that was closer to Marley's. Armstrong used the selling techniques that they had in the USA and appointed approved contractors, usually small firms. Although Dunlop also appointed two or three larger nominated contractors, the firm sold and fixed largely under its own name, and using its own contracting staff. This was an important difference from Marley who, although selling and fixing under its own name, actually used independent firms of small contractors. Dunlop's Len Griffiths thought that these independent sub-contractors were more cost effective than their own in-house contracting organisation. 'They were always able to be the lowest price so really they raced away and they became, I would say, the biggest producers in the UK'. In addition to operating through its own sub-contractors, Marley also established a close relationship with the larger builders. 'Not only are Marley Floor Tiles fixed by Marley craftsmen, but also twelve hundred builders buy and lay Marley Tiles with their own fixers specially trained in the method of laying by our technical staff.'[11] This was an early attempt to distinguish between the the large contract, which was appropriate for Marley's own supply and fix organisation, and the smaller job, which the builder could do with his 'Buy and Lay' service. Side by side with this were Approved Flooring Contractors who were developed in the early 1950s as a means of penetrating the replacement flooring market. However, Marley Tile's own supply and fix teams represented the sharp edge of the selling drive and it was not until the floor company gained control of its own selling in the 1970s that the Approved Flooring Contractor scheme became part of the mainstream distribution policy.

Commitment to the local authorities

Marley's early sales were concentrated on the local authority housing market; Dunlop tended to keep out of this sector concentrating instead on schools or higher value projects. This possibly reflected a view on where they wanted to position themselves in the market, but there may also have been a gentlemen's agreement. Marley had the advantage of being able to utilise its extensive roofing tile contacts with the local authorities. Owen Aisher: 'My Uncle Dick played a very important part in getting us specified with what was then the London County Council; we were laying tiles $\frac{1}{8}$ inch thick, in the cheaper

---

11 *The Marley Tile (Holding) Company* Annual Report, *1953*.

grades. That gave us the volume.' Another large contract in those early days was the flooring for 2,000 prefabricated bungalows in Northern Ireland (built by Hawker-Siddeley). 'I remember, I went over there with a young chap called Pike to lay a floor in the Stormont building for the architect; obviously before he did anything he wanted to see what it was like. So Pike and I burnt the midnight oil, made sure the screed was all right, laid the tiles; next day we presented ourselves to Mr Aitken. We had to quote figures relating to the wear and tear conditions that they had experienced in America over a number of years. I remember him getting a brick and dropping it. Fortunately it didn't land on its corner and so he said "Oh, it seems to be alright" and gave us the order for 2,000 houses.'

That first LCC contract proved the basis for a series of contracts on other LCC estates during the 1950s. Other important early local authority customers were in the Medway towns, Rochester, Chatham and Gillingham; 'we knew the builders, we knew the architects, we knew the local authorities'. Those early years were dominated by local authority work for there was very little private building. However, as building controls relaxed, a new market beckoned and Marley responded with a different structure. Eventually, Marley had different salesmen selling to flooring contractors; for the large part, these people were sub-contractors, completely dedicated to Marley products, and trading under the Marley name. To the domestic customer, the floor layer had all the appearance of being a Marley man and the estimating and invoicing all came out of Marley. However, that was not an exclusive arrangement and Marley did also sell to general flooring contractors trading under their own names.

It was not long before Marley was taking the floor tile overseas. The first market was in Holland and Marley recruited agents in Amsterdam, Rotterdam and The Hague, followed by Luxembourg and Belgium, all around 1950. By the time the 1951 Group accounts were published, the Chairman could boast of exporting to 30 countries; exports then accounted for around 20% of floor tile sales and provided the platform from which Marley launched its overseas manufacturing – of which more later. Owen Aisher and Laurence Brady made frequent trips to the Low Countries and then Germany, guiding, instructing and even laying floors themselves. 'We took a lot of the tiles over in a motor car (broke the springs). It was fascinating to go over there and play such a part in the development because people in many of those countries had not seen the product and they wanted to know about it.'

The story of the Little Man Kneeling

One of the overseas agents, a Dutch flooring contractor called Vervoort, was to leave a lasting impression on Marley in the form of the universally known logo – the little man kneeling. Having found what he wanted, Sir Owen duly wrote for permission to use it.

28th May 1954

PERSONAL
A. Vervoort, Esq.,
Messrs. A.N. de Lint N.V.,
Stationsweg 91,
The Hague, Holland.

My dear Vervoort,

    Over the years we have tried to popularise the slogan 'Cock o' the Walk'. In Germany we have a Seal, but the general consensus of opinion is the more we see of your beautiful cut-out of the man laying tile, the more we think perhaps that is the most universal sign, with the greater likelihood of being understood in all countries. Would it be possible, if the Company wanted – and I would yet have to get the other Directors and executives to agree – to use your little man as the Company's trademark in all advertisements?

The reply came back by return.

Directie
N.V.A.N. DE LINT   *June 1st 1954*

O.A. Aisher Esq.
The Marley Floor Tile Comp. Ltd.,
London Road.
Riverhead, Sevenoaks
PERSONAL   *Kent – England*

Dear Mr Aisher,

    I am both pleased and flattered through your letter, in which you mention the idea of using our [picture] as a trademark, to which I gladly consent. I hope the 'little man' will be able to be a good mascotte for the company.
    From my son I hear, that he is very happy with his work and he and his family appear to like life in England very much. I hope that he will succeed to fulfil the place you intend for him and thank you very much so far for what you have done for him.

A Vervoort, designer of the Little Man

Sir Owen remembers Vervoort, an amateur artist, telling him where the idea for the logo had arisen. 'We had a huge floor to do, and we had to do it between Friday night and Monday morning; we had six or seven floor tilers and the foreman lined them all up and they went across the floor all kneeling down. I came in and took a sketch of it, of the tiler laying the tile.' At first, the little man was just used as the "N" in "Marleytile Nederland" but it was soon adopted to represent Marley across the Group; the 1954 accounts showed the "little man" on the cover for first time.

The fight for Harrietsham

Responding to the market-place with characteristic enthusiasm, Marley quickly decided to build a second factory. Leighton Buzzard was still one of the key roof tile factories, which meant that Marley could not extend the floor tile plant; more volume meant another plant elsewhere. The natural choice was Harrietsham where the site was still lying vacant. The intention had been to sell it after the roof tile factory closed but war intervened and so, fortuitously, Marley had a large site at its disposal. Marley applied to the Board of Trade for permission but to their dismay it was refused. The reasons are not wholly clear but the refusal led to another battle of willpower which Marley eventually won. When Marley had received the Leighton Buzzard factory back from the RAF, it was heavily dilapidated, and Marley appears to have gone about its task of renovation and installing floor tile machinery without applying for permission. Fred Hardy thinks that when the Board of Trade realised too late what had happened it was not best pleased, particularly over Marley's use of scarce dollars to import fibre.

Fred Hardy's determination came in: 'I looked at the rules and regulations, and there was nothing that would stop us putting the plant in the factory'. Marley was able to point to the fact that it had made floor tiles (the Berger ones) before the war and however different in composition, a floor tile was a floor tile. The Board of Trade countered by refusing to grant an import permit for the asbestos. Fred Hardy continues: 'Most people would have said at that stage – forget it. Owen Aisher said carry on, this is the sort of chap he was. If you'd taken any notice of him you'd never have applied for building permission or anything else; he just used to say, "oh we'll get over that when the time comes."' Fred Hardy kept going back to the Ministry; they must have been interesting conversations. Eventually the outburst: 'Look, we are going to do it and we shall do it with or without you. And even if we use bloody sawdust we will do it.' Indeed, for a brief time Marley did use sawdust, but in the end Marley secured the asbestos it needed – from Russia! Sir Owen: 'I went over to Russia, saw the chap, and he came over, had a look around and then we got it; once we got it, the Canadians complained and we could then get Canadian.' In September 1951, the floor tile plant was installed at Harrietsham and the first tiles came off the line in May 1952. However, Marley never did get permission to knock the factory down and rebuild it; it had to fit the new plant into the old building.

The Harrietsham plant was run briefly by Dick Eyres (who had started in Roof Tiles in 1947) but he was scheduled to go to South Africa to run the new flooring plant at Nigel. An advert for a works manager brought a response from Geoff Barrett, then production manager at a glass works in Bilston, Staffordshire: 'I assumed it was for roof tiles, and I felt I just wanted an outside job after working by those furnaces. I applied for the job thinking it might be for Burton-on-Trent.' By Christmas 1953, Marley had its new works manager. At the time the decision to install a plastics line at Harrietsham had been made, work was well advanced at Leighton Buzzard on the vinyl tile. (Vinyl has become accepted within resilient flooring as shorthand for polyvinyl chloride which is only one of a number of compounds containing vinyl.) The plan was to produce the vinyl tiles at Leighton Buzzard, 'bashing out the cheap and cheerful tiles' at Harrietsham. The Harrietsham plant was similar to that installed at Leighton Buzzard, except that Harrietsham had two K6 machines, twice the capacity of Leighton's K4s; the tiles were still hand punched. The factory was run on two shifts – from 6–3 p.m. and from 3–1 a.m. 'We used to have to bus our labour force in from all round the country districts and Maidstone and Ashford particularly because of the labour shortage in that area.'

The Leighton Buzzard and Harrietsham factories were run independently by their works managers, reporting to Dennis Knight. Knight had been recruited by Fred Hardy in 1950 from Bata (the Czech shoe company) where he had gained experience of rubber technology and calendering. Dennis Knight sadly died in 1975 but is well remembered. 'He was the head office man; he had a unique personality and he was very good with figures... he had a curious way of getting his ideas across but you would never feel any resentment. He had a good personality and was highly intelligent.' Dennis Knight in turn reported to Fred Hardy; at that time, of course, production and sales were strictly separate, virtually all output was transferred to Marley Tile's contracting division.

The vinyl tile arrives

The early asphalt tiles had limitations in colour and flexibility. With its pitch base, the asphalt tile had of necessity to be dark, brown or black; coumarone resin could be used to produce a wider, though still limited, range of colours but it was an expensive and not wholly satisfactory solution. The asphalt tiles were also difficult to lay; they were brittle and needed heating before they were laid. Owen Aisher described his approach: '... we used to have tables where they laid the tiles for a minute or two, with a gas fire underneath. In America they didn't do that – because most of the houses were centrally heated.' The search for a superior binder was inevitable and was in mind almost before the first asphalt tiles had come off the production line.

The major breakthrough came with the introduction of PVC as a replacement for LTP which gave a much greater degree of flexibility and strength. Although PVC had been in use in Germany before the war it only began to be used in Britain on any scale after the war, finding its way onto the consumer market through such products as shower curtains, "plastic" raincoats, etc. Peter Amsden remembers Laurence Brady talking to him in the laboratory in Riverhead: '... the future, Amsden, is going to be with polyvinyl chloride, which didn't mean a thing.' Polyvinyl chloride, a high polymer (or chain of molecules) of vinyl chloride, was not an easy product to work; it needed very high temperatures and even with the addition of plasticisers it did not flow easily. The answer came from the American chemical company Geon who had produced a PVC copolymer by adding small amounts of vinyl acetate to the vinyl chloride in the polymerisation process. This produced a PVC which was less viscous at lower temperatures and which could therefore be calendered at lower temperatures. Marley was now on the way.

The USA does not seem to have been as ready a source of technical information as it was with the pure asphalt tile. Sir Owen clearly had the vinyl tile on his agenda on his next visit to the States (January to March 1949). Evidence of vinyl was there to be found but little sign of it being in regular commercial production. The diary records Sir Owen's first factory visit: 'Not interested yet in vinyl tile'; to the Asphalt Tile Institute – '... did not or could not say much about the vinyl tile, said only asphalt dealt in'; walking around

Dallas after dinner – 'Noticed quite a few hard rubber tile floors. I am sure that if we could make a similar tile in vinyl we would do well'; visits to Goodrich Chemical to discuss their vinyls; hearing that 'a vinyl tile made from scrap is being made in Alabama' and even that Johns-Manville had made a vinyl tile ten years previously – 'man from J.M. has some laid at home on wood in bedrooms with scatter rugs only. It was mainly a question of price – how little could be used.'

Despite Sir Owen's attempt to draw on the US, and Brady's efforts in the laboratory, Dunlop appears to have been first on the British market with a vinyl tile under the Vinylex name followed by Marley in 1950–51 under the trade name "Marleyflex". Armstrong did not successfully produce its "Excelon" vinyl tile in the USA until 1952. The vinyl tiles were introduced as a top of the range product with better colours, increased flexibility, greater resistance and, of course, a higher price. 'These tiles, even in their early form, were an immense advance over asphalt tiles. They were much more resilient, and resistant to grease, and could be manufactured in an almost unlimited range of colours. Initially, prospective customers found it difficult to accept that vinyl tiles did not have the disadvantages of asphalt tiles. Nonetheless... vigorous selling, particularly to local authorities who were already buying concrete roofing tiles, eventually won the day.'[12]

Although more expensive to produce, the vinyl tile could be made $\frac{1}{16}$-inch thick instead of $\frac{1}{8}$-inch which made it a lot lighter 'and we could export it like fun.' At home, the old "asphalt" and the new "vinyl" tile sold side by side but to different markets. The council houses would have the cheaper, thicker, tiles based on the LTP and coumarone binders while Marleyflex was targeted to private housing and commercial users; gradually, these distinctions blurred and the vinyl tile became the standard product.

Marleyflex had a wide range of colours, including the light end of the spectrum. Marley's 1953 accounts featured colour pictures for the first time and there proudly displayed was a range that included red, green, buff and grey. These were self-colours, but more common were the tiles with flashing or marbling in them. Marbling was produced by adding broken up pieces of different coloured tile during the calendering process; it is inserted into the "nip" between the two calender bowls and is dispersed so that it looks like marbling. This had its own production problems in that one of the common causes of tile rejects was too much or too little marbling. (This was eventually overcome in the 1980s by the introduction of the "scratching" process.) To the consumer, the finish of the marbled tiles had greater visual appeal and they also showed dirt less; to the manufacturer they had another important advantage – they disguised shade variation more than the plain tiles did.

The product remained constant for at least another three years: Marley

---

12 Plastics Today, *no 29.*

Marley floor tile displays from 1954

Standard Floor Tiles, the original asphalt tile in its A, B, C or D range (later sold as Econoflex when an additional amount of PVC was used to replace the synthetic resins used in the C and D ranges); and the Marleyflex vinyl tile. However, the mid-1950s saw a new generation of products introduced, and the manufacture for the first time of a sheet or roll flooring able to compete head on with linoleum. The first new tile that was introduced to complement Marleyflex was the Homelay which came on to the market in the summer of 1955. It was thinner and more flexible than Marleyflex and was targeted at the domestic customer and marketed through the retailers; their great advantage to those householders 'who like the idea of "having a go" ' was that they needed

Homelay floor tiles

no heating before laying. Exhibitions were held in Barkers, Gamages and Selfridges and by March 1956 Marley was selling Homelay through 1,000 shops. The 1956 Group Accounts featured Homelay Floor Tiles benefiting from the the 'Do-it-yourself enthusiasm sweeping the country... Our "Do-it-yourself" programme with Marley Homelay products has established itself over the whole country'. Other tiles that followed were the almost solid vinyl Marley de Luxe, a higher quality of Marleyflex, launched at the 1957 Building Exhibition and then a pressed tile called the Terrazzo; this was made from calendered sheet which was chipped up and put in a press.

Sheet flooring

One of the most important benefits arising from the introduction of vinyl was that it enabled the floor tile manufacturers to produce sheet flooring. This might seem surprising in that the calendering process first produces a sheet out of which the floor tiles are punched but, as we have seen, the first formulations barely had the flexibility to support individual tiles, let alone continuous sheet

Marley Floor Tiles exhibition stand from 1958

– in that linoleum reigned supreme. Continued experimentation eventually enabled Marley to produce a formulation which retained both its strength and its flexibility after it had been calendered, allowing it to produce a new generation of sheet vinyl flooring. An essential feature of the sheet flooring was the much higher proportion of PVC binder.

Marley's first commercial sheet flooring, Marleytred, was developed (at Harrietsham) during 1954 and launched in the December of that year. Although it was calendered, it was not made in a continuous process. A filled calendered PVC film was made on the three bowl calender and then taken to a laminating machine where it was laid on top of a hessian felt base, passed under infra-red heaters and then straight into an embossing nip, where a deep embossed pattern was put on and the PVC film laminated into the jute fibre. The process had its technical difficulties; one particular problem was that the infra-red heat which was applied to the material to soften it before it went through the embossing nip, would often ignite the fumes given off by the plasticisers. Marley persevered for a time but production of Marleytred on the laminater had been stopped by the end of 1957. By then, however, Marleytred was being made by an entirely different process – the spreader.

The spreader acquired its name because the process involves spreading the vinyl formulation, in the form of a paste, on to a base sheet; in the case of

Marleytred a hessian felt but, eventually fibreglass. The roll of base sheet was fed into the spreader and the mix of almost pure vinyl was poured on top and spread before going into an oven for drying. After the vinyl was spread it was embossed to create the pattern. The single colour was whatever pigment was put into the vinyl but Marleytred was the first time that Marley had produced a flooring with a pattern.

It was sold heavily into the retail market, in 48-in. and 24-in. widths, 12 colours and 2 embossed designs. It was one of Marley's first ventures into heavy marketing of a consumer product with heavy advertising in women's magazines and the national press. The 1956 Holdings accounts reported that 'Marleytred is now established as a floor covering that gives comfort, quietness and "the look of luxury". A thick felt surfaced with tough vinyl plastic, in various colours and embossed designs, Marleytred is sold in many furnishing and floor-covering stores.' In fact, there were over 2,000 shops selling it and among prestige contracts was one to floor the whole of Woburn.

Marleytred had been a half way stage requiring a lamination process; the wear surface was made on a calender before the spreading process was developed. The experimentation continued, enabling Marley to produce a fully calendered vinyl flooring, to be known as Marleyflor; also in contrast to Marleytred it would be a thin sheeting with a printed, not embossed, finish. Following the American example, a bitumen impregnated paper or felt was used as the backing with a thin calendered vinyl sheet providing the wearing surface; unfortunately Marley could not overcome problems with the adhesives. 'We could undoubtedly have done it today but at that time adhesive technology was limited and we couldn't get an adhesive that could stop the Marleyflor from shrinking at the edges. It looked fine, rolled up fine but you lay it on a floor and within say six or nine months you got a black border down each edge where the Marleyflor had shrunk. If you could have used a solvent based adhesive then you could have stopped it shrinking, but you couldn't use one on a bitumen based floor because bitumen dissolves very readily with the solvent so you would have got black sticky bitumen underneath. You had to use a water based adhesive but none of the water based adhesives were good enough to stop the Marleyflor from shrinking.'[13] Production of the Marleyflor was only distributed on a limited basis before being given up until it was possible to manufacture it with a PVC backing.

In this case, every cloud had its plastic lining; the calendered vinyl film that provided the wearing surface for Marleyflor proved a commercial success on its own, not as a flooring medium, but as a surface covering (table tops, counters, etc) better known to the world as Marleyfilm. Because the film had no bitumen backing and was being used on different surfaces, it was possible to

---

13 *Denis Moss interview.*

Marleyfilm

Laying Marley floor tiles

use it with a solvent based adhesive. Marleyfilm was launched as a retail product in August 1956 and was a resounding commercial success; it was the first Marley product to be intensively advertised on the new medium of commercial television. Within two months, production had to be increased to two shifts and production of Marleyflor was "retarded" to accommodate the additional demand; by the middle of 1957, production was running at over 10,000 yards a day. Marleyfilm enjoyed considerable short term success but was soon overtaken by more sophisticated products such as Fablon and Contact, and Marley itself followed up with MarleyDecor, a more flexible material which incorporated designs as distinct from the marbling of Marleyfilm.

The technical team continued its work on Marleyflor and eventually a new backing material, including scrap PVC, replaced the bitumen paper; the vinyl sheet (otherwise known as Marleyfilm) was bonded to the backing under pressure on the calenders. Denis Moss: 'I can remember taking the little roll that I had made on the laboratory calender to Sir Owen and Laurence Brady and rolling it out on the floor and how delighted they were with the product.' Marleyflor was re-launched in the spring of 1958. It was produced in three thicknesses, 30 colours and sold into both the contractual and retail markets. Marleyflor was advertised to the domestic customer as easy to lay; a mark of the competition that vinyl sheeting still faced from traditional floorings was the claim that it could be laid 'as easy as lino'. It was particularly used where people wanted a floor without seams, e.g. hospitals, and where you could "cove" it (turn it up at the sides); to make the larger widths, the joints were welded with similar material. Probably three-quarters of the sales were made to industrial, commercial and public contracts, with the balance to the domestic market.

Purchase of Wallington Weston

The whole scale of Marley's calendering resources changed in 1956 when Marley bought the West Country firm of Wallington Weston, a business with long-standing experience of calendering rubber and plastics. 'The original company was formed in 1896 by two chemists who left an international rubber group, to set up business manufacturing rubber wheels at Limpley Stoke. Within a few years they moved to St. John's Mill, Frome, and in 1946, the company came to its present site at Vallis Mills.'[14] Robin Aisher remembers first seeing it with Sir Owen: 'We drove down on a very foggy day to Wallington Weston, stayed at a little hotel outside the town and the next day went into this old mill where all these people were squirting paint filled with solvent onto beach balls. What it also had was calenders. Anyway, father said we are going to buy it – this is the new technology. That was what we really bought, a business that had calenders.' In April 1956, the whole of the Wallington Weston share capital was purchased for £125,000, satisfied by £25,000 in cash and 333,333 "A" non-voting shares.

Wallington Weston had been losing money and was an inexpensive purchase – the consideration was equivalent to no more than 12% of Marley's pre-tax profits in that year – but it brought with it larger calendering capacity than Marley hitherto possessed, specifically the three and four bowl calenders that were necessary to produce the very thin flooring and to print; indeed, later purchases of 98-inch calenders were the largest in Europe. Dennis Knight was sent down as managing director leaving Howard Knock behind in charge of floor tile production; Jack Aisher was also closely involved at Wallington Weston. The existing product range was an odd mixture of plastic and rubber products including play balls, rubber foam mattresses, plastic sheeting and injection rubber mouldings for the aircraft industry. But more than anything, Wallington Weston was to prove central to Marley's development of Consort, probably Marley's most successful flooring product ever – of which more later.

One of Sir Owen's early visits to Wallington Weston provided a clear illustration of his attitude to Trade Unions – they could represent the men, but

14   *Marley Limited* Jubilee Brochure, 1974.

not at his expense. When asked what one particular office was, he was told it belonged to the shop steward; 'They're the rules round here and we have to do it.' The response was immediate: 'Move it outside, about a hundred yards away; every time he wants something he has got to go out in the cold and come in again. We're not having it on our premises. That was the end of him.'[15] Sir Owen was by no means opposed to the Trade Unions but he imposed strict limits on their influence. 'I said anyone could join a Union if they wanted to though we are not going to make them. They could put their signs up on the board but they couldn't hold meetings in the Company's time and they couldn't go around collecting money either.'

Flooring minority acquired from the family

While the purchase of Wallington Weston was under negotiation, the capital structure of Marley Floor Tile was rationalised. The substantial family interest in the flooring business was becoming untenable and proposals were drawn up to to buy out the personal shareholdings. In March 1956 the 49% minority, held largely by the Aisher family, was acquired. After independent advice on the terms, a total of 2,181,723 non-voting Marley shares were issued compared with 5,000,000 shares (voting and non-voting) previously in issue. If that was the value of a 49% minority then it implied Marley Floors in total would have been worth 4.45 million shares compared with an enlarged group total of 7.2 million shares. It seemed a generous price and the extraordinary general meeting called for 26th March 1956 did not go smoothly. In particular, [Sir] Godfrey Mitchell, Wimpey Chairman and old friend of Sir Owen, and two other shareholders 'spoke against the Resolution at some length.'[16] Despite this intervention, the purchase was approved. By this time, the shareholdings were much more widely spread than the original three Aisher brothers, Brady, Hardy and Stoker.

---

15 *Sir Owen Aisher interview.*
16 *Minutes of the EGM, March 1956.*

Transferor	Marley shares allotted
O A Aisher	411,818
O A Aisher and others	411,818
R H Aisher	171,818
J E Aisher	171,818
O A A Aisher	108,349
Mrs J F Aisher	152,727
Mrs E E Aisher	152,727
F L Brady	57,512
Mr L Brady	11,640
Mrs M A Brady	4,363
F G Hardy	36,436
Mrs J Hardy	36,000
C N Vokins and Mrs J Hardy	36,000
J W S Stoker	43,200
A W Smyth-Pigott and Mrs B M Stoker	21,818
A H Aldridge	13,363
F L Cooke	13,309
F L Cooke, Jason Smith and J E Aisher	87,272
F L Cooke, Jason Smith and Mrs E E Aisher	87,272
Mrs K Ogden	32,727
Mrs W J Moss	32,727
Mrs P U Leckie	16,363
Mrs M A Mitchell	13,363
Mrs S G Simpson	13,363
Mrs M J Ward	11,640
National Provincial Bank	23,280

Source: Minutes of the EGM, March 1956

The purchase of the minority and the acquisition of Wallington Weston provides a useful stopping point to review the financial progress of Marley Floors. The table that follows shows the financial performance of Marley Floor Tile from its formal incorporation in 1948 to 1957, the first year after the acquisition of the minority 49% from the directors. The growth in sales was dramatic, from the £286,000 in the first full year as a corporate entity to ten times that amount in 1957. After the early losses Marley moved rapidly into profit, earning pre-tax profit margins of 20% and more for several years. This was not sustainable and gradually came under pressure, the reintroduction of purchase tax in January 1954 being a particular blow. By 1953, the last year before the introduction of purchase tax, floor tiles accounted for 22% of group pre-tax profits, rising to 24% in 1955 when roofing tile profits came under pressure. The true contribution was probably higher for the distribution and contracting profits derived from flooring were being earned within Marley Tile Co while the overseas operations, based on flooring, were now beginning to make a return.

The following table below clearly shows the rapid growth of sales through the 1950s; all the home sales were channelled through the roofing company's contracting division until 1954 when a modest direct sale business was started by Marley Floor Tile. Because of the internal transfer pricing the profits figures may not accurately reflect the performance of the Company – it is believed, for instance, that Marley Floors was probably losing rather more, and for longer, than the early accounts show.

Marley Floors early growth (£000)

Sales to:	1948	1949	1950	1951	1952	1953	1954	1955*	1956	1957	1958
M. Tile	17	267	619	682	940	1,304	1,270	1,576	1,179	2,064	2,038
Home customers							203	317	261	476}	782
Exports		18	80	131	97	162	172	213	137	266	}
Sundry		1	14	4	3	3	2	5	18	33	23
Total	17	286	713	817	1,040	1,469	1,647	2,111	1,604	2,888	2,843
Profit	−22	54	178	191	191	242	169	338	−91	248	324
Margins, %		19.1	25.3	23.4	18.4	16.5	10.3	16.0		11.6	11.4

*19th March to 31st October. New company with same name formed following the acquisition of the minority holding.
Incorporated 1st March 1948.
Source: Marley Floors Accounts

The money comes in

We saw earlier the dramatic growth in roofing tile profits after the war as housebuilding activity recovered and the new factories came on stream, with the embryo flooring operation eventually adding its contribution. Housing completions in 1954 reached a peak of 348,000, a level not reached again for another ten years. The Marley Tile (Holding) Company earned its first million-pound – plus profit in 1953, just exceeding it in 1954. As with the housing market, this too represented a peak but one that Marley was to recapture within only three years.

The Marley Tile (Holding) Company: pre-tax profits (£000)

1946	1947	1948	1949	1950	1951	1952	1953	1954
42	83	135	240	387	389	552	1,110	1,123

Source: Holding Company Accounts

The dramatic growth in profits enabled Marley to repair the damage the war had done to its finances. The final arrears of preference dividend were repaid out of the 1949 profits and the Company was then able to resume payment of an ordinary dividend. This paved the way for the issue of permanent capital in the form of another preference issue – a £200,000 issue at 6%. The issue was underwritten by the Industrial & Commercial Finance Corporation and the Prudential for 6d a share and the brokers to the issue, De Zoete & Gorton, received a further 3½d, terms viewed with some degree of envy by the author. The proceeds served to refinance the earlier £200,000 loan from the ICFC which had, in turn, been raised to avoid breaching the banks' borrowing limits.

Welcome though it was, Marley's needs were not going to be satisfied by £200,000 and, almost as soon as the preference money was in, the directors were facing fresh pressures on finances. Jack Aisher had been appointed to the Holding Company Board on his return from wartime service and, with Fred Hardy now in charge of production, Jack had been taking prime responsibility for finance. In the summer of 1950, he set about a comprehensive review of Marley's finances, presenting his findings to the Board in July. The Board's response was immediate: 'after consideration of our commitments on Fixed Assets and Working Capital requirements it was unanimously resolved that until further finance was obtained no additional capital commitments must be entered into. It was further decided that immediate steps should be taken by Mr J E Aisher, with the help of Mr Cullen, to explore the possibilities of obtaining additional finance for the Marley Tile Company Limited and The Marley Floor Tile Company.'

The discussions on fund raising dragged on, long outlasting the capital expenditure resolution of July 1950 which was rescinded in April 1951 'as other procedures for dealing with this form of expenditure had now been adopted.' An important preliminary was to obtain the consent of the preference shareholders to allow Marley to raise its borrowing limits from £500,000 to £1 million, which was done at the Annual Meeting in June 1951. Throughout the year there were meetings with Price Waterhouse, Marley's auditors, and the merchant bank Phillip Hill & Partners and then with Lloyds Bank. By the beginning of 1952, no agreement had been reached on the method of funding and Marley was back to talking with ICFC and the Prudential. Eventually, in June 1952, now two years after Jack Aisher's report, Marley's bankers suggested a meeting with stockbrokers W Greenwell. Agreement was soon reached that a debenture issue was appropriate and on October 1st an application was made to the Capital Issues Committee. In July 1953, a £750,000 5% First Mortgage Debenture was offered to shareholders and the general public; applications totalling £14,180,000, or 19 times the issue, were received.

Combined then with the cash generation from the business, which had taken equity capital up to £2½ million, the preference and debenture issues had eliminated net short term borrowings. Marley had thus established a sound financial base from which it was to embark on one of its most vigorous and widespread periods of expansion. The first international steps had already been taken in Europe and South Africa while at home Marley was beginning the experimentation with wider uses of the new plastic materials which was to take it into plumbing goods and then motor components.

Part 4
Marley goes overseas

Sir Owen travelled extensively between the wars. There were visits to the United States where, in a private capacity and in partnership with other British firms, he built houses in New York State. Closer to home there were journeys to continental Europe and, on one occasion, even to Russia. When the time came for Marley to establish itself overseas after the war, Sir Owen already had extensive experience of the market place, and clear views as to how and where he could transplant his UK expertise.

The choice is flooring

The shape of Marley's extensive overseas manufacturing interests was eventually determined in the 1950s when the Aishers chose to develop not the concrete roof tile that had been the foundation of their domestic success, but the newer plastic flooring business. Sir Owen had thought long and hard about the prospects for concrete tiles overseas. In 1937, a patent application had been obtained in the USA for a "continuous drive" tile machine.[1] At the Board meeting of July 1st 1940, the directors agreed 'to proceed with the USA Application... for making "Westwold" tiles', negotiated a new price for the supply of sand to Leighton Buzzard, and then sat back to listen to Sir Owen's

---

1   *Marley Tile (Holding) Company minutes, September 1937.*

report on his visit to the USA: 'Mr O A Aisher referred to his discussions with Ludowici-Celadon Company regarding the proposal to co-operate with them in the manufacture and sale of our tiles in the USA and after a general discussion thereon it was agreed that Mr Aisher should write this Concern confirming his talks and suggestions to them on this proposal and obtain their reaction.' It was another 40 years before Marley finally began roof tile manufacture in the States.

Europe was another possibility for the concrete roof tile but Sir Owen took the view that Marley's supply and fix distribution methods could not be transposed on to the Continent. He argued that the trade unions and craft guilds in the roofing industry were too powerful to allow Marley to control all the downstream operations and without supply and fix, Sir Owen was not going. In contrast, plastic flooring, as a completely new product, was thought to give greater opportunities to Marley's supply and fix philosophy. An additional factor in favour of plastic flooring was that by 1950/51, Marley had already developed a lively export trade giving it the confidence of an existing customer base.

Even as the new Harrietsham factory was coming into production, Marley was forming overseas subsidiaries to develop the process and over the next ten years a network of plants was developed – if not around the world, then at least across Europe and into the extremities of the Southern hemisphere. Germany had the first plant to become operative, in November 1953, closely followed by South Africa in June 1954. Later came Finland in 1957, Austria 1959, Italy 1960, New Zealand and Brazil in 1961.

Although the Aishers expressed a clear preference for flooring in their early overseas expansion, it was not to the total exclusion of the concrete roofing tile. Indeed, technically, the first overseas investment was actually in Eire when, following a chance yachting encounter between Sir Owen and the Chadwick brothers, Marley made its initial investment in Concrete Products of Ireland in 1948. However, the historic association of Eire with the home market and the existence of a ready-made business meant that CPI was never properly representative of Marley's overseas strategy. The first concrete roof tile plant that Marley built overseas did not come until 1957 in Southern Rhodesia and, for 20 years, that remained the only country which Marley opened up via a greenfield development of roof tiles rather than by flooring or acquisition. Subsequently, there were attempts to graft the concrete roofing tile on to existing overseas businesses, with mixed success. A German plant was built in 1958 but Marley could never make it pay and it was eventually sold; before that sale, Marley bought into a French clay tile business (1968) that was seeking to diversify into concrete tiles but, there also, competition was acute. In contrast, the later introduction of the roof tile into South Africa (1971) contributed to the outstanding success Marley had in creating a rounded building materials business in that country. To complete the picture, Marley moved into the two missing Dominions in 1960 with the purchase of an Australian concrete products business and a Canadian flooring wholesaler. Within ten years of building that first flooring plant in Germany, Marley had established a network of investments around the world – Europe, Australasia, South Africa, South America and Canada; only the United States lacked representation. By the early 1970s, approaching half of Marley's sales were being derived from overseas markets.

The Eternit connection

The individual overseas ventures all have their special history and interest, as befits a Marley business, and it seems appropriate to let the story of the principal countries be told separately. Before that, another story needs to be told, that of Eternit – a name more familiar than the organisations which control it. Much of Marley's investment in Europe in the 1950s and 1960s, and then in South America, was done in association with organisations trading under the Eternit name. There are several geographic Eternits, of which the Belgian, Swiss and French are now the more important; they are all independent of each other but linked together by common history, trading agreements and, probably, cross shareholdings. Marley has been in partnership with different Eternits in different countries, sometimes separately, sometimes together. Some explanation of the different Eternit organisations helps put Marley's overseas ventures in context, but the story is an interesting one its own right.

It starts with a man called Ludwig Hatschek, born into a brewing family at Tesetice, Moravia (now the Czech Republic) in 1856. After the Prussian-Austrian War of 1866 (lost by Austria), the family emigrated to Linz in upper Austria, where Ludwig's father, Philip Hatschek, owned a brewery. Ludwig did not get along very well with his brothers and sisters and so was paid out his share of the capital, and in 1890 he became the new owner of an asbestos spinning mill in the little village of Schoendorf near Voecklabruck. This mill produced seals, brake linings, asbestos ropes and insulation panels.

Daily output at the mill was only a few kilogrammes and Ludwig Hatschek needed to find new products. Asbestos cardboards already existed, but he wanted to invent a roofing material, hard like stone and inflammable, as many roofs were still covered with straw. The board machine already existed and after seven years of experimental work, Ludwig Hatschek finally succeeded in producing asbestos-cement; the importance of his invention was the ability to produce asbestos-cement on an industrial scale. In 1901 he was granted a patent and the protection of the brand name 'Eternit' (from the Latin *eternum*, i.e. eternal).[2] The patent expired in 1918 but the brand name is still protected

---

2 *Another early name for the product, and one still used today, was Uralite, derived from the source of the asbestos in the Urals.*

today. Ludwig Hatschek died in 1914; control of the Austrian Eternit-Werke Ludwig Hatschek, as it is now known, remained in the family and it is currently managed by his two grandsons, Fritz and Rupert Hatschek.

Shortly after the patent had been obtained, Ludwig Hatschek began to licence the new process overseas. Eternit Niederurnen was founded in 1903 in the Swiss canton of Glarus by local industrialists. After the First World War, Niederurnen was taken over by Ernst Schmidheiny, then a cement manufacturer, to form what we know as Swiss Eternit. That original factory has grown into one of the largest building materials groups in Europe; the Schmidheiny interests also include Holderbank, the world's largest cement company. Later, Swiss Eternit formed a German Eternit (recently sold to Belgian Eternit) and it is also understood to hold shares in the other Eternit companies.

In 1905, Alphonse Emsens' family formed Eternit Belges which again became a multi-national combine and probably the largest of the Eternit companies; its flooring subsidiary, Fademac, was formed in 1948 and later became a Marley partner. In 1904, a French Eternit had been formed by an M Lanhoffer but his company was taken over by the Cuvelier family around 1920, probably with the support of the Swiss and Belgian Eternits who also became shareholders. Not part of the Eternit grouping itself but also becoming involved in France was the Pierard family, who owned a flooring company called Dalami. Jumping many years in the story, Dalami went into liquidation and was taken over by French Eternit, with Jean Louis Pierard joining the company.

Although Eternits were formed in other countries, they do not concern us here. The only other name to be introduced is that of Oesterheld, a German employed by Hatschek in the early years: 'One day, he left the company all of a sudden, nobody knew the reason for it. There must have been a serious quarrel between him and my grandfather.'[3] Oesterheld went back to Germany and began manufacturing asbestos-cement under the name of Fulgurit; he never took out a licence. It was Fulgurit that became Marley's first partner in Germany. Swiss, Belgian, French Eternits and Fulgurit; these are names which cross our path repeatedly in charting the development of Marley's partners in its post-war growth overseas – in European flooring, in French roofing tiles and in South America.

At an early stage, Marley Werke of Germany, then partly owned by Karl Oesterheld's Fulgurit, Fademac and Dalami formed a loose association, a grouping later extended to include Johns-Manville of America. In the case of the European companies, there were cross holdings. In 1962, Marley bought out the 20% holding that Fulgurit owned in Marley Werke and then sold 15%

---

3 *Fritz Hatschek correspondence with author.*

to Fademac and 10% to Dalami; in turn Marley purchased the same percentage shareholdings in the other two companies. This was clearly seen as part of a strategy for the emerging Economic Community – 'This will strengthen our position in the EEC'.

In South America, Marley had flooring joint ventures with Fademac (Belgian Eternit) in Brazil and Argentina; Swiss Eternit were minority shareholders in the Brazilian flooring company and Marley's main partner in that country for the manufacture of concrete roofing tiles. 'It all became a little bit incestuous at the end of the day in the sense that we were partners with some and not with others, and we were competing in some countries and not in others.'[4]

Manufacturing in Germany

Marley had contacts with Germany before the war in that the Aishers had bought certain of the roof tile colour pigments from I G Farben. Immediately after the end of the war, Marley was quick to resume old contacts and look for new opportunities. Fred Hardy had been over to buy wood wool machines almost as soon as the war ended, and Marley Tile minutes record Sir Owen's absence in Germany on business as early as October 1945. The contact with I G Farben was a man called Jansen and he began supplying pigment again to Marley Tile; he used to visit Marley every year and became a personal friend of Sir Owen. As Marley's floor tile business developed, the search for export agents was on and Sir Owen naturally turned to his friend Jansen for a recommendation. The suggestion was one Karl Oesterheld of Wunstorf, Hanover. As we saw earlier it was Karl Oesterheld's father who had worked at Hatschek's Eternit factory before returning to Wunstorf to set up his own company, Fulgurit. Oesterheld was a larger than life character and Mike Evans, Managing Director of Marley Werke from 1966, remembers some of the stories. 'He was a hunter of great enthusiasm and he used to go and shoot elephants. He had an ashtray that was an elephant's foot and things like this in this office. He was also Honorary Consul to San Salvador, so his office was also the Consul's office (the consulate in Hanover of San Salvador) so he was known as Herr Konsul. He had his own plane which at that time was quite extraordinary and the story goes that, if he wanted fish for lunch he would fly to Hamburg. He was obviously quite a showman – what I knew of him confirmed that.'

Karl Oesterheld's Fulgurit proved a natural sales agent and the

---

4 *Trevor Aisher interview.*

arrangements worked well to the point where a manufacturing base in Germany could follow. In June 1952, Deutsche Marley Floor Tile GmbH was formed with a share capital of DM 400,000 of which Oesterheld had 51% and Marley Floor Tile 49%. The articles of association carefully distinguished which products Deutsche Marley was allowed to make: 'the object of the company is the manufacture, laying and sale of floor and wall tiles, insulating sheets and similar products'. Fulgurit's share was paid in cash but Marley's contribution was largely satisfied by the transfer of 'a secret process' for manufacturing floor tiles. The Marley Werke sphere of interest was confined to the territory of Germany but, whether out of sensitivity or foresight, that was defined as the frontiers of 31.12.1937. Marley purchased spare land from Fulgurit, adjoining its main works. The title to the land was not without its ambiguities for the local farmers believed they had a right of way and during the early years they drove through the Marley site with their tractors to the fields; 'they called it the "Bauernkrieg" – the war of the farmers'. Whatever, Fred Hardy ordered the plant and construction went ahead, and at 10.15 a.m. on November 3rd 1953 the first floor tiles left the belt. Karl Oesterheld was the General Manager of Marley Werke with decision making very much concentrated in his hands. This may have proved less satisfactory than Marley had anticipated and very shortly after production started, there were proposals to buy out part of Oesterheld's shareholding, thereby switching majority control to Marley. This took place in July 1954 at which point Ernst Uhde, one of the Fulgurit managers, became the General Manager for Deutsche Marley.

As in the UK, Marley quickly moved to build up an extensive contracting organisation to complement its manufacturing facilities and the group accounts published in December 1954 reported that Marley had 'a well established sales and fixing organisation in all the leading centres in Germany'. An interesting reflection of the times was that of the 150 employees on the payroll in 1954, most were refugees from East Germany. The early years brought rapid financial success for Marley with sales rising from DM, 2m in 1954 to DM, 25m in 1957, while pre-tax profits rose from nothing to over DM, 3m (then equivalent to £260,000). This was despite manufacturing problems which necessitated Marley sending over Peter Amsden, Paul Nemet and Ivor Prewitt. Peter Amsden was surprised at what he found: '. . . to my amazement, having heard so much about the efficiency of the Germans, I found them extremely rigid, incapable of switching from making an A series on one machine to a C series on another; they seemed to resent the British too. There was still a lot of wartime attitude about.' That was only a hint of the troubles that Marley was to experience later in Germany. From the 1957 contribution of DM 3m, profits steadily declined, until substantial losses were incurred in the early 1960s. Competition was certainly intense as new entrants came in to what had been perceived as a growth market. Pegulan was set up after the war by a Doctor Ries who had originally been a manufacturer of rubber and plastics in East

Germany before the war; this was an aggressive successful business and was eventually bought out by BAT. The major linoleum manufacturer was DLW who entered the plastics flooring market shortly after Marley, also providing strong competition and in addition there were Dunlop and Armstrong as in the UK together with DASAG (Deutsche Asphalt). Relationships with Pegulan became tense when Marley Werke's company chemist moved to Pegulan in 1959 taking with him 'the company's secrets'; criminal proceedings were started and damages sought from Pegulan.

Marley did not find it easy to exercise effective management control in Germany. Ernst Uhde, previously one of the Fulgurit managers, was appointed General Manager for Deutsche Marley in 1954 but it was felt that he remained closer to his old German boss than his new English ones. Sometimes the clashes could be funny. Uhde wore a monocle and on one occasion came into the factory when John Kenward was production manager. 'Uhde looked at the tiles coming off the line and said 'these tiles are no use – you can't sell tiles that have got bubbles on the surface – it's all scrap material'. John looked at the tiles and said "Herr Uhde, I think if you clean the condensation off your monocle you will see that the tiles don't have bubbles on the surface".[5] The Marley Tile minutes constantly reflect the dissatisfaction with the performance of the German business and it is clear that language was one of the complications. Eventually John Kenward took over as Managing Director in 1962; he had a German mother and had married a local Wunstorf girl but there was still an objective of selecting a German deputy 'capable of becoming a general manager... but it was emphasised that he should always be under the supervision of an Englishman.'[6] In fact, despite two years of searching, Marley failed to find the ideal local candidate; meanwhile, the losses began to mount up. Not only was the competition in the flooring market becoming acute, particularly with the growing use of carpets, but Marley was also having to contend with the problems in its newer concrete roof tile company and its shops, both discussed separately.

In 1966, Mike Evans, then aged only 31 and working in Marley's retail business, took over from John Kenward but it was not until the closure of both the roof tile operation and the shops in 1970 that he was able to engineer the slow rehabilitation of the German subsidiary. After those closures, around a third of turnover came from the Spacesaver door (introduced in 1960), just ahead of the traditional floorings business following which came rainwater goods, which Marley Werke first started manufacturing in 1962. As if the failures with roofing tiles and shops had not been enough, Marley had to contend with the decline in the German market for resilient floorings. More worrying, Marley's own market share was also falling. 'Our effectiveness as

---

5 Mike Evans interview.
6 Marley Overseas minutes, November 1963.

flooring contractors was getting less because of the wide range of flooring which we needed to supply and fix for customers. During the early years the tilers would cover virtually the whole area of a block of flats with vinyl tiles and so that was relatively easy to control. But if Frau Schmidt wanted to have some carpet in this room and some parquet in that room, you had to order those quantities from a supplier – very difficult to control. Of course, having been the aggressive manufacturing and contracting company, the flooring contractors were not all that easily persuaded to buy on a supply only basis from Marley; there was enough of the product to be had from other manufacturers.'[7] These were not problems which were different in principle from those experienced in the UK but Marley was not able to sustain the market share necessary to dominate the market as it did in the UK, and it is also fair to say that the German flooring market diversified more quickly than had been the case at home.

The Consortium: new joint ventures

Shortly after Marley Werke's Hanover plant became operative, Marley was negotiating in Finland for the formation of a local company to make Marley tiles. Kymarno AB was formed in 1956 with a manufacturing and licensing agreement from Marley. Marley took a 20% interest, paid for with its licence fee, the balance being owned by Oy Nokia; helped by staff from Leighton Buzzard, the Finnish associate started production in April 1957. Austria was another small market, but it was a natural extension of Marley Werke's sales territory. A separate selling subsidiary had been formed in 1956 but in 1958 the imposition of increased duties on imported flooring products encouraged Marley to build its own flooring plant at Linz, entering production the following year. The following year, 1960, Plastica Italiana commenced production. Marley was the largest shareholder with 40% and provided the technical know-how and the management supervision; Fademac and Dalami had 25% each and Johns-Manville 10%. This provided the practical experience of working together which preceded the exchange of shares with Fademac and Dalami in 1962. At that point, Marley had direct or indirect manufacturing interests in the flooring markets of Britain, Germany, Austria, Belgium and France. Given the extent of overseas investment in flooring perhaps the surprise is that Marley contented itself with no more than a 10% trade investment in France but Sir Owen had his reservations: 'I think we were sensible enough to think of it as a much more difficult country'.

As the relationship between the joint venture partners developed, it

7 *Mike Evans interview.*

became increasingly formalised until eventually it was recognised as a 'consortium'; it had formal meetings, joint investments and, on occasions, even a common strategy. Indeed, in 1967, there was even discussion of a proposal to merge the Consortium's European interests into a joint company: 'OAA informed the meeting that he had been asked by M A Emsens to consider the consolidation of all their interests in Europe under a single company. In preliminary discussions he had had with M Pierard, Mr O A Aisher had expressed a willingness to participate in this scheme if this would be of any benefit to all members from a trading, finance or tax point of view. A further meeting was to be held with M Emsens and M de Cartier when Mr O A Aisher intended to ask for proof of the benefits to be derived from the scheme before any further negotiations took place.'[8]

The possibilities considered by the Consortium ranged around the world. The 1960s started off with negotiations with Osman Ahmed Osman & Co of Cairo on the formation of a floor tile company in Egypt, followed by proposals of varying degrees of seriousness for flooring plants in India, Japan, Israel, Turkey, Greece and Colombia. Nearer to home, a Spanish company was formed, this time bringing in the Spanish company, Uralita. A flooring factory was proposed for Seville but agreement on a majority vote did not augur well for the project and it was abandoned at the end of 1965. However, where the Consortium was successful in establishing its presence was in South America and significant investments were made in Argentina and Brazil.

The decision to manufacture vinyl flooring at Jacarei to the East of Sao Paulo in Brazil, in partnership with Fademac and Dalami, was taken in 1960 with Marley subscribing for an initial 26% holding. Early losses were incurred, partly due to difficulties in coping with Brazil's hyperinflation, and the partners were clearly frustrated at their ability to exercise control from a distance: 'In respect of most administrative matters Eternit as well as Marley are complaining of lack of coherent information. OAAA should write to Fademac Belgium expressing misgivings about the Brazilian business and also warning that the current financial problems of Marley will forbid further remittance of funds or undertaking of guarantees.'[9]

The position showed little improvement and by 1968, the Brazilian company was on the verge of closure. At the Marley Overseas Board meeting, John Pollard reported on 'the conclusions reached at the recent Consortium meeting, where a final decision as to whether or not to continue in Brazil will be taken on the presentation of the year end profit and loss account. He emphasised the Marley attitude throughout had been that the Brazilian business should be closed down and there was no change in this view.'[10] That

---

8 *Marley Overseas minutes, July 1967.*
9 *Ibid, September 1966.*
10 *Ibid, January 1968.*

must have represented the low point; the management began to gain a firmer grip on the business and the Brazilian economy started to boom. Fademac was the only manufacturer of significance in the Brazilian vinyl floor tile market, covering the whole of that enormous country through 90 distributors, most of whom had regional exclusivity. (No supply and fix work was carried out.)

Roof tiles in Europe

One of Redland's undoubted successes has been its German concrete roof tile business where it dominates the roofing industry. On its own admission, Redland attributes its success to a partnership with the right man at the right time – Herr Rudolf Braas. One of the stories in the Marley folklore is that Herr Braas approached Sir Owen Aisher with a proposal of partnership but Sir Owen turned it down because he wanted at least 50%. Herr Braas went on to see Redland and the rest is history. There certainly does seem to have been some meeting between Herr Braas and Marley but whether it ever led to firm proposals is difficult to say. Whatever, the Redland/Braas partnership was formed in 1953. Eventually, Marley decided to build a concrete roof tile plant itself and in January 1958 the first plans were minuted for a new plant at Griesheim near Darmstadt in south-west Germany; the first roof tiles were made on May 28th that year. The roof tile business never made a profit. Marley was no longer leading the way for by that time Braas was well established. The location of the Marley factory appeared less than satisfactory: 'Uhde came from the Darmstadt area and this is why the roof tile business was set up there because he, in fact, wanted the head office of Marley to be near his home. He never did move to the Hanover area and his ambition was apparently to move the head office of the business down to the Darmstadt area and so that was one of the advantages of buying a piece of land to put the roof tile plant on. As it happened, it was also putting it in the middle of all the roof tile operations which Braas were setting up. One of the reasons that it failed, I think, is that it was absolutely surrounded by one competitor who was able to squeeze the life out of the business.'[11]

Sir Owen had had his reservations after the war about the suitability of the Marley integrated manufacture and the supply and fix system on the continent and his reservations proved correct. By the time Marley established its contracting operation, Redland was well entrenched with the merchants. 'They were much stronger, the merchants in Germany, much more organised than they were here... we didn't stand a chance, frankly.'[12] Marley struggled

11   Mike Evans interview.
12   Trevor Aisher interview.

with its one plant for years; the comparison with Redland was particularly irksome and it became a matter of pride. 'It was agreed that it would be a terrible admission of defeat for Marley to cease roof tile production at Darmstadt, but this must be seriously contemplated.'[13] Opinions at that meeting varied widely from spending to automate the plant, to closing Darmstadt and opening a new modern factory in northern Germany 'aimed at securing a good slice of business capable of withstanding any future Braas or other competition'. Eventually the overseas board turned down the expenditure at Darmstadt but agreed to build a new roof tile factory in the Ruhr and in November 1965 the main board gave the go-ahead for a factory at Dusseldorf. Before a satisfactory site could be found the proposal was put on hold and the factory never did get built.

The tone of the minutes became bleaker as the years rolled on: '... considerable discussion on the future of Darmstadt where the factory equipment is ageing and thus the business is becoming less competitive in the factory compared with Braas... with the current losses, further capital investment is unattractive. It was common ground that nobody wishes to admit defeat in Germany but an end to roof tile manufacture at Darmstadt, if not elsewhere in Germany, must be in the foreseeable future. Rees... would make quiet enquiries... to see if there would be any exterior interest in the business.'[14] 'The problems of massive competition from Braas in the Griesheim area and high haulage cost if the selling area was expanded.'[15] 'Rees referred to the narrowing circle of Braas factories around the Darmstadt area and it was appreciated that the long term prospects must be bleak.'[16] In the end, Marley admitted defeat and production ceased at Darmstadt in 1970. The plant and equipment was sold to Braas for D M 1.7m, and in the following year the site was sold for D M 3.45m.

Opportunities in France

Darmstadt may have offered little but hope but it was sufficient to encourage Marley (just) to examine other roof tile possibilities in Europe; indeed, Marley's market leadership in the UK naturally produced approaches from other parties. In 1963, five years after the start of roof tile production in Germany, Jack Aisher was reporting on the possibilities of production in France – 'considered but not met with enthusiasm'. The idea was better received in 1967. At a meeting of the Marley Overseas Board in July, young Owen outlined the

---

13 *Marley Overseas minutes, January 1964*
14 *Ibid, July 1968.*
15 *Ibid, June 1969.*
16 *Ibid, July 1969.*

negotiations between Marley's D J G Dicks and the Societe Commercial D'Affretements et de Combustibles (SCAC) with a view to forming a roof tile manufacturing company in France; he suggested that as a preliminary it was thought that roof tiles from Darmstadt would be exported into eastern France.

It was clear from those minutes that France was not viewed as an isolated investment proposal but part of a European strategy: 'it was agreed that... expansion of roof tile business throughout Europe is to be encouraged, preferably by entering into partnership on a joint venture basis with some existing local company. Whilst it was agreed that controlling interest in any venture is ideal... there was no reason why a minority interest should not be taken'. Trevor Aisher was asked 'to explore'. However, despite the wish to develop on a broader front, the new investment was to remain confined to France; indeed an approach from a clay tile manufacturer in Austria for a joint venture in that same year was turned down.

Trevor Aisher remembers the enticements to enter the French market: 'We had been approached by a number of people over the years who kept coming to Riverhead and saying "Look, we want to get into the roofing business in France, would you be interested?" ' – it never led anywhere. One approach which did nearly succeed was from a Monsieur Pux of Maison Phenix, a prefabricated housebuilding company with a factory near Rouen. The September 1967 minutes showed that discussions had progressed as far as the formation of a new company with Maison Phenix (60% Marley, 40% MP) for the production of roof tiles a few miles north west of Paris. '... for various reasons we didn't sign the agreement, it fell through. We then heard of Monsieur Bisch, he came on to the stand at the Building Exhibition in England – he had been told to come and see us. He had a clay tile works at Strasbourg which was an old family business, and he had opened up a concrete tile works at Lyon (Seyssuel), built it with Keller equipment and was having all sorts of problems trying to get it to work, he was going broke.'

In May 1968, Marley agreed to take a 41% shareholding in Les Tuileries Bisch for £422,000 though the deal was not actually concluded until January 1969. Central to the agreement was a new joint venture between Marley and Bisch with the intention of building up to four or five factories across France. Also coming in as a partner at the request of Bisch was Phenix with a 5% shareholding in Les Tuileries Bisch. The initial shareholding in the new concrete tile company was 39% to Bisch, 31% to B M Financial (a Bisch family company), 20% Marley and 10% Maisons Phenix – hence the name Tuileries BMP. The management was to be provided by Bisch with technical assistance from Marley.

The first task was to get Seyssuel working properly; a resident Marley engineer was appointed but the problems ran deep – Marley Holdings minutes of November 1969 detailed the death of the technical manager, removal of the factory manager, lack of a chief mechanic, strikes and a lack of knowledge!

Against that background, it is not surprising to discover that the relationship with their Bisch partners was not wholly comfortable and Marley needed to ensure it had greater managerial control. The Marley Overseas Board meeting in September 1970 witnessed 'considerable discussion' on the future of the French business. 'Due to difficulties with the introduction of concrete tiles, profits have not been ploughed back and the clay tiles side is now suffering from lack of capital expenditure. It is becoming apparent to the Bisch management that the concrete plant at Seyssuel will have to be scrapped as it cannot be made to work effectively although Mr T J Aisher emphasised that with more sophisticated machinery, more sophisticated labour will be essential... arising therefrom Monsieur Bisch was wavering between offering Marley a small percentage of his shareholding, sufficient for control to pass to Marley, to offering his entire shareholding. Agreed advantage to get control but leave sufficient with M Bisch to give him incentive.'

In the event, Marley subscribed for new shares at a cost of FF 3 million and bought a few shares from M Bisch personally at a cost of FF 300,000; the net effect being to give Marley 74% of the main operating company at Selz and 64% of the concrete tile company, at that point controlling only the Paris factory. Marley was then able to take over complete responsibility for concrete roof tile manufacture leaving M Bisch to deal with clay roof tile manufacture and the sales for both sides. Archie Orme became joint general manager with M Bisch.

The workforce at Bisch's Selz clay tile plant were also concerned about Marley's intentions. At the Bisch Board meeting on 10th November 1971, Monsieur Roess of the Works' Committee 'stated that he wanted to know what was the intention of the MARLEY GROUP in respect of the future of the SELZ Factory. He feared lest the commercial policy be pivoted essentially on the sales of concrete tiles. He went on to remind the Board that Selz was profitable whereas the Seyssuel concrete plant had been in loss since it opened. Five days later, John Pollard (Marley representative on the Bisch Board) had to issue a Memorandum for all the staff at Selz.

> At the request of the Delegates to the Central Committee we confirm to you the statements made on November 10th by Mr Pollard, Director and Financial Manager of the Marley Company at the Meeting of the Board of Directors of Tuileries Bisch.
>
> Mr Pollard, having expressed his surprise concerning rumours of closure of the factory, stated:-
>
> 'The Marley Company has substantial holdings in the Share Capital of Tuileries Bisch the greater part of which holdings relate to the Selz factory. For this reason alone it is difficult to imagine that the Marley Company should not take the greatest interest in the Selz factory which constitutes one of the most important units in the Bisch Group.'

Mr Pollard further stated that Marley has investments in many other materials than concrete tiles and he is convinced that our earthenware tiles will continue to hold their place on the market.

The difficulties we have encountered are due to a number of factors and more particularly to the national, local and trade situations... There has at no time been considered the closing of the Selz factory and there is no internal or external factor of which we can at present be aware to cause us to envisage any such eventuality.

The staff might have relaxed more had they known that Marley was eventually to pull out of the concrete tile market in France and that the Selz factory, much expanded, would become one of the most successful of Marley's overseas investments.

In the meantime, Tuileries BMP was pressing on with the original plan to build a new concrete roof tile factory at Fontenay near Paris, which became operative at the end of 1971; it was followed by a plant at Harnes near Lille, and another at Thouars in the Loire in 1974/75. The potential of France to the concrete roof tile manufacturers was the high market share still in the hands of the clay tile producers; with the example of Britain across the Channel and now Germany next door it was thought only a matter of time before concrete took control of the French roofing market. Inevitably, this attracted others into the industry. In 1969 French Eternit had indicated 'a desire to participate in Bisch' but Marley was not interested. Next year, Eternit France, Eternit Belgium, Seric and Comptoir Tulier du Nord et Tuileries de Beauvais announced that they were forming a new company to make concrete roof tiles in France. Beauvais Tuileries brought its new factory at Ons-en-Bray (25m tile capacity); Seric a similar sized plant at St Just-de-Claix; Eternit France and Belgium planned to put into production in 1971 two factories of the same type and the construction of another production centre was decided upon near Grenoble. With Redland also present, this would have caused problems even in a fast growing market but as the French showed a marked reluctance to desert their traditional, and picturesque, clay tile the result was financially disastrous.

The pressures arising out of the industry's overcapacity were compounded by continued technical problems at the new factories and the divisions of control between Bisch and Marley. The remaining Bisch family interests were bought out by Marley in the Summer of 1974 for FF 6 million. In November, John Pollard had to submit a depressing report to the Marley main Board: 'Bisch is now one of our leading investments with £6½ million tied up... we are having a bad experience with Paris, which is still not off the ground. If Thouars and Harnes take as long to become viable, the financial consequences will be serious. In this event, we would be unable to further subsidise the business from the UK due to the new exchange controls recently introduced by the Labour government. Since Marley became interested in

Bisch, tax losses of FF 15 millions have been incurred. This note is to draw attention to the need for an early improvement in cash flow...' In fact, Selz was continuing to trade well with profits of around FF2 million in 1974 and Seyssuel made not far short of that; the damage was being done by the three new concrete factories which had lost over FF7 million between them that year. Unfortunately, the losses were to increase yet further; Selz with 23 million tiles a year and Seyssuel with 11 million were able to achieve viable volumes, but falling activity in the building industry meant that the newer factories had come on stream too late.

Ireland

Although technically part of Marley's "European" operations, Concrete Products of Ireland never played an integrated part in Marley's European strategy; it was a another product of Sir Owen's travels and, for obvious historic reasons, it was regarded as an offshoot of Marley's mainland activities as much as anything else. In practice, it had a life of its own and for much of its history CPI was a quoted public company with Marley as no more than the majority shareholder. Marley disposed of its holding in 1987 but for most of its 40 year association with Marley, Ireland was an important (indeed, sometimes the only) contributor to "European" profits.

Ireland had always been a natural market for concrete products, lacking any significant reserves of coal to burn clay, and between the wars small companies abounded. William Thomas Chadwick had established a small builders' merchants business at Talbot Place, Dublin in 1902 – Chadwicks (Dublin). He was an agent for Blue Circle Cement between the wars which inevitably took him into the local concrete products manufacturers. In 1930 he acquired control of one of these small customers who manufactured roof tiles and concrete blocks at Dolphin's Barn in Dublin; on August 28th 1931 that business was registered as a private limited company – Concrete Products of Ireland. In 1937, Sir Owen had been taking part in a yacht race and decided to call in to Dun Laoghaire with the intention of visiting a particular concrete works. By mistake the taxi took him to the Dolphin's Barn premises of Concrete Products of Ireland; the result was a chance meeting with Terence Chadwick, William's eldest son. Nothing came directly from the meeting but immediately after the war, in 1946, William Chadwick died. His sons, Terence and Finton, then came to Riverhead to see the Aishers. Sir Owen: 'We went over and had a look: it was awful. Anyhow, we helped them and in the end we had 30% of it for our help.' In more formal terms, a technical agreement on concrete products and roof tiles was signed in October 1948; CPI paid Marley £3,000 and ceded one third of the equity. The concession on equity did not look especially generous at that stage as CPI was still having difficulty in repaying its bank debts. Prior to formalising the agreement, CPI had introduced the Marley roof tile into the Irish market and acquired a 50 acre site at Lucan, Co. Dublin to relocate the manufacturing business. Following from Sir Owen's contacts with Besser in 1940, Terence Chadwick visited the United States in 1947 and brought back the first Besser block making machine which was installed on the new site. The following year the new tile making plant from Marley was ready and the share transfer could take place.

CPI expanded its roof tile and concrete products capacity to meet rising demand in Eire but the company was also able to profit from its association with Marley by marketing the latter's more diversified range of products. Thus, in the early 1950s, CPI began selling flooring and later extrusions. In the early 1960s discussions began on Marley acquiring a controlling interest in CPI. In January 1965 CPI bought the other part of the Chadwick family's building interests, Chadwicks Dublin, by then one of the largest builders merchants in Eire. An offer was made to the public of 25% of the shares and at the same time Marley acquired from the Chadwick family additional shares taking Marley's holding up to 51%. Sir Owen and Tom O'Sullivan joined the CPI Board. Profits in that first year amounted to £310,000.

The consolidation at the time of the public issue gave CPI a broadly based business: the Dublin factory was market leader for concrete roofing tile production in Eire; Chadwicks was one of the leading merchants in Dublin and CPI, was also distributing a range of UK flooring and extrusion products. Gradually these different businesses were expanded, for concrete products it was straightforward organic expansion, capitalising on the growth in the Irish building industry. Features which stand out are the investment in a fully automated block plant in 1973 and a new automated roof tile factory at Cork in 1974. In the light of the debate which was then beginning to intensify, perhaps one of the more interesting importations from the UK was the supply and fix organisational structure which was started in 1967.

Marley's flooring and extrusions range sold well in Ireland providing useful added volumes for the home plants. Flooring remained distribution only but CPI installed an extrusions plant of its own and Marley Extrusions (Ireland) started production in 1967 with three employees; the factory had to be extended twice and by 1980 was employing over 80 people.

Africa – a mini-Marley in the making

As in continental Europe, Marley's entree into Africa was through the export of floor tiles. The initial contacts were made through Dick Aisher and agents were appointed in South Africa and the Rhodesias. Jack Aisher remembers the

South Africans coming to England to obtain the franchises for this new flooring product: 'A chap called Lionel Brazier from Durban came over to England and met Dick and Dick made a deal with him where he could have the franchise for Natal. Shortly after that, a fellow called Leopold came over and we were also approached by Arden Scott Timbers.' Demand rose rapidly in the early 1950s and Marley enjoyed a good export business through its agents but import restrictions soon dictated that Marley establish local manufacturing facilities.

Encouraged by the agents, Jack Aisher was sent out to South Africa in 1953: 'I was commissioned to go over there more or less with a blank cheque on the basis "you make your mind up whether you think we ought to build a factory" and I had an introduction to Philip Sceales.' Philip Sceales was a partner with Bowman, Gillfillian & Blacklock, solicitors and the South African agent for Marley's British lawyers, Freshfields, who introduced him to Marley. He became the first Chairman in South Africa and he remained so for over 30 years until he retired in 1984. 'We went and looked at land. The difficulty was getting anywhere where there was electric power and we finished up by going to a place called Nigel on the East Rand. Laings were over there and I saw them. Literally I bought the land [June 1953], talked to Laings about it; the factory was built and the whole investment was, I think, something like just under £100,000. We took a young fellow called Dick Eyres to run the plant.' The first tiles came off the line at 10.55 p.m. on Sunday June 27th 1954.

The Municipality of Nigel had been anxious to have industry established in a town where the gold mines were coming to the end of their lives and went out of their way to let Marley have the land cheaply and to overcome the uncertainties over electricity supplies. They even signed an agreement that the municipality would guarantee power to Marley at the expense of domestic customers: 'on two occasions it was necessary for the street lights of Nigel to be extinguished so that the Marley night shift could operate without interruption.'[17]

The agents that Marley had first used for its exports played a particularly important role as they were not only the distributors but, trained by Marley, they also acted as the supply and fix arm of the business: in more formal terms than above they were K & L Timbers of Cape Town (in the same grouping as Arden Scott); L Brazier & Sons of Durban and Frank Wright of Johannesburg (run by Fritz Leopold). To tie them as part of the supply and fix operation they were allowed to purchase 20% of the new company. Marley was also fortunate in that the post-war emigration from Britain to South Africa had included tradesmen; there was a greater pool of experience available to the Company than might have been expected in a new market.

Initially, it had not been considered advisable to take a more active part in the contracting side of the industry. However, Marley found the working

---

17 *Marley Limited* Jubilee Brochure, *1974*.

arrangements with its three semi-independent distributors restrictive nor did they always work together smoothly: 'Those agents, we taught them how to do it [but] they were a nuisance because they wouldn't want to sell the tiles to anybody else, a typical merchant. So we bought them out and we did sell to everybody.'[18] However, it could not be done in a hurry. The first step was the agreement in 1956 for the purchase of the minority interests in Marley held by K & L Timbers and Frank Wright although Brazier's holding was not bought until 1965. More important than the mopping up of the agents' minorities in Marley was the purchase, in 1957, of the whole of the Frank Wright distribution and contracting business which covered Rhodesia as well as South Africa. The business was owned by Fritz Leopold; with the £72,000 consideration received for his Company, Leopold subscribed for 221,000 shares in Marley (Holding) giving him 2.8% of the parent company.

Until the mid-1960s Marley's concentration was almost entirely on its flooring products and the related contracting and distribution. The product range was gradually extended, often following lines previously imported from Britain – the manufacture of Consort in 1965 being a notable example. The distribution arm was substantial and was enlarged in scope by two acquisitions – The Trinidad and General Asphalt Contracting Company (a waterproofing business) in 1963, and three years later, Epping Timber Holdings which was bought from K & L Timbers, one of the three original partners. Epping's two active subsidiaries were builders' merchants and timber dealers which between them employed 800 people, managed by Eric Ismay who later joined the Board of Marley S.A. Epping was a substantial deal by Marley S.A. standards being valued at R3.6m including R1.0m of debt; its last accounts had showed sales of R1.9m and post tax profits of R324,000. The vendors accepted 200,000 Marley shares. Marley was at last in full control of its own distribution and contracting.

Epping Timber proved a bigger business than Marley needed, and they certainly had no lasting interest in the timber merchanting. In September 1968, but two years later, it was agreed that with the exception of the flooring business, Epping should be sold; in a complicated deal, Marley received a mixture of shares in Federated Timber and Barlow to a value of R3m. Shortly afterwards Barlow took over Federated Timber and then Marley's enlarged Barlow holding was sold for R5.45m; the whole transaction realised Marley a profit of around R3m.

Although Marley had been the first company to lay down a flooring plant, it was not an advantage it held for long. The market was expanding rapidly but with the experience of Europe and the USA to draw on, there was no shortage of competition – Dunlop; Gersud, a subsidiary of the French Gerland; Krommenie, a Dutch firm; and Poly-Flor (owned by the British James

---

18   *Sir Owen Aisher interview.*

Halstead) were the principal rivals. This led to periods of intense competition between manufacturers (who were probably two too many for the market place) interspersed with moments of "understanding" which were not untypical of the South African business scene. Thus, profits which had grown in fits and starts to around 140,000 Rand in 1961 and 1962, more than doubled to 350,000 Rand in 1963 as a result of more muted competition. There were even negotiations between Marley and Dunlop for a merger in 1964; although the talks were abandoned, some production sharing did develop – for instance, Dunlop manufactured Marley's requirements of Marleyflor.

Attempts to stabilise the market brought little lasting success and another pricing war developed in the late 1960s which resulted in Marley acquiring two of its weakened competitors. Gersud (Pty), with 12% of the roll flooring market, was bought in 1969 and its production facility at Cape is still in use today. Poly-Flor Products was acquired in 1970 but it was closed down and the plant installed on the Nigel site. Gersud was bought for R410,000 but it was a contentious purchase not wholly supported by the parent company. Marley (Overseas) minutes recorded concern as to the extra burden on the management which was already stretched to capacity. The immediate financial costs were greater than expected; Marley had expected Gersud to lose R500,000 but when the accounts were produced the loss turned out to be R1.25m. However, the acquisitions did consolidate Marley's position giving it half the market for resilient floorings.

The product range expands

By the mid-1960s Marley was gradually beginning to draw its wider UK range of products into South Africa. Extrusions and retail, both new divisions in the UK were early additions. Trials of rainwater goods were made in the spring of 1966 and by the autumn a separate division was formed to sell and install plumbing goods – now one of South Africa's strengths. In line with the Marley philosophy of getting closer to the customer, a presence had also been established in retailing; by 1966 some half-dozen shops had been opened and questions were already being asked about their losses. Indeed the poor performance in the retail division continued for some years until they were eventually closed. Whatever the policy from Head Office, it is unlikely that the local management had the same enthusiasm for retailing which threatened to bring the Company into direct competition with its customers. The long distances involved in serving the South African market, or series of markets, and the Government policy directing commercial traffic onto a less than reliable railway system, meant that Marley had developed its network of regional depots to a greater extent than in any other country. They are more than depots, they are business centres where all the selling is done and the

Manager is part of the community. He is selling to all the shops; every little furniture shop is going to have Marley goods in it – we saturate the retail market. So while there was a policy from overseas that we should have shops, there was an absolute block in South Africa against doing anything to upset our High Street customers. [Our shops] would only sell at prices that were above other retailers; you could say they became mainly showrooms for the convenience of architects.'[19]

Perhaps surprisingly, it took some time before a roof tile factory was built, possibly because other manufacturers had already established a strong market position. The first investigations into the possibility of building a plant dated back to 1966; main Board directors raised it periodically on their visits but it was not until 1971 that a plant was finally opened at Olifantsfontein in 1971. Sales growth was rapid, reaching 10 million tiles a year by 1976 and by 1980 Marley was installing a second roof tile line. One thing that was agreed was that Marley would not contemplate setting up a fixing division. Where supply and fix work was taken it was 'with the express condition that the fixing would be carried out by an independent contractor.'[20] In fact, some of the large builders preferred to give contracts on a supply and fix basis so Marley was drawn into it in certain regions but it never became a philosophy in its own right.

Rhodesia

Prior to introducing its roof tiles into South Africa, Marley had built a plant in Southern Rhodesia. Marley Tile Co. (Private) was registered in Salisbury, Southern Rhodesia on 8th February 1957 as the vehicle for Marley's first overseas concrete roof tile plant. Joe Waterman, previously manager of the Storrington factory, was sent out to manage the new company and supervise the construction of the plant. It was a good test of Marley ingenuity. The sand resources were in the bush 13 miles outside Salisbury; the access road had to be built during the rainy season and the Nyrongo River bridged. The factory was built four miles outside Salisbury and the tile making machinery, made by Marley, and the sand washing and grading plant all had to be brought round the Cape as the Suez crisis had shut the Canal. Eventually, the first Ludlow tiles rolled off the production line on 19th July, a year ahead of Germany.

Denis Hunt, who was to play a key role in the development of Marley's business in South Africa, had been an area sales manager at Burton when he was asked to go to Rhodesia as the sales manager shortly after production commenced. 'A typical Marley approach. I had just got back from my holidays when Ben Rees, who was in charge of the Midlands area at the time, phoned

19 *Denis Hunt interview.*
20 *Marley S.A. minutes, June 1971.*

and said they would like to interview me at Sevenoaks but they would like to know first whether I wanted to go. Take my time and talk to my wife about it and would I please ring back at 9 o'clock the next morning and let them know.'

The intention behind the move into Rhodesia had been to use the Salisbury plant as the base for sales throughout the Central African Federation of Rhodesia and Nyasaland. Unfortunately, increasing dissension within the Federation prior to its break-up caused people to start leaving the country, houses were left empty and the building market collapsed to the extent that the factory was closed in 1959. Sales of tiles continued in a modest way out of existing stocks until a few years later Marley itself tried reviving the market by putting up a few houses in 1965. Denis Hunt recalls: 'We were amazed: about two or three hundred people came to look at them and it just got going again and other builders started building.' The factory was re-opened but then in 1965 UDI was declared by Ian Smith. The factory was kept going throughout the whole of the UDI period by Len Jones and Frank Butler, and indeed still operates today, but Rhodesia never became more than a peripheral interest of Marley. It did, however, nurture Denis Hunt, the man who was to develop the South African subsidiary into one of the leading building material companies in the country, as Managing Director from 1973 to 1986, and Chairman since 1984 when Philip Sceales retired.

Although the late 1960s and early 1970s were successful in that the base of the operation was broadened, it was a period of low financial returns and the parent company came close to parting company with its offshoot. The dissatisfaction was clearly apparent in the minutes and appeared to come to a head in 1971. Thus, the parent company minutes of July 1971 recorded the '... lengthy discussion on the problems of South Africa which Mr J E Aisher summed up as being mainly of management although assessing the nature of the weakness is difficult'. In November, Bill Courtney, who was now becoming more closely involved in South Africa reported back on his recent visit, expressing dissatisfaction with the efficiency of the business, indicating that he intended insisting on much tighter controls operating throughout the whole business. Eventually patience ran out and, in July 1973, an agreement was reached to sell Marley S.A. to Abercom Investments. The price was to be £5.6m in cash and shares which would have given Marley 10% of the Abercom capital. Marley's interest in the Rhodesian Company was also to be sold, for £1.3m.

The financial press was positive on the benefits to Abercom. 'On the basis that the Marley operations here have performed poorly in comparison to those of the parent in the UK, this makes sense. But in the hands of Abercom, Marley's flooring and roof tiling operations could start turning in some good results.'[21] Against South Africa's pre-tax contribution of £317,000 in the

---

21 South African Financial Review, *27th July 1973.*

Denis Hunt

financial year June 1972, and net assets of £5.1m, it looked a good deal for Marley as well. In the event, the sale of the Rhodesian company was blocked by the UK authorities under the 1965 Southern Rhodesia Act and since the sales were interdependent this effectively ended the whole transaction. Blocking the sale proved a blessing in disguise: under Denis Hunt's leadership, South Africa blossomed over the next ten years and became one of Marley's leading profit earners.

'Never play two up with an Australian'

Sir Owen first visited Australia in 1956 and friendly relations had been established with Reliance Industries of Sydney. Reliance manufactured concrete roofing tiles, pre-cast and pre-stressed concrete products and also had interests in ready mixed concrete, so it was a business that Marley understood well. The first formal reference to Reliance came in the Marley Holdings minutes of September 14th 1960 when there was a lengthy report on Australia and the decision to 'ratify' the purchase of 70% of Reliance; the choice of words clearly indicated a Board approval after the event. In the following year, the 30% minority was acquired for the issue of 153,000 Marley shares. Looking back on it, Sir Owen's view was that 'Probably the worst place we ever went to was Australia, it was a long way away and we never did any good there: never play "two up" with an Australian'.

The honeymoon lasted a couple of years and the usual thoughts were voiced about introducing plastic products and opening shops. The reckoning came in time for Christmas 1963 when the directors of Marley Overseas 'expressed their astonishment at the discrepancies discovered by the auditors and their disquiet that Mr Hamilton as Managing Director should not have given any indication or warning of the auditors report which he must have known about when he attended the last meeting'. A year later Fred Hardy was sent to Australia to close the business. His arrival was less than auspicious – there was a strike when he got off the plane. Fred Hardy thought that although there was much wrong with the business, it could be put right and it was better to do so before trying to sell it. Putting it right involved sending out Rod Hewson from the UK as General Manager but this in turn led to wholesale clashes with the Australian directors. Anybody who was anyone took legal advice and in May 1965 a formal letter of protest was sent by the Australian directors to each of the Holding Company directors. At the Board meeting of 12th May it was agreed that Marley was 'unable to accept the advice tendered'. The Reliance directors resigned the next month followed by their Chairman in September.

Slowly Marley set about reconstituting the Australian management team. Fred Osborne, a lawyer and Minister of Navy in the Menzies Government, was appointed Chairman in March 1966 and Rod Hewson remained as General Manager. The business was slowly rationalised, particularly roof tiles, and significant write downs made on old plant. Problems began to re-emerge in the early 1970s. Aggravated by labour troubles, profits halved in 1970 and fresh thought was given to the future of the Company. With the return of the roofing tile subsidiary to profit, discussions were even held in 1972 on the possibility of a local listing but this was soon abandoned. Later that year, discussions began with Concrete Industries (Monier), in which Redland held 50%, and in June 1973 Marley Reliance was sold for A$6.7 million (£3.7 million).

Prior to its purchase of Reliance, Marley had been exporting flooring from the UK into New Zealand, an exercise that was cheaper than local manufacture; however, the New Zealand Government, keen to increase local manufacturing activity persuaded Marley to establish a manufacturing base on the understanding that imports would be limited. 'Following our policy of obtaining a larger share of the world's market, your Company has acquired a site in Auckland and will shortly commence the erection of a floor tile plant. We have had a sales Company in that Country for three years, but its activities have been limited due to that Government's policy of restricting the imports of flooring products.'[22] Once the floor tile factory became operational, Marley bought the contracting firm of John Weston of Auckland with whom Marley had been associated for some years. 'Following the pattern we have adopted in the UK and elsewhere, it was considered advisable to enter the flooring contracting business'.[23]

The flooring business was a success in its early years; it had reached full capacity in 1962 and had to be extended. However, before long New Zealand presented its own particular brand of management problems as a visit by Fred Hardy in 1964 highlighted: 'owing to the rather complicated religious opinions of a certain sect, to which most of the managers belonged, it meant the senior

22 *Marley Tile (Holding) Company Accounts, January 1960.*
23 *Ibid, December 1961.*

management had been drastically reduced by resignations this year'.[24] Reinforcements were sent out from the UK and slowly the operations were expanded again; new flooring ranges, including roll flooring, were introduced and the manufacture of rainwater goods commenced in 1968. New Zealand Flooring also began a substantial exporting business in 1968, selling into Australia, South-East Asia and the Indian Ocean.

Carpets in Canada

Before the start of the Second World War, Sir Owen had traded in the USA as a housebuilder, and had patented concrete tile making machines. Despite the discussions referred to earlier with Ludowici-Celadon on the possibility of local manufacture, Marley did not succeed in entering the US market until the very end of the 1970s. Long before that materialised, however, Marley had acquired a Canadian business. Sir Owen had had discussions with Flintkote with a view to buying a floor tile factory in Canada but the transport economics deterred him. In 1957 Jack Aisher visited the country with a view to acquiring an interest in a floor contracting business and building a Marley floor tile plant but again those discussions were abortive. When Marley did move, in June 1960, it was for the purchase of a wholesaling business only – McMahon & Company of Winnipeg; 'a building materials wholesaling business with branches covering the most important western areas. We consider this the most advantageous way of entering this important market and although it is unlikely for the present to have a material effect on the products manufactured in our existing plants, we shall take every opportunity to introduce those where they do not conflict with our local trading arrangements... This old established family business originated by selling binder twine to prairie farmers, and now services about half... of Canada. McMahon's today are the largest distributors of floor coverings in Western Canada and market a number of allied materials.'[25]

At regular intervals, consideration was given to supporting the distribution warehouses with a manufacturing base and immediately after the McMahon acquisition the Marley trade name was registered in Canada. In that same year discussions were held with the Clopay Corporation (from whom Marley licensed its Spacesaver folding doors) and Marley progressed as far as drawing up heads of agreement for the manufacture and sale of rigid PVC products in the USA. However, the economics never looked right and instead Marley concentrated on developing the McMahon operation eastward, a strategy started by the purchase of Imperial Carpet Distributors Limited of

24 *Marley Overseas minutes, March 1964.*
25 *Marley Tile (Holding) Company* Annual Report, *1960.*

Sam Fabro, of McMahon & Company (right)

Toronto in 1962 and continued warehouse and depot construction. By the 1970 accounts, the Chairman was able to report that 'in 1970 we shall be completing our new warehouse at the Winnipeg headquarters and will then have a chain of modern depots throughout the country'.

The problems of control

The twenty years between Marley establishing its first German plant in 1953 and the international oil crisis in 1973 was a period of rapid international economic growth. Marley certainly participated; the Aisher drive had ensured representation in all the significant markets around the world with the exception of the United States. In 1972, Marley's overseas sales totalled £45 million out of a Group total of £101 million; inclusion of overseas associates would have increased the overseas percentage. Yet Marley did not enjoy the financial returns that might have been expected. The 1972 Accounts revealed overseas profitability for the first time.

Although the UK profits were abnormally depressed in 1971, the overseas contribution was as high as it ever had been; even then it relied heavily on the quoted Irish subsidiary, which had made approaching £1 million

	1971			1972		
	Sales (£m)	Profit (£m)	Margin (%)	Sales (£m)	Profit (£m)	Margin (%)
UK	50.0	5.89	11.8	56.5	8.13	14.4
Overseas	34.3	1.02	3.0	44.6	2.66	6.0

Source: 1972 Holding Company Accounts

in its own right in 1972. In part the answer goes back to the original decision to choose the new flooring product as the vehicle for overseas expansion. Marley was undoubtedly successful in establishing a network of flooring subsidiaries and associates around the world. Unfortunately, by the time Marley had achieved its target, the market was suffering from overcapacity as consumers moved on to carpeting as a preferred flooring. Public recognition of this problem was given in the 1968 Group Accounts: 'We have considerable investments overseas which in a number of countries have not so far yielded a return comparable to what we have achieved in the UK. Germany, Austria and South Africa have suffered from over-production of nearly all the products we are concerned with, and demanded a fresh approach in marketing in order to maximise profits. We are confident that through our depots and shops this can be attained.' However, it is interesting to note that the only two overseas markets where Marley has retained a flooring presence are South Africa and Brazil, both of which possess significant lower income populations within their society.

Geoffrey Jones' study of British multinationals suggest Marley was not alone in failing to achieve the same performance overseas as it had at home; its experience was reminiscent of many who had ventured abroad before the war. 'British managers... had to learn by experience how to control and manage capital over distance and in alien conditions. The persistence of family firms and loose holding companies in the United Kingdom helps to explain why this learning process was a slow one. Multinational business is typically more difficult to conduct than domestic business, as it requires a considerable extension of managerial control. If domestic management structures were defective, it was not surprising that their foreign activities were inadequately managed.[26]

Marley also suffered from a belief, not uncommon in British companies, that what works at home works abroad; examples can be found in the text but there was an overriding belief in the need to replicate the UK contracting philosophy. Thus, in the Group Accounts for 1957: 'It has been your

26 *Geoffrey Jones*, British Multinationals: Origins, Management and Performance, *London, 1986, p 14*

company's policy in both roofing and flooring products to take an active part not only in the marketing but also the contracting side of these industries'. Ten years later, this was being tactfully questioned by the Marley Overseas Board: 'The long term problems for Marley in Europe being created by the static or even decreasing, floor tile market in face of competition from tufted carpet was discussed... Whether, in the long term, it is wise to put much effort into the expansion of contracting depots, unless they can be profitably adapted to some other product in the event of continued decline of floor tiles, was questioned. All were agreed that change in Europe is likely to be substantial and commitments to the products and methods of the last decade during the next is likely to lead to disaster.'

In personal terms, too, Marley was unable to find, in those early days, the strong characters, the businessmen, that created the domestic businesses. Control from the UK was not always consistent and, again, Geoffrey Jones makes it clear Marley was not alone. 'The usual form of parent control over foreign subsidiaries came when a director or official from Britain was despatched on an investigation or special mission... This system had a high capacity for disruptive and inconsistent management, even if it did offer peripatetic directors an escape route from British winters. Nevertheless it was a system which survived in some firms beyond the Second World War.[27]

In 1963, Marley formed a separate Overseas Holdings company to achieve a greater degree of formalised control over the overseas investments; in the Chair was Owen Aisher Junior with Denis Knight, John Pollard, Tom O'Sullivan and Peter Wilson on the Board. One of their first recorded comments was that there was no general system of control on overseas capital expenditure and far wider discretion was given to general managers overseas than in the UK. It was also true that decisions could still be made directly by senior directors not on the Overseas Board. In practice, there was intermittent decision making from the UK, but without systematic control. 'We used to get accounts in and raise queries with the overseas companies on the accounts but it was difficult to get someone really interested in the business aspect of it... We didn't have a dedicated Overseas Board... they all had other responsibilities. To some extent there was a hands off attitude to the overseas companies. Certainly, on the accounting side, one only went over there if there was a problem... I think what they missed more than anything was the overseas companies had hardly any contact with the UK except for perhaps a visit of a main Board director. They didn't see any of the line management that much. Therefore I think some of the main Board had no idea what the line management of the overseas companies were thinking.'[28] Marley's most successful overseas investment in that period was Concrete

27 Jones, p 13
28 *Denis Rigden interview.*

Products of Ireland which had a clearly defined local management and, because of its location and language, a much closer relationship with the home business. Of the portfolio of overseas companies discussed so far, the ones that eventually proved most successful for Marley – Germany, South Africa and Bisch in France – were all ones which acquired a local managing director with a clear mandate from the UK and consistent support from a main Board Director.

Part 5
Marley widens its base

We have taken Marley's story up to the early 1950s, at which time it was still largely focused on tiling the roofs and floors of Britain. 1954 represented the peak in the post-war housebuilding recovery and although the next twenty years did see higher levels of activity, it was never significantly so. It was, however, a period of considerable increase in consumer purchasing power and of technical change and innovation. Of the changes within the building materials industry, few can have been as far reaching as the introduction of plastics and it was through the use of plastics that Marley sought to widen its sphere of interest, eventually spreading as far as the motor industry. Parallel to that, the Aishers also sought to extend the philosophy of creating their own market, successfully embodied in the supply and fix contracting business, into the development of its own merchanting and do-it-yourself retailing business. At the same time, Marley was creating an overseas business with representation in five continents.

The product development was driven by Sir Owen's own thirst for new ideas, fed in turn by continued travelling around the world, and no great inhibition over using whatever he found. Fred Hardy remembers the flood of suggestions coming through to him: 'He would read all these books and things and see what other people had done. I've never met anyone who would read like he did, he read everything. He would come in the morning with a pile of books under his arm, with memos "see page this; why haven't you done this?"

And every morning you would have a batch of stuff on your desk; if you read through it all it would take you a couple of days.' But for all Fred Hardy had to bear the frustration of too many bright ideas per square inch, he is in no doubt of the encouragement that Sir Owen also gave to everyone else within Marley to innovate. 'The Governor was an absolutely first class chap to work for insofar as he never handicapped you, he always encouraged you to do what you wanted; he encouraged you to go and do something fresh.'

Even though Marley had its share of problems in later years, that innovative ethos was still evident in the late 1970s. Mike Armstrong (later Finance Director) joined the Company in 1978: 'Looking back, one of the biggest pluses of all was a free and easy management style which allowed – indeed encouraged – people to do what they thought needed to be done. There was very little interference and... people were encouraged to come up with ideas. I am quite sure that this style was responsible for the constant stream of new products which Marley introduced for so long.' Some developments were more home grown than others. There is little doubt that the plumbing extrusion business was born out of that atmosphere of experimentation in the Harrietsham laboratory whereas automotive components, for instance, was a product of Sir Owen's sailing contacts in the USA. Equally, on the distribution side, the merchanting business grew naturally out of the depot system whereas the move into retail followed Sir Owen seeing a do-it-yourself shop elsewhere. But whatever its source, once the new product area had been identified Marley had the ability to move rapidly – and on several fronts.

From flooring to extrusions

Although Marley Extrusions rapidly developed a life of its own, its early development was largely as an adjunct to the flooring business. When Geoff Barrett arrived at Harrietsham at the end of 1953 to run the new flooring factory he found them making skirting board by pressing the raw material; 'then we had to extrude little feature strips to go between the tiles and we had one little extruder making that'. It was decided to try extruding the skirting board and a new small extruder was bought; in 1954, Marley began extruding 2-inch and 4-inch black skirting boards. The immediate labour saving was staggering: 'we could extrude it with one chap rather than lots of girls in the press shop.'[1] John Austin was put in charge of the department and started to produce a number of small auxiliary products including threshold strips and hand rails for staircases. Another product which featured in reasonable quantity

1   *Robin Aisher interview.*

Marleythene   *The first extruder machine*

early on was Marleythene, a polythene pipe for external water distribution launched in the autumn of 1954. Its market was agriculture and market gardening but Marley also had its first success in domestic plumbing where Marleythene was used as a cold water service pipe and, in a few cases, as waste pipes and rainwater downpipes. Sufficient progress had been made to justify the formation of a separate Extrusions Company in October 1955 but even at that stage the product range had not achieved a clear identity; it was the equivalent of an active mind, turning from idea to idea as opportunities presented themselves.

One of the new products leaves us with an amusing historical footnote. Marley became the biggest manufacturer in the UK of hula hoops, a craze which swept through the country in 1958. Fred Hardy remembers the telephone call from Sir Owen in America: 'One night he phoned up saying "What do you know about hula hoops? It's the craze out here – you had better start making them." I said "What are they?" and Owen said "Round hoops like we used to bowl as children and you put them round your body and wiggle them and they keep going round". I said "Go into the shop, buy one, cut it six

Hula hoops

inches either side of the joint and put it in the post to me". It came a couple of days later and I saw it was made of high density polythene and we had a die made and managed to make the product. Within two days we had made a hula hoop. We had some little laboratory machines making vinyl hose which we couldn't sell because it was more expensive than the rubber product. So we stuck an extrusion tool on the end of the machine and we pushed out hula hoops in large quantities. We also sent the tool to Germany and South Africa and we became the largest manufacturer in the UK, South Africa and Germany. We couldn't make them fast enough; we made them in all colours and we made a lot of money.' Harrietsham was turning out 4,000 to 5,000 hoops a day but the craze vanished as soon as it had come and Geoff Barrett was left with a warehouse full of stock: 'I used to have to give it away to get the warehouse empty; I was giving it to schools for two years after'.

The first rainwater goods

It was yet another odd turn of events, no less strange than making hula hoops, which led to the breakthrough into rainwater goods. Around 1957, Geoff

Barrett received an enquiry from a farmer in Blackpool who was tired of his chickens pecking through galvanised water troughs – could Marley make a plastic one? 'We developed a hard plastic which wasn't easy, but from the knowledge we had on making handrail, which was a reasonably hard plastic, still PVC, we developed a harder one that was self supporting; just a U-shaped bit of extrusion. It got developed by John Austin and one or two others and that was supplied to this farmer in Blackpool. We made a good profit out of it and then the competition saw it and cut the price. From the chicken trough, I thought we could make a gutter. What we did was to make a pipe and split it, just opened it up and that was the gutter. We had the pipe, we had the gutter, all we had to do were the swan necks and so on.'

Marley was by no means the first to extrude plastic pipe; high density polythene, for instance, had been available since the early 1950s. The possibility of extruding PVC had been well recognised but it presented more serious technical problems and Marley was one of the companies trying to master the challenge. Marley would not claim to be the first to produce an extruded PVC pipe; uPVC pipes were being extruded by Osma, one of Marley's later competitors, and were being used in Germany for above ground drainage. Osma had also introduced a glass fibre gutter but that had technical problems. Where Marley did pioneer, and can rightly claim a first, was in the introduction of a rigid PVC rainwater gutter.

One of the early problems to be overcome in the manufacture of extruded rainwater goods was the natural tendency of unplasticised PVC to discolour on exposure to sunlight; the technical solution was the addition of the correct stabilisers to the polymer. Denis Moss offered an interesting distinction between the development philosophy of Marley and that of the PVC supplier, the more conservative ICI: 'When PVC rainwater goods were first being considered, knowledge of the effect of long term weathering was sketchy indeed. ICI had carried out some exposure tests but these were limited, as were our own. I believe that this development shows a basic difference between the Marley approach at this time in comparison with that of ICI in that we took a calculated risk when we went into the manufacture of PVC rainwater goods with limited knowledge of the long term effects of weathering on the product, whereas ICI would not have considered such manufacture without having carried out an extensive, ten year duration weathering programme.'

The early extrusion machines were limited. There was only one manufacturer in the UK, Windsor, making an extruder that was strong enough to extrude uPVC (unplasticised PVC, often referred to as rigid PVC) and as they had not designed or marketed the extruder for that purpose it was left to the Marley engineers to do much of the development. So much of the early work was pioneering. PVC itself was a relatively recent plastic and not the easiest to use; any attempt to form it had necessitated the use of plasticisers to make it workable but the end product, like plastic sheeting or floor tiles, was not rigid. But extruding PVC without that plasticiser was really more than any existing machinery could cope with. Marley's learning process was paralleled at its main rival Key Plastics (later Key Terrain) which had been formed by Michael Collins in 1957 to mould fittings in a variety of plastics. 'PVC is a bad conductor of heat. In my day we started with just ram machines, there were no such thing as screw [feeds]. What happened was, the outside [of the PVC] burnt up and the middle wasn't cooked.'[2] Marley's early application of the Windsor extruder to uPVC helped in turn to stimulate machinery manufacturers who began to see the new market opening before them.

Moving away from straight extrusions further tested Marley's skills. The gutter and the downpipe were both straight extrusions but what of the pipe that joined them which needed to have an S-bend to go round the corner of the eaves? An initial attempt was to fill a pipe full of sand and get a former to bend it round but 'the outside used to burst and the inside used to crinkle'. Eventually the "rocket machine" was produced. 'We realised that if you put a hot spring inside [the pipe] it heated the plastic; you could then put the hot spring in a jig that made it into a swan neck shape. You then blew cold air over it and pulled the spring out. That was fine so we then had a huge machine which you put lots of these coil springs into, a hot oil machine, and we called it the rocket.'[3]

Getting the S-bend to form was the final hurdle solved and Marley exhibited its new product at the 1959 Building Exhibition. 'We always went to the Building Exhibition but it was decided it was worth a risk of putting on this newly developed PVC gutter and downpipe, which was very crude. They were just overwhelmed with enquiries. They couldn't give us enough money to buy extruders after that.'[4] Until extrusions, the introduction of new products had typically come from the top, frequently from Sir Owen himself; indeed, if there was a criticism, it was of too great a flow of ideas and suggestions. However, in the case of extrusions, the ideas had been generated from down the line, and there was not always full backing from Head Office. Marley's success at the Building Exhibition changed all that.

Late in 1959 the resources of the Division were strengthened with the recruitment of Peter Wilson. Peter Wilson, who was to become a main Board director, had come from Hoover bringing with him a strong technical background on toolmaking and the compounding of plastics and a small team was put together to work on the problems the new products posed. The ability to work with the new raw material had to be learnt and there was little that Marley Floors, with its totally different formulations, could do to help. PVC

2   *Michael Collins interview.*
3   *Robin Aisher interview.*
4   *Geoff Barrett interview.*

itself is unstable and can break down as it is processed; Peter Wilson is in no doubt that Marley's ability to process rigid PVC was a key factor behind their early market leadership. ICI produced the basic PVC polymer but the PVC has to be compounded with inhibitors that ensure that the material does not embrittle under ultraviolet light, strong sunlight; that it does not change colour; and that it does not deteriorate over time. Using Swiss compounding machines Marley developed formulations that were specific for their new rainwater goods – and without much support from the chemical companies. 'ICI, years later, admitted that they were very lax in not coming up with information as to how we could achieve it and we achieved it by blood, sweat and tears really.'[5]

The production process also needed to change rapidly and, in particular, move beyond the simple extrusion of pipe to the moulding of the more complicated shapes that were essential if an effective rainwater goods system was to be marketed. To begin with, the components and fittings were made in primitive fashion. We have already described the swan necks, or S-bends; there were also 'hoppers' which gathered the water from the end of the gutter, feeding it into the downpipe. The hopper, and other components, were formed out of flat sheet and bent by hand. They were crudely made, lacked the precision of cast iron, and sometimes even leaked. The need for more sophisticated methods of manufacturing components was well recognised at Marley and the team knew that moulding was the answer.

At the start of the 1960s there were few people that could mould PVC; fortunately, when Peter Wilson had been at Hoover he had been involved in the moulding of the first cleaner bodies in plastic and had visited the USA to see their new process: 'with great difficulty, we moulded some of the first parts in PVC but we could only mould two or three before the machine burnt up. By the time I'd got to Marley, and became aware of the German development on PVC (and PVC is very much a German development), I was able to see the dramatic change in machine design to enable us to mould the PVC and that was the breakthrough.' The injection moulding machines that Marley imported from Eckhert Ziegler in Germany were the first rigid PVC moulding machines to be used in the UK. Ironically, although the Germans had pioneered the injection moulding machines, they had not turned them to the production of rainwater goods, leaving the way open to Marley.

The Eckhert machines were introduced in 1960 and although it took a long time to get them working properly they had a dramatic impact: '... it was unique and it enabled us, ahead of anyone else, to mould PVC parts for rainwater goods in a way that nobody had ever visualised. It surprised everybody as to how accurate it was'.[6] Just to state what may be the obvious,

5   *Peter Wilson interview.*
6   *Ibid.*

the extrusion and the injection moulding machines are quite different. The extruders are continuous process machines, pushing out the formed product (in Marley's case typically a pipe) in a continuous length. The moulding machines take the PVC granules and squirt them into the mould under heat and pressure; the mould is opened and the individual component is produced. Peter Wilson also developed a machine to make the hoppers which was a combination of vacuum forming and drape forming based on equipment in use at Hoovers.

The need for a system

Rainwater goods were not a series of isolated products: they had to work together as a system and water could be a cruel examiner. Marley had to find an answer, therefore, to the expansion and contraction of the gutters. Having abandoned mastic jointing, a favoured early solution was to bolt the lengths of guttering together as was traditional with cast iron guttering, but this made no allowances for the far greater coefficient of expansion of a plastic gutter under the heat of the sun. Denis Moss remembers a trial set-up of a bolted section and another section using the newly developed notch and clip on the Central Research building at Riverhead: 'When the hot sun played on the sections the bolted system expanded and buckled. Sir Owen came over to inspect the trial: he looked at it and walked off saying "you've rigged it!". But we knew then that he would no longer insist on bolting.'

Eventually, the answer was found in a sliding joint which allowed movement. A notch was put into the gutter around which a clip could be attached. A neoprene rubber pad was stuck inside the socket (or female end) of the gutter and into the socket and the surface of the spigot (or male end) could slide over the socket as it expanded. Even when moving, the spigot stayed tight onto the rubber pad as it was held under compression from the external clip; there was therefore a watertight joint which allowed for expansion and contraction. 'We thought about patenting the device but no one had ever tried patenting a notch in the past. The Americans had been facing the same problem and their solution was to use a hopper head above the downpipe which took the gutter and the gutter could move across the hopper head, but this was too expensive a solution for the UK.'[7] In the end, Marley patented its system which lasted for sixteen years.

By 1961, Marley could claim a workable system, the gutters and downpipes produced on extruders, the components made by injection moulding and the parts fitting together and carrying off the rainwater as efficiently as the cast iron or asbestos cement products they were hoping to replace. PVC rainwater goods were on their way and they served as a model

7   *Fred Hardy interview.*

for an extensive use of extruded PVC products both outside and inside the house. The building trade was being offered a precision product. It did not need painting and it would not rot. The alternative was asbestos cement which needed painting; or cast iron which was heavy and expensive and also needed painting. However, it would not have been the building industry if there had not been pockets of resistance. Peter Wilson: 'I can remember vividly, supplying Birmingham City Council with rainwater goods and being called up there to look at some problems and in actual fact the plumber who was installing it said that it was the biggest load of rubbish he'd ever seen. It would never get anywhere. You could burn it with a blow lamp and he ripped it off the building and threw it to the ground below and trampled on it. And we said to him that that proves the point. You've ripped it off the roof, you've thrown it from the roof onto the ground, you've trampled on it and it's as good as the day it was made. He was lost for words because it proved the point. Whereas, if it was cast iron or asbestos he could never have done that.'

Although supply and fix never had the grip on plumbing that it did for roofing tiles and flooring, it was used in the early days of rainwater goods. In 1962, Marley formally announced that 'they can now undertake to supply and fix their rainwater goods as well as supply only'. Sir Owen put it succinctly: 'Don't forget when we first made gutters we had to supply and fix them

Placing sealing compound and hooking strap for jointing on to the back edge of gutter socket.

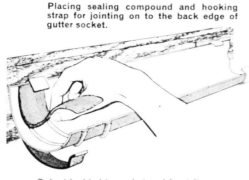

Spigot bedded in socket and front flange of strap snapped over between rolls of socket and grooves of spigot to complete joint.

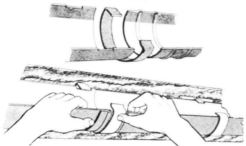

Flexible joint system for vinyl gutters, from 1960

because the trade didn't know how to do it but within six months the plumbers realised that anybody could do it and we stopped.' The supply only sales force continued to operate within Marley Tile's contracting division and it was not until 1970 that the selling function was completely transferred to Extrusions itself.

In seeking to strengthen its market position, Marley had been talking to Burn Brothers (London) but, in the event, Key Terrain (then part of Reed) bought the business. It was an interesting strategy: Burn Brothers had a virtual monopoly on the design and installation of cast iron drainage in the London market, and were very close to the old London County Council who were strongly influential then in the setting of building specifications. Michael Collins: 'I could see that was the thing to do to get quick penetration because London was the critical market. In those days the LCC drainage specifications were accepted in every part of the globe that had red ink on it. In those days, unless you had LCC approval for the product, you would never get a British Standard because they sat on the British Standards Committee and they waved a big strong arm.' Eventually, Key Terrain found itself in conflict with its other merchant customers and disposed of Burn Brothers. We will see later how Marley developed its own plumbers' merchanting business.

With the product range beginning to win acceptance in the trade and sales increasing rapidly, investment in new manufacturing capacity was necessary. In 1962, Marley authorised the expenditure of a quarter of a million pounds for investment in a new tool room. The Extrusions management team had convinced the main Board directors of the need to have their own independent toolmaking capability to enable them to develop new products rapidly. 'We had to have our own toolmaking capacity to manufacture injection moulds and all the dies; we couldn't go outside and get the expertise and that was another major breakthrough for the company because there was very little engineering expertise within the group because it was an entirely new technology. That also pushed the company forward at a tremendous rate and in fact [it] became one of the largest toolmaking operations in the south of England in the industry. Every new product range that had to be brought in required tooling so that we could manufacture it ourselves without anybody knowing what we were doing, doing it quickly, having it ready on time... building in the best technology and, again, we were ahead of the field.'

The table that follows shows that even from its early days Marley Extrusions, though small, was growing rapidly but still only in a modest way. Once the rainwater goods were established as a soundly based system, the sales started jumping to more significant levels. One feature which will by now be familiar is that largely all the product was sold to Marley Tile's contracting company for distribution. There was also a brief introduction of a supply and fix operation to show the plumbing trade it could be done, but it lasted no more than a few months. It is not easy to interpret the profitability that Marley achieved in the early days with all the output being sold at internally agreed transfer prices. Clearly the period 1959–1961 when Marley led the market into PVC rainwater goods saw profit margins jump to the 20–25% range; with selling profits taken elsewhere this probably understated the true returns. However, Marley's lead did not last long. In Marley Tile's March 1962 minutes we find the first discussion of competition in rainwater goods and a 'reluctance' to consider price reductions. Profits in that year halved and although they bounced smartly back again in 1963, it was the first indication of the periodic battles that would be fought within the extrusions industry over the next three decades.

Extrusions financial record

£000	1955*	1956	1957	1958	1959	1960	1961	1962	1963
Sales									
Inter-group	12	56	110	154	226	411	535	761	1,301
Customers		3	5	10	5	10	21	59	54
Total	12	59	115	164	231	421	556	820	1,355
Pre-tax profit	(14)	6	13	28	58	104	102	57	123

*6 months

The wider plumbing market

Once Marley had demonstrated what could be done with PVC products in rainwater drainage it took not a lot of imagination to look for ways of widening the product range: the whole of the pipework moving water around and away from the house was being made from traditional and, to the plastics industry, replaceable materials. The next market segment to be addressed was that of waste and soil pipes; these are the pipes which remove the waste water and sewage from within the house, the pipes that lead directly from the individual appliances (bath, water closet, etc) and through to the external stack before discharging into the underground drainage.

Marley had pioneered the development of PVC rainwater systems, establishing a leadership which it still retains. But Marley was soon just one of a number of companies determined to exploit the new growth market of plastics for the building industry and, if Marley had taken the lead in rainwater goods then it is fair to credit Key Plastics with the first soil pipe system. Marley developed its own 4-inch vertical stack; launched in 1963, the November Marley Tile minutes recorded their 'extremely good acceptance'. Marley continued with the socket and spigot connections, inserting rubber rings in the joints, which were standard on its rainwater goods system. In contrast, Key used an all socket system with solvent welding. However, although Marley made its own soil stacks, Key supplied Marley with the smaller waste pipes that connected the appliances to the stack and these were marketed under Marley's name as a complete system, until Marley later had its own manufacture fully on stream.

In 1961, Marley Plumbing Division was started at Riverhead to design and develop new products, prepare technical literature and give marketing support to the contracting sales branches of the Marley Tile Company. The design of the new plumbing products was put into the hands (not to mention the house) of plumber extraordinaire, Geoff Marsh who joined Marley Extrusions in 1961, subsequently becoming Technical Director of Extrusions and President of the Institute of Plumbers. Mention his name and it will not be long before *Water For Six* is mentioned; a remarkable document, it details the daily records of every water-related appliance in Geoff Marsh's house and the water usage of himself, his wife and four young children, taken throughout the whole of 1965. 'The incentive to embark upon a laborious task of this type originated from a feeling of concern about the lack of published data relating to basic plumbing problems. Quite often plumbing technology appears to vary between the extremes of practical guesswork and theoretical assumption… in order to successfully interpret the requirements for new plumbing products, there is a need to become directly involved in the study of existing systems.'[8] This then was the drive behind Marley's search for new plumbing products.

The introduction of Marley's own range of waste pipes might be thought a simple matter of using the rainwater goods extruders with appropriately smaller dies. Unfortunately, there was a small but important difference – the water temperature. It only rains cold water but the outflow from the wash basin and the bath can be hot, sufficiently so to soften a uPVC pipe which is being run at full bore. Marley developed a pipe using chlorinated PVC which had a higher softening point. Although chlorinated PVC could be extruded it was difficult to produce injection moulded fittings because of the effect that the chlorinated material had on the dies. 'Therefore we decided to mould a thicker PVC fitting to go with a thinner cPVC pipe and in that way we made a modified uPVC system which was capable of withstanding these hotter temperatures.'[9]

Other companies were looking at different solutions to the temperature problem, including polypropylene and ABS (acrylonitrile butadiene styrene). Both had the high temperature properties required but Marley regarded ABS as more fragile, losing impact strength when left exposed to the sunlight; polypropylene could not be solvent welded and required a ring seal method

8   *G J W Marsh,* Water For Six, *1971.*
9   *Geoff Marsh interview.*

which Marley preferred not to use at that stage. 'We decided that because of our knowledge of uPVC it would be best to offer chlorinated PVC which has good characteristics inside and out with thicker PVC fittings'; that gave Marley a range of plumbing products all based on the same basic plastic raw material.

From the development of Marley's own waste pipe system, it was a natural progression to cold water distribution and, in 1967, to what Marley hoped was going to be another major breakthrough – a hot water system. On the 10th November the *Financial Times* reported: 'Following the introduction last year of a waste drainage system made entirely of chlorinated pvc, Marley Extrusions has developed the material further with improved properties – claimed to make it completely non-toxic, even when in contact with boiling water... As a result, Marley Extrusions is to introduce a domestic hot and cold water system with pipes and fittings (including an expansion joint) in sizes of half, three-quarter and one inch. This, together with a new four inch underground drainage system, will be shown at the International Building Exhibition at Olympia.'

In the event, it was the casual aside about the underground drainage product that contained the winner; the hot water system never saw commercial sales and even today Marley does not produce a hot water system (although one or two systems have now been marketed by other companies). Although Marley came close in the 1960s, continued research testing was unable to solve fully the problems of expansion, contraction and the leaching out into the water of certain of the constituents of the PVC, and "hydraulic knocking" in the pipes. Marley was not unaware of the potential claims against the Company if they were found responsible for failures in a domestic hot water system! It was formally abandoned in May 1969.[10]

Marley goes underground

The underground drainage products were, however, a great success and provided Marley with its third leg of water related products after rainwater goods and cold water distribution. The traditional product for underground drainage in the UK was the clay pipe, virtually all in the control of Hepworth Iron who manufactured at very competitive cost. The battle with clay was a fierce one which continues to this day; the underground clay pipe is the only traditional product that has been able substantially to withstand the inroads made by plastic.

Marley was again one of a group of companies which introduced plastic underground drainage in 1967; the product had been put on the market in Germany and Marley took encouragement from the development work which

10   Marley Board Report, *69/20.*

had been done there. 'There had been concern about whether uPVC pipe under ground loading would flatten but German work showed that if the pipe had the right wall thickness, the bedding and backfill round the pipe and on the top would equalise the pressures and there wouldn't be undue distortion, and therefore uPVC was a possibility for an underground drainage system.'[11] But it was the local authorities who were responsible for the building regulations and they had to be converted to the new material, again with the old London County Council playing a leading role.

Marley sought to differentiate itself from the competition by the development of a "rodding system". Access to a clay underground pipe was via an access chamber (the thing under the manhole cover) which was expensive to construct. In 1961, well before plastics had appeared on the scene, a Joint Committee sponsored by the Building Research Station called for cost-saving alternatives to conventional underground drainage systems. The Committee recommended that rodding points could replace manholes for general maintenance. Marley undertook extensive fieldwork in 1968 and launched their new system the following year. Marley 'became the first Company to successfully develop and install an all-British uPVC sealed access drainage system in this country.'[12] It meant substantial savings for the builders because every time there was a change of direction in the pipe, they could install a rodding point instead of an expansion chamber; Marley put the cost of a rodding point at only 22% of the cost of a conventional manhole. This compensated for the higher manufactured cost of the plastic pipe, which Marley put at some 40% above the rubber jointed clay pipe.

Despite this encouragement, Marley had to accept that it was not only using the new material but also breaking away from the existing codes of practice relating to manholes and access. Sales of PVC underground pipe had begun in 1969, but Marley still awaited its first Agrément Certificate. In May 1970, the Board report on Extrusions clearly expected its imminent publication: 'Underground drainage, including the above ground rodding system is now being specified and deliveries are slightly in excess of the budgeted level, builders are anxious to use the system because of the savings in installation costs but some authorities continue to insist on the Agrément Certificate. We anticipate this being available within the next two weeks and we are informed that the tests being carried out by the Building Research Station have been successfully completed. New brochures dealing with rodding and installation in some detail are nearly completed and we should be in a position during the next month to apply an all out effort behind the selling of the system.' However, a year later, Marley was still waiting: 'The draft Agrément Certificate is now in our possession, is comprehensive and states that

11   *Geoff Marsh interview.*
12   *Marley trade advertising, May 1973.*

installations are expected to have a life in excess of fifty years... The major savings can be achieved through the rodding point which eliminates costly manholes. We are facing the fact that this will be a hard sell. The tools for the six inch system are now complete and materials are going into stock. Our programme on underground drainage is now virtually complete and no further major expenditure is expected for some time.'[13] In June 1971, the breakthrough for which Marley had been striving was achieved and Agrément Certificate No. 71/99 was published for 4-in bore pipe. 'Results of the tests described above indicated that the Marley Rodding Point Drainage System provides effective access to domestic underground drainage and as such is a suitable alternative to traditional manholes. In carrying out the rodding tests it was found possible in all cases to clear blockages from drains without damage to the material or the drain.'[14] By the end of 1971 most local authorities had approved Marley's rodding system.[15]

Marley's competitors were tending to follow more closely the traditional designs, offering injection moulded access chambers. Marley's sealed access system was not accepted by all authorities, which was limiting its opportunities for securing volume. In 1975, therefore, Marley purchased a machine large enough to mould chambers – a 3,000 ton moulding machine from Cincinnati USA, the largest in the country at the time and a far cry from those original Eckhert and Zeigler 150 ton presses.

Although there were three clear product ranges, all related to water distribution around the house, the 1960s saw Marley introduce a diverse range of other plastic products, some, but not all, connected with the building industry. These ranged from cladding and soffits at the beginning of the decade to plastic window frames which Marley began to develop in 1969. Innovative though these new products may have been, Marley Extrusions' fortunes, as it moved into the 1970s, still lay in its three water-related product ranges; the baby of them all, underground drainage, was then achieving the level of success originally seen when Marley had introduced its first rainwater goods system. The Extrusions minutes over the next two or three years paid ample tribute; in 1971: 'This year has seen the emergence of the soil system as a major contributor to profitability'.[16] In October 1972 Marley claimed as much as 60% of the plastic underground drainage market[17] and a measure of the speed of growth was recorded by the statistic of 60 miles of pipe delivered that month – three times the previous year's level.[18]

Competition remained intense. Marley had a number of powerfully

13 *Marley Board Report, May 1971.*
14 Agrément Board Certificate, *no 71/79.*
15 Marley Board Report, 72/7, *January 1972.*
16 *Ibid, 71/100, December 1971.*
17 *Ibid, 72/216, 1972.*
18 *Ibid, 72/194, November 1972.*

backed competitors: Key Terrain was part of Reed International; Osma (part of Shell), and Bartol, supported by the clay manufacturer Hepworth. There were also a host of smaller companies and in 1969 Marley was able to identify as many as 18 competitors. Despite the fact that 1968 was a record year with profits of £897,000, the sales reports were complaining of fierce competition. Any fast growing market where there are a handful of key players, all determined to hold or improve their market position, is vulnerable if market growth slows. A decline in the housing market created the competitive background which was responsible for Extrusions' profits more than halving to £385,000 in 1970. However, by then the increased penetration of the clay market by plastic drainage systems was raising the base level of demand and that coincided with the start of one of the strongest periods of demand ever seen by the housebuilding industry. By 1973, the pressure of competition and the growing sophistication and therefore capital cost of the machinery, had reduced the number of competitors from 18 to 8 – only two of which were regarded as 'serious competition'.[19] Profits responded accordingly and in that year reached a new peak of £1.7 million.

Marley and the motor industry

The Davidson connection

Of all the diverse paths followed by Sir Owen's fertile mind, none took him further away from his roots than Marley Foam (recently renamed Marley Automotive Components). Originating yet again from the family's yachting interests, Marley became one of the leading international suppliers of plastic based interior and exterior components to the car industry, receiving a series of awards for excellence from the car companies in the 1980s. The story began in the late 1950s when the Aishers were looking for new sails for the *Evaine*, a potential trialist for the Americas Cup. Robin Aisher went to Marblehead on the New England coast of America near Boston where Ted Hood was a sail maker. Through Ted, the Aishers met his father, 'Professor' Steadman Hood and his brother Bruce. Bruce Hood was a schoolboy friend of Paul Casey whose mother, Virginia Dee then ran the local family company Davidson Rubber, already approaching its centenary.

In 1954, Bruce Hood went to work for the Davidson Rubber Company and Professor Hood, who had just retired from Monsanto Chemical Company, became a part-time engineering consultant for Davidson in 1956. (Paul Casey:

19 *Ibid*, 73/85, June 1973.

' "Professor" was a nickname that Bruce and I gave him because of his combined inventive qualities with occasional absentmindedness.' Sir Owen was more pithy: 'You never saw such a mess, he couldn't boil an egg that chap; anyhow, he could invent things'. In 1957 Bruce Hood, who had been put in charge of new product development, invented a unique product for Davidson Rubber Company – an integral armrest for the motor car. This armrest consisted of vinyl outer skin covering a polyurethane foam body and strengthened with a metal insert.[20] Bruce Hood was granted patents in the US and internationally and between 1957 and early 1959, Professor Hood helped Bruce and others at Davidson to prepare for large scale production of this product.

The first armrest orders received at Davidson were from Ford and General Motors for their 1959 models, including Ford's Mercury and GM's Buick. These orders were, interestingly enough, greater in their combined sales volume than Davidson's total sales of other products. The first armrest to be produced and installed on vehicles appeared in the summer of 1958. Shortly after they appeared on the market, Davidson was approached for a licence by Otto Happich, the Chief Executive and major shareholder of Gerbruder Happich GmbH of Wuppertal. Davidson commenced negotiations with Happich for its first foreign licence around the middle of 1958. In the summer of that same year, Professor Hood went to Europe for a combined business and pleasure trip; the business was with Happich where he continued Davidson's negotiations and transferred some of the technology. His next destination was England for Cowes Week to pursue his interest in sailing and the family sailmaking business. It was then that he renewed his contacts with the Aisher family, fortuitously at a time when Marley was actively seeking to expand its plastics technology.

Once Sir Owen realised what else had brought Professor Hood to Europe he moved with typical determination: 'I had a look at it. I said "Who is going to do it in England?" He said "I don't know" and I said "We will" '. Fred Hardy remembers Sir Owen bringing Professor Hood to Riverhead. 'At the lunch he said that Bruce Hood and Paul Casey were making armrests for Fords. The Professor pulled an armrest out from his pocket. Owen asked me if I could make it and I said "Yes you can make anything if you want to". Owen said "Don't you think we ought to get into it". I agreed to have a go.' From then on, Marley was in a new industry.

In fact, Marley had got in just in time. Davidson Rubber had not been

---

20 *Paul Casey provides a more detailed technical description: 'The armrest consisted of a rotationally cast vinyl plastisol skin made in a unique electro-formed mould with a grained surface. A metal insert was inserted into the plastisol skin and a two component polyurethane was introduced into the skin which at this point was retained in an aluminium mould. The prepolymer polyurethane, when mixed with a catalyst, immediately started foaming in an exothermic reaction and within a period of a few minutes, cured, so that the armrest in pretty much its completed finished shape could be removed from the aluminium mould.'*

looking for an English partner. 'Happich in fact had encouraged us to license his sun visor licensee in Great Britain just as we agreed to do in Italy and France. However, because of Aisher's immediate interest and the very prompt lunch at Riverhead, we withheld extending the Happich licence to their English licensee until Marley could fully consider the matter. In the Fall of 1958 Owen Aisher came to the States on yachting business. He... visited Davidson in New England to see the production of the armrest and the early development of other foam products including cushions. At this point Owen confirmed his desire for a Davidson license.'[21]

Commercial agreements are not always simple but Marley's early relationship with Davidson proved so tempestuous that it is a wonder that it ever survived let alone prospered. Sir Owen decided to send some of the younger executives from Marley Floors to America to negotiate, but on their return there was not complete confidence that they had obtained the best terms for Marley. Nevertheless, in February 1960 the Marley Tile minutes recorded that a licence agreement had been reached with Davidson Rubber Company of Massachusetts covering the use of moulded urethane foam and related techniques. The agreement also had in it a clause which allowed for the renegotiation of the royalty if Marley was unable to make a reasonable profit – a clause that was later to lead to legal action.

One of Marley's undoubted strengths was the ability to move quickly once an opportunity had been sensed. Well before formal agreement had been reached, the Marley Tile minutes of July 1959 record the purchase of additional land at Harrietsham and a successful planning permission for a proposed foam project. In April 1960, but two months after the licence was signed, production started and Marleyfoam was launched:

> MOULDED Polyether Comes to UK. For the first time in Britain – moulded polyether produced on a countrywide scale. Called 'Marleyfoam' it is being made primarily for the furnishing trades. This moulded polyether is a lightweight, odourless foam in an integral skin, and can be moulded into any shape to meet specific requirements ...[22]

A supporting quotation from the March issue of the American *Journal of Commerce* followed. 'The polyethers are the strongest flexible foams widely available. They can be stitched, quilted, tufted, cemented, hog-ringed, stapled, tacked and stretched 4–5 fold without tearing... they are about half the weight of foam rubber.'

Although the attraction of the Davidson licence lay in the potential for supplying the fast growing motor industry, the furniture industry offered a market with a shorter order cycle and therefore a more immediate return on

21 *Paul Casey interview.*
22 Marley News, *July 1960.*

capital. Marleyfoam cushions were originally based on polyester but were soon replaced by the higher quality polyether;[23] its practical advantage was that it could be moulded into any shape. Prior to that, foam cushion manufacturers had produced an extruded slab and cut it to size. However, the Davidson technique covered far more than the moulding process for it integrated the foam with a vinyl skin (for exterior finish) and metal reinforcement for strength. In that way a strong, lightweight component with an acceptable finished look could be produced for both the motor and furniture trades.

Enter the Ford Consul

Sir Owen had recognised the potential for foam within the motor industry but the length of the car model replacement cycle meant a slow start. Nevertheless, Marley was once again pioneering product innovation in the UK. The first foam trim installed in a car was the armrest for the Ford Consul Classic two-door model, made at Harrietsham in 1961. In the furniture industry, the foam could be hidden beneath the upholstery but the car industry required a different solution. Marley moulded the foam directly on to a metal insert (which provided rigidity) and then bonded it on to a thin vinyl skin which served as the exterior finish. Fixing holes were pre-formed in the moulding – a simple forerunner of the complicated mouldings which were later to be made.

A very small mention in *Marley News* that summer paved the way for what was to prove a complete transformation of the car interior: 'One of the big advantages [foam] has over traditional materials is the freedom of design it gives, moulds of practically any shape being a feasible and practical proposition. Another important asset is its light weight'. That, of course, was written before the various oil price crises and the greater concentration on fuel weight ratios. By the end of 1961, armrests for the Ford Classic were followed by the Vauxhall Victor and now there were two further advantages to claim – safety, and the supremacy of the assembly line. The safety claim rested on the soft finish and absence of sharp edges or hard spots; this may have seemed of minor importance in an armrest halfway down the side of the door but once Marley began manufacturing crash pads at face level then the safety feature took on a new meaning. The assembly line advantage on the armrest was also relatively modest in the beginning; it just meant that the component had already been assembled and could be bolted straight onto the car. However, as the mouldings became more complicated over the years, stretching to complete dashboards, the motor manufacturers increasingly relied on Marley Foam for whole sub-assemblies in which other components were fitted into the Marley moulding before delivery to the assembly line.

---

23 *Both polyester and polyether are types of polyurethane.*

THE NEW FORD

INCORPORATES MARLEYFOAM

The Ford Consul Classic

Within two years, Marley was supplying Ford, Vauxhall, British Motor Corporation and Jaguar; production of armrests and instrument covers was running at around one million items a year. The 1962 accounts were able to report that 'The Marleyfoam rotacast foam filled armrests are now standard equipment on most new cars and the British motor industry is making increased use of our moulded cushions as well as crash pads and armrests'.

'Never have a court case in Massachusetts'

Marley was selling a new product into, for Marley, a new industry. For the first two years Marley Foam made no money on armrests, although it did on cushions on which the royalty was duly paid. Neither was Marley's endeavour to earn a return from the motor industry helped by the presence of two other British manufacturers who were copying the Davidson process but not paying a royalty; the 1960 agreement did not require Davidson to stop this competition. The cry of 'no patent, no pay' could be heard in Riverhead, and to force the issue Marley ceased the payment of its own royalties on the justification that it was not making profits. Davidson initiated action with the American Arbitration Association in Boston and Fred Hardy went out to fight the case. Davidson argued that Marley had drawn up the accounts to produce losses but despite providing figures from Price Waterhouse, Marley failed to win its case; the arbitrators suggested the two parties tried again to reach agreement. In response, Fred Hardy gave notice that it was cancelling the licence agreement and refused to deal with the Davidson lawyer. To enforce the arbitration award, Davidson went to court in Massachusetts to obtain certification of the arbitrators' award. (Sir Owen: 'I learnt afterwards you should never have a court case in Massachusetts'.) Still no royalties were forthcoming and Davidson was faced with prospect of commencing litigation in the UK.

Eventually Paul Casey came over to the UK and he and Fred Hardy were able to reach an amicable agreement, finally confirmed over the telephone with Sir Owen. The new agreement was signed on August 5th 1963 and confirmed in the Marley Tile minutes of September 1963. In May 1964, Marley Foam minutes 'reported on the terms of an agreement with the Davidson Rubber Company... it was resolved to ratify and confirm the previous sealing thereof'. This confirmed the licence for the UK, Australia and South Africa and agreed that Marley would pay Davidson 1% for interflow of knowledge between the two firms; this compared with a 5% royalty on the armrests under the original agreement. Since then there has been a strong working relationship between the two companies. Indeed, it is doubtful if Marley could have achieved the success it has without the support of Davidson. The next year, Marley was able to claim that: '... we have strengthened our position as the leading manufacturers of moulded armrests, cushions, crashpads and other interior trim features for the furniture and automobile industries'.[24] Looking back thirty years later, Paul Casey remembers with wry humour the first dinner party given by his mother and grandmother for Sir Owen and his wife: 'Mrs Aisher warned my mother that we should be careful in our licensing programme with the Europeans lest they take advantage of the two nice but naive young men namely Bruce and Paul. Later when we were in bitter litigation we weren't so sure that it wasn't easier to deal with the Europeans than the English.'

Other Davidson licencees agreed contemporaneously with Marley included existing Happich licencees under its sun visor patents in Italy (Gallino) and France (Maglum). (Marley now refers to Hutchinson in France and Fiat in Italy.) This was followed by Mitsuboshi (*sic*) Belting Company in Japan, Nylex in Australia and Aeroplex in Mexico. Marley had taken the view that there was insufficient business in South Africa or Australia to justify production ('we can export cheaper') and it therefore gave up its Australian and South African licences. Although never formally part of the agreement, a feature of the Davidson relationship became the understanding that any licencee could inspect any other licencee's factory and have access to their know-how. This, and the annual Davidson conference have helped to develop close links between the Davidson licencees and this is now being taken further by Marley with its recently announced cross-border joint ventures.

In August 1956 Peter Winfield had joined Marley as a chemist straight from university and after little more than a year with Floors he was transferred to the Marley Foam management team. He was made a director in November 1964 and was soon the Managing Director, a position he held until his early death in 1982. Peter Winfield was one of Marley's ablest executives and built up Foam to be a leading supplier to one of the most demanding group of industrial customers in existence.

Although Marley gained its first Ford order in 1961, it had not proved

24 *Marley Tile (Holding) Company Accounts, 1966.*

easy to convince the UK motor industry of the virtues of the new foam products. Marley soon discovered that showing the UK subsidiary of a US motor company what its parent company was doing did not immediately bring out the order forms. It was here that the working relationships with Davidson came into their own. 'Davidson was so strong in America; they knew all the top people in the motor industry. Paul Casey would come over to the UK and visit the manufacturers with us – they would take more notice of him. He had a letter from [the motor manufacturers'] top people to our top people. It all worked very smoothly.'[25] Peter Winfield's father was also a senior executive at Ford which no doubt also helped to open doors.

During the 1960s, the motor industry's requirement for a low-cost interior product, lighter than the traditional alternatives, and able to be simply incorporated on to the assembly line, led to an inexorable rise in the amount of non-structural plastic used within the motor industry. The foam concept became more acceptable and gradually insinuated itself into more expensive models; getting into one's car today, it is hard to remember the days of polished wood dashboards. The range of components increased, stimulated by an increasing concern with safety standards especially in the American market. 'New Government safety regulations in the USA have already made a considerable impact on car design in the UK and will hasten the trend towards the ideal of the all-padded car interior. As a result, sales... are being increased by the introduction of new padded units, including door panels.'[26]

Marley Foam established itself as a clear market leader in the UK, so successful that it needed fresh challenges. 'Overall it can be stated that we have achieved such a major share of our potential markets that we cannot expect to maintain this rapid expansion without extending our sphere of activities, either by marketing our existing products in the [EEC] or by the introduction of new products in our range.'[27] Looking back on 1971, Peter Winfield reported the sale of 4.5 million armrests, with a market share up from 85% to 99%; and 1.3 million crash pads, where the market share had risen from 50% to 65%. As Chrysler and British Leyland both made crash pads in-house, Marley's share of the free market in that product was actually as high as 85%. In both cases Marley had benefited from competitors leaving the business. The balance of sales at that time was in hot and cold cure cushions, car floors and door panels. The cushion business was the only disappointing one and Marley withdrew from the fiercely competitive hot cure market in 1974.

25 *Fred Hardy interview.*
26 *Marley Tile (Holding) Company Accounts, 1966.*
27 Marley Board Report, 71/90, November 1971.

Closer to the customer

Marley's contracting business was born of a need to move closer to the end user, the builder. The philosophy was taken a stage further in the 1960s with the development of Marley as both a retailer and a builders' supplier. Marley opened its first shop at 29 London Road, Southampton on the 2nd July 1959: '... it is hoped to gain valuable experience from this experiment that may be used as a guide to the company's future policy regarding retail outlets. The shop is intended to promote the goodwill and sales of all MARLEY products by having available a comprehensive display of all types of materials manufactured by the various companies in the Group. Supply and fix orders are dealt with, retail sales are executed and information and literature are readily available from the shop manager and his staff. The shop also acts as a distribution point for the local stockists who are encouraged to make full use of the facilities available.'[28]

The rationalisation may have followed the event. Jack Aisher remembers how he first discovered Marley was in retailing: 'Owen came back one day. He'd been yachting and he said "I've bought a shop". He hadn't really, but he jolly nearly had, at Southampton. Well we put a Marley chap in but he wasn't a retailer; we put another Marley chap in but he wasn't any more successful. I remember sitting down with Dick and Fred and Owen all together in the old office and someone said, let's admit the fact, we're tile makers, we don't know our... when it comes to retailing. Eventually they decided to advertise and Tom O'Sullivan answered.' He was then the manager at Woolworths, Stratford East, where he was their youngest manager of a large store. When Marley found out how much O'Sullivan was paid relative to their own executives it caused some consternation but eventually he arrived – at a salary of £3,250 – Marley's highest paid executive. It was to be one of the most significant recruitments Marley made. Tom O'Sullivan built Marley's retail business up to be one of the largest in the country until it was eventually sold in 1986 for £94 million. Apart from hosting Marley's first shop, Southampton also produced Ted Lansdowne, who eventually became managing director under Tom O'Sullivan, and David Quayle who was employed by Marley before going on to found B & Q.

The new Marley retailing philosophy was expounded further in the 1960 accounts: 'What is a Marley shop? Firstly, it enables the public or the trade to buy any Marley product, and to arrange for any contractual service that may be required. Flooring products alone would justify these premises... But supplement these flooring products with wall tiles, surfacing materials, folding doors, cement mixes, concrete products, foam cushions etc and it will be seen

28 *Marley Tile (Holding) Company Accounts, 1959.*

The first Marley shop, in Southampton

that a Marley shop can be a very useful store for Mr- and Mrs- Public to visit.

'More than a shop – a showroom. The premises have been laid out to function as a display area, in which the architect and the builder, as well as the man in the street, can see the goods and obtain any information required.

'More than a shop and a showroom – a distributing warehouse. It would be impossible for the normal stockist of Marley materials to hold anything like a complete range of Marley products. The retailer who hitherto may have been handling a limited selection... now has an immediate source of supply... Far from competing with existing retailers, it has been found that the extra facilities have resulted in increased business for the local retailer as well as for the Marley shop.'

Thus, there was a range of functions expected of the Marley shop: what you and I would expect of a shop; display facilities to support the manufacturing units; and wholesaling. In practice, the range of Marley products was not that extensive particularly when the concrete roof tile is excluded. Not too much of a living could be extracted from bags of MarleyMix concrete and foam cushions; the reality was that Marley's shops were specialist outlets for resilient flooring and that from one manufacturer.

At the time the Marley shops were first being developed, the resilient flooring market was still growing rapidly and, perhaps even more important as far as the High Street was concerned, it was becoming more of a fashion product: Marley pushed ahead rapidly with its retail units. The plans were on a grand scale: in August 1960, with only 7 shops then open, the Board of Marley Werke was being told that the intention was to have 300 shops in total. By 1964, there were over 60 shops and the 'retail business is capable of opening a new shop every fortnight'.[29] The earlier Marley Werke minutes were an indication that the concept was international and even then Marley was claiming 11 shops open on the continent.

Knowing the large do-it-yourself retail centres that now dominate the trade, it is hard to remember how small those first shops were. The 1963 Holding Company accounts provided an illustration for shareholders of a typical conversion of an 18ft. × 25 ft., seed merchants in Brighton: '... a new area was built on to make full use of the site depth and provide a covered parking space [singular!]. The shop is now 18ft. wide and 80ft. deep'. The decade finished with 184 shops and Mansfield as the last in the then programme of openings.

Marley was never slow to experiment with different formulae and, when Cyril Lord collapsed in 1968, took over the individual shop franchisees under the new name of ''Floorshops''; within months Marley had around 200 of these small units but they were not particularly successful and were gradually closed down during 1969 and 1970.

The 1970s brought a crucial change in strategy. There was a swing towards larger sized stores, a trend seen in other branches of the retail trade. But more important was a change in philosophy on the product range. Although Marley had widened the selling base to include its range of carpets, it had still confined itself to Marley products. It was not enough – the customer demanded a wider range of choice. Despite the rapid physical expansion and the growth in sales to almost £6 million, Marley's shops were losing money. A Board report in 1969 recognised the problems of a narrow range but still sought to correct it within a Marley manufacturing framework: 'The advantages our competitors possess are ability to cut prices and show greater selection. We cannot do anything about prices but we intend to increase our range of traffic generating merchandise to assist in achieving the very necessary higher level of sales. We will endeavour to concentrate on products that Marley could manufacture.'[30]

Marley had first experimented with its product range in a do-it-yourself

29 *Ibid, 1964.*
30 Marley Board Report, *69/70, 1969.*

shop at Bromley, but the shop was too small to be effective. In the spring of 1970, Marley chose its Redhill shop, able to stock a more extensive range of merchandise in the fields of walls, floors and ceilings, and presenting it as a self-service display. 'The aim is to make the shop profitable by the increased sales obtained by the additional products whilst at least holding the sales of Marley goods which, although they must be in a smaller display, should be exposed to a greater traffic flow.'[31] The experiment was adjudged a success and in September, the Board authorised the start of a programme of 23 conversions to the new Homecare formula. Those were completed by December and the Board then agreed to convert the remaining units to Homecare by March 1971.[32] The Holding Company Accounts published around that time made it clear to shareholders that Marley had set out to make that fundamental change from being a High Street distributor of its own products to an independent retailer. 'We have closed some of our smaller shops during the year and have increased the range of merchandise in the remainder to include complementary materials from other manufacturers. In our shops division we are now actively engaged in converting most of our shops to become 'Homecare' units, which sell goods produced by others as well as those made by Marley... This is improving the results financially and has also increased the sales of our own manufactured goods.'[33] By 1980, Marley's own products had fallen to around 15% of retail sales.

The strategy of widening the product range served to focus on the issue of size. The trend to larger stores, or superstores, often located on sites outside the traditional High Street had started. Sir Owen himself had drawn attention to the inevitability of larger units in the September 1969 diary of his visit to Germany: '... in the modern world of marketing, larger premises are essential... more like a super-market. I would think that from now on, the days of the small carpet and floor shop are likely to be, if not numbered, severely restricted and as the super-market idea grows into more and more of the everyday things of life, so we must grow with it. Please see that O'Sullivan speaks to me about it when I get back'. This no doubt fell on receptive ears for by that time Tom O'Sullivan and Alan Foster had visited the United States. The reason for their visit had been to attend an NCR retailing seminar and, while they were there, had seen some of America's 'home centers'. These had evolved out of lumber depots; in the USA, with its preponderance of timber framed construction methods, and a greater degree of self-build than in the UK, the lumber store was naturally placed to serve a wider market – and it was large! O'Sullivan and Foster returned to the UK convinced that was the route Marley must take. Having established a substantial retail chain in the 1960s, Marley had to

31   *Ibid, 70/64, July 1970.*
32   *Ibid, 70/125, December 1970.*
33   *Marley Limited Accounts, 1970.*

Mike Evans

completely rebuild it in the the 1970s, as did Home Charm (now Texas), then Marley's principal competitor.

Retailing overseas

In the 1960s, the Marley Board strongly believed that retailing was not only a worthwhile business in its own right but that it also served to increase the throughput in, and therefore the profits of, the manufacturing subsidiaries. As such, it fully deserved to be transplanted across to Marley's overseas companies. The first moves came in Germany and in January 1961, scarcely eighteen months after the original Southampton shop was opened, Marley shops were opened in Kiel and Brunswick and the numbers were slowly built up. In 1964, Mike Evans, later to be Managing Director in Germany, was sent out to supervise the shops. Immediately prior to that, he had been responsible for opening Marley's first and, it transpired, only shop in Belgium. 'There was one retail outlet in Belgium which I had the privilege of opening – on the 1st of January. Sir Owen and Tom O'Sullivan and Owen Junior arrived at the end of the first day's trading for a Consortium meeting on the 2nd January and I had to meet them and I did it in great fear and dread because the turnover in the first day had been 42 Belgian Francs, which even in those days was very little money. Someone had come in and bought a tin of polish and that was the only thing we sold. [It] remained a one off operation in Belgium because it was very difficult to get off the ground. I was just the man from the UK who was sent over to help set it up.' (The shop was eventually closed in 1968.)

Proposals had also been drawn up as early as 1962 to move into Holland; nothing was done for some while but in 1966 there were suggestions of a joint venture between Marley, Fademac and Eternit Holland. David Quayle, then living in England but supervising Belgium, moved to Benelux; by then, Quayle had been with the shops division for five years in England rising from sales assistant to Sales Promotion Manager at Head Office. The plan suggested three shops opened in the first year; the first shop on its own for six months. 'If the shops are to be successful within two years they must sell, apart from Marley/ Fademac/Eternit goods, other attractive retail lines sold under names other than Marley. We would want to brand under the Marley name as soon as the number and turnover of shops permits.'[34]

The Benelux move was followed in 1967 by the opening of the first of the Austrian chain of shops, in Vienna, and in 1969 there was even a shop in Budapest. Across the other side of the world, shops were being opened in South Africa and New Zealand, although these were never pushed as assiduously as those nearer Sevenoaks.

In April 1967, Sir Owen visited Germany and prepared the way for a substantial expansion of retailing based on an operating structure of six shops for every depot. 'He [Evans] and the managers can decide where the shop must be; some with accommodation for dealing with local tilers, storing etc and it looks as if about 20 such are wanted to start with, so 120 shops... This could and must give a turnover of about £5 million.'[35] By January 1969, Marley was able to report to shareholders that Germany 'now have 30 shops and another 12 nearly ready'.[36]

Unfortunately for Marley, the German retail expansion was not nearly as successful as it was proving at home and the earlier ambitious plans were soon abandoned. In 1970 it was proposed that the future policy for Marley Werke should be 'To extricate the company from shops and depots at minimum cost'.[37] Later that year all 30 shops were sold to a subsidiary of Hoechst for DM 1.5 million. The problems faced by Marley's German retailing business were often the same as those faced by Homecare in the UK; it is not easy to see why one failed and the other succeeded. Mike Evans had been sent to Germany because of his retail experience; looking back, he observed that 'there was the problem that we were selling mainly products that we didn't make and the products that we did make were not necessarily a logical range of goods to offer in a retail outlet – to have rainwater goods together with floor coverings and folding doors and some corrugated translucent sheet and floor polishes. It was a little bit of a hotch-potch which was then supplemented by products which were brought in. But of course you always, as in the UK, had to keep one eye on your retail customers who, if you cut your prices on something would be furious... obviously we did it in Germany less well than we did it in the UK because it was never really a profitable business.'

---

34 *Undated budget, Marley files.*
35 *Sir Owen Aisher Diaries, April 1967.*
36 *Marley Tile (Holding) Company Accounts, 1968.*
37 *Marley Overseas minutes, March 1970.*

Marley persevered longer with its Austrian retail business and by 1976 there were 19 Homecare shops spread across the country and plans to double the amount of retail space. That did not stop it losing money and there were discussions on selling or closing it. This would, however, have incurred substantial redundancy costs and so Marley persevered. Eventually, it was brought back to profit and the business was sold to the management in October 1986 having valiantly outlasted Marley's domestic commitment to retailing.

The consequences of expansion

The widening of Marley's base, both by product and country, had consequences for both financial resources and the management structure. As Marley had successively raised preference shares, debenture and then a £1 million Unsecured Loan Stock, the next fund raising exercise had to be in ordinary shares. There was a small hurdle to be cleared first. Although it had brought in no additional capital, Marley had created a new class of non-voting shares in 1955 via a three for two scrip issue; this would have facilitated share sales by the Aisher family without reducing their percentage voting control. The non-voting 'A' shares were also used shortly after for the acquisition of the minority holding in Marley Floors, and the purchase of Wallington Weston and Lomond. By 1960, less than 17% of the equity capital was entitled to vote.

Eric Cook

Even then, institutions were not over keen to subscribe to new equity without a vote and the opportunity was taken to enfranchise the "A" shares (with a 1 for 20 compensating scrip issue to ordinary shareholders). This facilitated a two for five rights which raised just over £3 million for the Group in October. Marley once again had net cash in its balance sheet and its ordinary shareholders' funds of £8.9 million were complemented by £500,000 of preference capital and £1.8 million of long term loans.

In 1960, Marley and the Aisher family suffered the loss of "Mr Dick" who died at the age of only 52, after 37 years with the Company. Dick Aisher had been responsible for all Marley's sales and marketing and these came under new control just at the time when the development of a wider product base was set to place added pressure on the Group's centralised approach to selling and contracting. Initially Richard Aisher Junior, Dick Aisher's only son, was given responsibility for the southern half of the country and Eric Cook was brought down from the Glasgow tile factory to to take charge of the north. Eventually, Eric Cook took sole control of Marley Tile's contracting and selling functions.

This reorganisation was followed by new appointments to the holding company board. The Marley Tile Company acted as the main operating company and senior management like Fred Hardy and Laurence Brady had long been represented. From November 1958, Owen Junior, Brady and Hardy had attended all holding board meetings but without voting rights. Until 1960, the directors of the ultimate parent, The Marley Tile (Holding) Company, consisted only of members of the Aisher family or of the original BAT non-executive directors. In January 1961, Jack Aisher was appointed to the new post of Deputy Chairman and Owen Aisher Junior, Francis Cooke, William Cullen and Fred Hardy were all brought on to the holding board. (Cooke had been the family adviser on tax and financial matters and Cullen was a non-executive director from Price Waterhouse; he died the following year.) Fred Hardy's position as the senior non-Aisher, though clearly understood within the company, was now on public view.

Part 6

After Macmillan: roofing and flooring

The roofing industry matures

Marley completed its post-war construction programme with the opening of Beenham in 1954. Two decades of economic growth lay ahead yet, for the concrete roof tile industry, the mid-1950s marked a turning point. The period of frenetic expansion which had started in the mid-1920s taking industry production to 6 million square metres in 1935 and trebling to 19 million square metres in 1954 had come to an end. Housing completions of 348,000 were later exceeded but not for long periods of time and, with two-thirds of the pitched roof market already secured, concrete's ability to gain further market share had the obvious mathematical limitations. But if the volume growth that lay ahead of Marley was to be only modest, the changes in the business were substantial. The introduction of a new generation of automatic tile making machinery, factory closures, and new works transformed production with speeds increasing from 52 plain tiles a minute to 120 large tiles. More significant, and with important consequences for Marley, the structure of the market changed as repair work or 'strip and retile' gradually increased in importance until it finally became a larger market than new housing. Marley's supply and fix, for so long the strength of the company, lacked the flexibility to respond fully to the new class of business and Marley increasingly found itself competing with its potential customers. Market share reached a peak of over

55% in the mid-1960s from which point Marley found itself holding off increasingly powerful competition from Redland. After prolonged internal debate and a variety of compromise measures, Marley slowly changed its own contracting organisation and introduced a completely new marketing and distribution system — a development which will be fully discussed in a later chapter.

After the opening of Beenham in 1954, Marley did not build another greenfield concrete roof tile works in the UK; instead, existing works were modernised and capacity acquired from other smaller producers. Up to this point, acquisitions had been made primarily to take competing local manufacturers out of the market; Shurdcrete and Buckland were mentioned in an earlier chapter. This policy continued. In May 1956, Marley acquired Lomond Tile Company of Dunbar for £30,000 cash and £80,000 worth of "A" shares; production stopped in November 1957. The deal must have cost more than money: the managing director and minority owner was H G Butcher who had previously been a salesman with Marley.

Two years later, in May 1959, The Barnstaple Brick & Tile Company was bought for £62,500 cash. In that case we know that the Poole works was delivering into the West Country and Barnstaple was undercutting on price. Marley had considered putting a works at St. Austell based on china clay waste but it was not technically feasible. Eventually Barnstaple was bought; the factory was in poor condition 'falling to bits and dangerous' but Marley installed some new machinery to try to keep the factory operational at minimal cost. However, it never became a successful plant and production ceased in February 1968.

With more quotations due to follow from Trevor Aisher, a brief description of the management changes that brought him into the story must be interpolated somewhat arbitrarily into the chronology. In January 1961, the senior directors of Marley Tile, effectively the main operating subsidiary under the holding company, stood down from the subsidiary Board: Owen Aisher Senior; Sir Owen and Jack Aisher; and the two ex-BAT directors, Aldridge and Hartley. In their place came some of the next generation of Aishers — Robin, Trevor and Richard — with Fred Hardy as Chairman. Trevor Aisher was placed in charge of all roof tile production, a position he was to hold for almost thirty years. Trevor Aisher was Jack Aisher's eldest son, born in 1935; after National Service he joined the roof tile company in 1955 as a trainee at Riverhead, later moving through sales. At the age of 22 he was made works manager at Aveley following the sudden death of the previous manager. The next four years were all spent in manufacturing until he replaced Archie Orme, who was becoming more involved with Head Office administration and some of the newer subsidiaries.

Returning to the sequence of factory development, the first clear exception to buy and close came in 1965 when Newlay Tiles of Dewsbury was acquired specifically to give Marley a presence in the South Yorkshire area; it was purchased for only £97,000 in cash and considerable new investment in plant was required to bring the works up to standard. South Yorkshire had been developing fast and Marley was at a disadvantage over transport costs, the nearest factories being Burton, Delamere and Ebchester. Marley had looked for some years at possible sites and did find a quarry near Harrogate with a hundred acres but were unable to buy it. Then Newlay came to ask Marley if there was any interest in buying it. Newlay had started as a block maker before going into tile manufacture 'and like many of them ran for two years and then got into trouble.' Trevor Aisher remembers going up to look at it: 'it was... a real mess but was situated on a good site, right in Dewsbury on the edge of the canal. It was about six acres with reasonably good buildings. We agreed to buy it on the basis that we would run only one production line, which allowed us to manufacture in an area where we had for many years been weak, and suffered a considerable amount of competition from Sandtoft. Because they were local and could give a better service than we could from Ebchester and Burton, they were growing and we were not.'

Reference is inevitably made during this book to the position of Redland, Marley's main competitor. However, mention should also be made of the privately owned Sandtoft Tileries, and its subsidiary Goxhill, who have a substantial presence in the Yorkshire market and adjacent areas. Originally a brick manufacturer, Sandtoft started making clay tiles in the 1930s, diversifying into concrete tiles in 1954. By 1980, according to the *Monopolies Commission Report on Concrete Roof Tiles*[1] Sandtoft had three factories with a capacity of 44 million tiles (actual, not plain tile equivalent); 12% of the national market but perhaps as much as 40% of the local market in its Humberside area. With Sandtoft claiming to sell on a combination of price and personal service, there was an overriding need for Marley to establish itself in that area. It is no surprise that both Marley and Redland have made acquisition approaches to Sandtoft.

In the post-Beenham decade, the concrete roofing tile virtually completed its rout of the traditional clay product against a less favourable market background. During the second half of the 1950s the housing market was in decline; the 1954 peak of 348,000 completions gradually fell until it levelled out at around 270–280,000 per year in 1958 and 1959. Of some compensation for the pitched roofing industry, the share of the private sector increased from 26% to 54% during this period. Helped by increased penetration of the market, concrete roofing tile production fell by less than 10% between 1954 and 1958. However, concrete continued to draw demand from clay and was ideally placed to benefit from the next housebuilding boom. Housing completions had stabilised remarkably close to 300,000 a year in the early 1960s until there was

1 Monopolies Commission Report on Concrete Roof Tiles, *1981.*

an almost instantaneous jump to the 400,000 a year level; the change effectively came in 1964 when completions rose from 299,000 to 374,000, slowly rising to a peak of 414,000 in 1968. The whole of the building materials industry enjoyed boom conditions and in 1964 and 1965 concrete roof tile production exceeded 32 million square yards (around 27 million square metres). By 1965 its market share exceeded 90% for the first time; clay was left with 6.6% and slate a mere 3.3%.

GB production (million square yards)

	1954	1955	1956	1957	1958	1959	1960	1961	1962	1963
Concrete tiles	22.8	20.3	22.1	21.4	20.6	23.4	25.6	26.1	25.9	24.2
Clay tiles	9.1	8.0	6.5	5.7	4.8	4.6	4.2	3.8	3.7	3.5
Roofing slates	2.8	2.6	2.6	2.7	2.0	1.5	1.6	1.4	1.3	1.1
	34.6	30.9	31.2	29.8	27.4	29.5	31.4	31.3	30.9	28.8
Concrete, as %	65.7	65.5	70.8	71.8	75.2	79.4	81.4	83.4	83.8	83.9
cf. GB housing completions										
units (000)	348	317	301	301	274	277	298	296	305	299

Note: figures may not add due to rounding.
Source: Department of the Environment

The financial benefits to Marley were less obvious than in the previous decade and despite a doubling of sales, pre-tax profits showed no growth at all.

Marley Tile accounts

	1954	1955	1956	1957	1958	1959	1960	1961	1962	1963
Fixed assets (£m)	1.86	2.03	2.01	2.01	2.07	2.15	2.61	2.93	3.13	5.39
Sales (£m)	8.77	8.33	8.87	9.01	8.62	9.41	11.1	12.0	12.7	17.8
Pre-tax profit (£000)	935	489	570	864	720	827	752	930	966	892
Profit margins (%)	10.7	5.9	6.4	9.6	8.4	8.8	6.8	7.7	7.6	5.0

To every man a garage

During this period, Marley was also enjoying rapid growth in its concrete products operation. Surrey Concrete's original Guildford factory was joined by Cheltenham in 1950, following the takeover of Shurdcrete. Then the existing tile factories at Aveley and Poole were used as a base for two more concrete products factories. These four factories were integrated into a new, and for Marley, autonomous company: Marley Concrete in November 1956. Further expansion led to the construction of new factories at Chorley in Lancashire in 1963 and Carluke in Scotland in 1966. A wide range of products continued to be made; Marley was one of many companies offering similar products and one of the more familiar to reach the High Street was Marleymix, a dry aggregate and cement mix, first manufactured at Aveley in 1958 but later made on other Marley sites. Marley Homes had also been formed to incorporate the original Marlith wood wool business at Storrington and the factory there additionally made concrete slabs, stone walling and similar garden and patio products. With Storrington, Marley Concrete was operating out of seven factories in the late 1960s.

Marley continued to introduce new structural products and as well as the garages, other lines included factory buildings, municipal buildings, home extensions, village halls and clubs; Marley Concrete was even awarded the Royal Warrant in 1970. Profits grew steadily and by the early 1970s Marley Concrete was averaging profits of over £800,000 a year, or around 10% of the UK total. However, the Marley garage remained the mainstay of the company and, here, Marley was able to use its close relationship with the local authorities to its advantage. Unfortunately, in 1975, those local authorities were to deliver a body blow to Marley when local authorities were urged by the Department of the Environment to provide parking spaces not garages in its new developments.[2] This accounted for about half Marley's garage business.

Marley redoubled its efforts to sell directly to the private customer – a quite different approach. 'There was a tremendous amount of direct mail – selling capital equipment, which is what it was to home owners, isn't easy, so we had a very big advertising budget for our size and used to take lots of small spaces in the nationals on Saturday and Sundays and on the back of the *Radio Times*, in the glossies and the DIY magazines. Later when we had the gardening products, like greenhouses, in *Homes and Gardens, Good Housekeeping*, a whole range of motoring magazines.'[3]

Marley re-equips

The 1960s brought in a new generation of tile manufacturing technology to Marley; in particular the introduction of automatic racking, the most significant advance since the post-war introduction of conveyors. We described earlier the labour intensive handling of the tiles after they leave the extruder. It was not

2 *The Department of the Environment Circular* Housing: Needs and Action *was sent out to all local authorities urging that in an effort to save public expenditure and divert more resources to new housing, garages should not be included in new housing schemes. The DoE pointed to the average provision of 0.96 car spaces per dwelling compared with a then average of car ownership among local authority tenants of 0.4 per household.*
3 *Bill Courtney interview.*

without perceived advantages. Archie Orme: 'Marley was able to do a lot in the early days because they did not spend a great deal of capital on highly automated machinery, they rode on the back of a lot of cheap labour. I can remember it being said many times that all the time you could make it by hand you wanted to hang on to it, because if you start putting machines in, other bothers come and it costs money. It wasn't a bad philosophy.'

However, as volumes grew, the labour problems became acute. There were limits to the number of lines that could be put into a factory and the demand was for plant to be run at faster speeds. Trevor Aisher comments on his experience as he took control of manufacturing: 'We had to operate these individual lines at faster speeds and the major constraint was labour. It became increasingly difficult to run plants at 65 to 70 tiles per minute on a manual basis because with three or four lines in a factory, we would physically run out of space.' The answer was to automate the handling and the machinery developed to meet that requirement was called automatic racking.

Automatic racking

Redland had begun to introduce automatic racking during the 1950s and there is some admission within the Marley ranks that Redland started to gain a technological lead at that time; attributable quotations would not be appreciated by their authors. Redland owed its technological position to Harold Carter, a Dorking engineer, who built tile machines for Redland just before the war and who became one of the triumvirate who ran Redland subsequently. The Chairman, Alec Young, described Carter as 'the most important figure in our history. It [his engineering] has been the foundation of our business'.

By the end of the 1950s Marley was actively investigating the alternatives open to it for automation. On one of his trips to Australia, Sir Owen visited Atlas which was running an automatic tile machine; this had been designed by H A Wilkinson, a one-time partner of Harold Carter and an early Redland Tile director; that visit gave him clear ideas on what could be achieved. Numerous visits were made to Germany, believed to be leading the field technically, eventually taking them to an engineering company called Keller. Keller had grown up as a manufacturer of clay tile and brick handling machinery but the growth of concrete roof tile production in Germany had taken it into that market. Keller developed a concrete tile machine and then a racking system based on its clay tile handling experience.

Marley bought a Keller machine with a view to installing it at Leighton Buzzard, but it was never taken out of the packing cases as it had a maximum speed potential of only 36 tiles a minute, which was well below the capacity required. It did, however, lead to the Engineering Department developing a

Marley automatic machine and the first racking plant, which was operated hydraulically and called the Mark 1, was installed in Riverhead in 1961. The main objective with this machine was that it would take all the labour out of the curing area, although Trevor Aisher remembers it with mixed feelings. 'It was, in a word, a brute, and it took at least eighteen months before we were operating at reasonable efficiencies.' The principle behind the Mark 1 was that as the tiles came from the extruder, they were automatically loaded onto the racks; the racks were then taken on a guided, though manually operated, truck into a large curing shed. The racks of uncured tiles were deposited and a rack of cured tiles taken out. 'One man and a racker did the work of eight to ten men. It was a very big step forward and allowed the company to increase machine speeds to roughly 90 tiles per minute.'

As the introduction of tile racking allowed higher machine speeds, Marley took advantage of this by introducing a new type of tile making machine, the drum machine. It provided a smoother, more continuous production process which enabled Marley to produce at a range of speeds between 30 and 100 tiles per minute. The original single link tile machines had a reciprocating action as one tile was pushed through the extruder and then the next; the action was smoothed out with the introduction of the second generation double link machine. The third generation machine now being used was a large circular drum with eight pushing arms. 'The drum rotated slowly and each of the pushing arms came through, pushed the pallet, and the next one came round and pushed another pallet. This rotating gave an almost continuous push rather than an intermittent push but it still wasn't absolutely constant velocity, there was still a slight slowing down and speeding up.'[4] It was not until the chain machine, introduced in the 1980s, that a completely continuous action was achieved.

The first drum machine was introduced at Glasgow for 15 × 9 in. Ludlow tiles, but there were problems and it was transferred to Burton. From then on there were continued improvements in that generation of machines. A Mark 2 Racker followed as soon as possible at Riverhead and further Mark 2 Rackers were built for Glasgow and Beenham in 1963/64; by the 1970s Marley was up to Mark 5. The rise in machine speeds permitted by automatic racking inevitably led to other changes in manufacturing technology. In particular, it prompted the switch from the press plate system of tile extrusion to the roller and slipper system mentioned in an earlier chapter. There had been experiments back at Aveley in 1957 but Marley's first roller and slipper plant was put into Riverhead in the early 1960s and, gradually, all the plants were converted during the 1960s.

The introduction of the faster extrusion machines and automatic racking

---

4   *David Trapnell interview.*

considerably increased the capacities of the modernised factories and this was particularly true of the closing years of the 1960s when there was a major investment programme. Demand had not increased commensurately and it was therefore felt that a smaller number of high volume, low cost plants could serve Marley's markets just as effectively, particularly as larger lorries were reducing unit transport costs; Marley prepared for its first substantial closure programme. Individual factories had been closed before, as with Harrietsham when it was replaced by Riverhead, or new acquisitions closed to remove competition, but not on this scale. At the beginning of 1970, Marley closed three roof tile works, Aveley, Bridgend and Storrington – though not without some internal disagreement. The economics of Bridgend had been altered by the opening of the Severn Bridge and it was possible to deliver tiles from Beenham more cheaply than they could be made at Bridgend. Storrington had grown up on a range of profiles which were no longer the leaders, e.g. Anglias, and the cost of converting the lines was considered prohibitive. There was however, more concern that Aveley, as a strategic factory with lines that could produce all the existing profiles, was being closed too quickly.

New designs

The launch of the Yeoman tile in 1952 was stated earlier to be the first of the large concrete tiles. These had advantages in reducing the cost of tiling the roof. The larger area to circumference ratio meant a smaller proportion of the tile being overlapped; the fewer tile courses on the roof, the quicker they could be tiled. The limitation to the tiles becoming yet bigger was the physical difficulty of handling them and the need for flexibility working up to abutments, chimneys and edges; thus the $16\frac{1}{2} \times 13\frac{1}{4}$-inch gradually became the normal size. Marley introduced a Ludlow Major, which took most of the original Ludlow business. There was also an entirely new type of profile introduced, the Modern of 1960, which was the first Marley tile to break away from the traditional clay profiles: 'A concrete version of the traditional slate'.

First and foremost the roof tile has to fulfil a function; it self-evidently needs to be watertight and it should also have a high rate of water run-off. As architectural design began to favour lower pitched roofs, i.e. less steep, the need to ensure rapid run-off of water became increasingly important. It was at this point that new concrete tiles were designed to achieve this. For the first time, a concrete tile was being designed on its own merits instead of being an ersatz clay tile. In 1963, the Modern was followed by the Wessex, designed for even lower pitches (15 degrees). Thus, for the rest of the decade, the range of profiles was concentrated on the large $16\frac{1}{2} \times 13\frac{1}{4}$ tiles – the double Roman Yeoman, the Ludlow Major, and the low pitch Modern and Wessex tiles; these were supplemented by the original small plain tiles and modest sales of the

Ludlow and Anglia tiles. At the end of the decade, the Anglia was followed by the large sized Mendip. The only other large tile to be introduced after that was the successful Bold Roll (re-using one of the pre-war names), an interlocking double pantile in Mediterranean style, which came in January 1975.

The large tile (now designated 413 × 330 mm) remained the standard while the industry continued to be dependent on new construction but once the re-roofing market began to emerge as an important customer, the industry had to reassess its ability to supply smaller tiles once again. This change in the demand for profiles partly lay behind Marley's acquisition of one more new factory, despite the earlier closures. Camtiles of Sawston, near Cambridge, was bought in 1974 from Sindell the builder for a nominal sum. They were producing two profiles manually and not making any money from that part of their operation. However, one of those profiles was a 380 × 230 mm tile (15 × 9 in.) then suitable for the growing London re-roofing market. Camtiles also gave Marley distribution advantages into East Anglia – perhaps now missing Aveley. Although modernised, the double-link tile machines in operation before the acquisition were retained and the plant was run on a low output basis.

In the same year, interesting proposals were put forward to build a small factory in the north of Scotland; nothing was done for a couple of years until in 1976 land was bought at Ellon near Aberdeen. There had been growing concern about the security of aggregate supplies at Glasgow and the possibility of running down that works was under consideration. In addition, Marley was having to import tiles from south of the Border into the Scottish market – never popular with local specifiers. In the event, the housing market was beginning to decline and Marley overcame its supply problems at Glasgow. The Ellon proposals were abandoned and Marley grouped itself around its ten tile factories; these remained its production base until the rationalisation programme that began with the closure of Leighton Buzzard in 1986.

In the marketplace, the concrete tile completed its domination of the roofing market by the end of the 1960s. After 1966 the statistics for roofing slates were not even considered worth publishing.

Unfortunately, Marley's own competitive position was coming under increasing pressure. Trevor Aisher reported his concern over loss of market share to his Board in April 1970. It had reached 57% of concrete during 1964 (possibly one of the highest figures ever achieved by the Company) but had fallen to 48% by the end of 1969. 'It was apparent three years ago that our market share would come under heavy pressure in view of the number of new factories being built by our competitors. However, the present decline is disturbing and in view of the current situation, efforts must obviously be made to arrest this trend.'

GB production (million square metres)

	1963	1964	1965	1966	1967	1968	1969	1970	1971	1972
Concrete tiles	20.2	26.9	27.5	25.9	27.4	28.6	25.9	22.3	27.8	30.1
Clay tiles	2.9	2.7	1.8	1.6	1.6	1.4	1.1	1.0	1.0	1.2
	23.1	29.6	29.3	27.6	29.0	30.1	27.0	23.3	28.8	31.3
Concrete, as %	87.4	90.8	93.8	94.0	94.7	95.2	95.8	95.9	96.6	96.3
cf. GB housing completions units (000)	299	374	382	386	404	414	367	350	351	319

Note: figures may not add due to rounding.
Source: Department of the Environment

Tile deliveries (000 square yards)

Year to October	1963	1964	1965	1966	1967	1968	1969
All concrete	23,652	30,385	31,793	30,657	32,315	33,433	30,147
Marley	13,152	17,454	16,451	15,884	16,447	16,980	14,607
% share	55.6	57.4	51.7	51.8	50.9	50.8	48.5

Source: Marley Tile Board Report, 70/29, April 1970

Although there was substantial growth in the size of the concrete roofing tile market in the 1960s, Marley's loss of market share had given it only modest volume growth. Indeed, following the housing boom of 1963–64, profits were erratic and, to be realistic, disappointing, culminating in only a marginal contribution when the housing market turned down at the end of the decade. It was not until the next, and virtually uncontrolled housing boom in the early 1970s that Marley Tile's profits moved to new peaks.

The golden years of flooring

Consort the winner

The years following the acquisition of Wallington Weston can rightly be described as the golden years of the plastic flooring industry. Technological advances in resilient sheet flooring had virtually killed the linoleum market. A boom in private housing; 'you've never had it so good'; the growth of consumerism; all meant brighter homes and an ever increasing flow of new flooring products, each designed to have more customer appeal than the last. Marley's flagship in the 1960s was Consort, produced at Wallington Weston as a competitively priced vinyl sheet flooring, but from 1964 sold additionally as tiles. Its range of attractive colours and patterns, "no-scrub" surface finish and low cost made it a market leader and Marley's best ever selling flooring. Sales grew rapidly and at its peak in 1964/65, reached 11.2 million square yards; its value exceeded the whole of the sales achieved by Marley's previous staple products – the Standard and Econoflex tiles. Not surprisingly, it became Wallington Weston's principal profit earner.

First, following its acquisition, the Wallington Weston works had been completely modernised and Marley sought to develop new uses for the calendering capacity. One of these was an improved version of Marleyfilm. It was a good rugged material but not particularly decorative. Denis Moss remembers Laurence Brady saying to him 'how about calendering and printing a decorative material to use in the same way'. Denis Moss made a sheet with a pigmented base and a clear film which had been printed on one side; these were then laminated together and sold as MarleyDecor, a printed version of Marleyfilm. The concept of a printed film, protected by a clear PVC wearing layer, was now accepted; it was to be the precursor of Consort.

The search had been on within Marley to develop a cheap and cheerful sheet flooring and there are some who suggest that the basic principles had been in sight when Wallington Weston was bought. Later, a visit to a German producer by Robin Aisher and Hugh Robinson, production manager at Wallington Weston, had shown that printed vinyls could be made. With the example of MarleyDecor before them, Hugh Robinson and Denis Moss were driving back from Wallington Weston. 'We were passing through Warminster at the time and Hugh said "I wonder what it would be like as a flooring if we put more PVC on the back." ' Experiments were made on the Wallington Weston laminators and Marley succeeded; they produced a solid vinyl sheet flooring with the patterned film protected under the clear vinyl wearing surface. Marley took out a patent describing the making of surface materials which were protected by putting the print between layers of PVC. Dunlop later contested the patent but were granted a licence by Marley free of royalties, the intention being to keep other manufacturers out of the market.

The difference between Consort previous sheet floorings was that the designs were not limited to what could be built into the sheet; instead, the design patterns were printed separately on plastic film and laid on top of the vinyl sheet giving a variety previously approached only in linoleum. Marley bought in the printed film to start with before making it at Wallington Weston. It was a winner: '... it looked good, it felt good. We had a printed flooring that you could cut with a pair of scissors. A woman could buy a 48" roll of flooring, take it home, lay it down, cut it with a pair of scissors, and she had a flooring that was very easy to clean. It was the first flooring that you could put down in a kitchen that was so easy to clean.'

In 1959 the new range was launched, described in the 1960 Group

Marley Consort

accounts: 'Marleyflor Consort is on the way to becoming one of the most popular roll floor coverings. Of solid vinyl, with a printed pattern which is topped by transparent vinyl film – so that the pattern is protected from wear – the floor covering is being made in an increasing variety of colours and designs. Launched by an intensive publicity campaign in the Home Counties, its success is spreading further afield.' Two years later it was described as 'our leading retail product'. While the Consort sheet flooring was doing so much for Wallington Weston, Marley Floors continued to dominate the market for floor tiles: the old A, B, C and D ranges, the latter two by then called Econoflex, were produced at Harrietsham and the vinyl based Marleyflex at Leighton Buzzard.

Wallington Weston was also chosen as the manufacturing base for another of those products peculiarly associated with the Marley name – the Spacesaver folding door. Designed for use in restricted space, the door slides on runners and concertinas against the door frame. The manufacture of the door was related to flooring in that the main components are manufactured from calendered PVC; the door consists of two layers of thick flexible PVC with a fibrous material sandwiched between them. Like so many other ideas, it

The Spacesaver folding door

stemmed from Sir Owen's overseas travels, this time to Cinncinati where he came into contact with the Clopay Corporation. In November 1958 Marley took out a manufacturing licence and the Spacesaver door became a steady seller for the next two decades – not only at home but also overseas; indeed, at one point, the folding door was the main product in the German factory.

In 1961, Robin Aisher, Sir Owen's younger son, was appointed Managing Director of Marley Floors (Wallington Weston, with its mixed product range, was always kept separate). Robin Aisher first worked at Marley for a three month spell in 1952 in between helping the British sailing team at the 1952 Helsinki Olympics (he won a bronze medal in 1968) and doing his National Service; he spent his time in the transport company 'taking engines apart and putting them back together again'. After serving in the Navy (and turning down a potential career in Naval Intelligence) he rejoined Marley to work in plastics. 'My last year at school, I devoted all my energies into finding out about this new product called plastic. I knew that my brother was up at Leighton Buzzard making flooring but there were other sides to plastic which excited me so I thought it would be rather good to enter the business.' During a five year training programme which moved him around the Group, Robin Aisher gravitated towards flooring until by 1958 it was his full-time commitment.

One of the more exciting new products to be launched by Marley Floors during the 1960s was a floor tile that could be laid easily by the amateur or do-it-yourself enthusiast as he was then becoming known. The tile was thinner than that made for the contractors and the adhesive was put on the tile in the factory, protected by a silicone treated paper; the tiles were sold into the retail market. They were featured by Sheila Black, the Woman's Editor of the *Financial Times*, in August 1967: 'The first time I ever laid Marley Tiles, I started by being thrilled at how easily we were getting this nice new floor. When it came to cleaning off all that superfluous, oozing black glue from the joints of the tiles, I felt rather differently. Having no floors to tile, I can only view Marley's latest offering with pleasure on behalf of others. The vinyl tiles are backed with peel-off paper which covers the strong glue. So one can lay them in position, cut them to fit the tricky corners, peel off and stick. In fact, they are called "Peel and Stick" and they are in colour with a slight flashing, each 9 inches square. They sell at about 10d each tile in most suitable shops.'

The Queen's Award

Innovation in floor tile production was not confined to the housing market. Little known by the public, but perhaps giving more satisfaction to its designers than any other product, was the Anti-static Floor Tile. For that, The Marley Floor Tile Company was given the Queen's Award to Industry in 1967, the citation being for technical innovation. The new tile was of particular importance to hospital operating theatres where, if static electricity caused sparking, the anaesthetic gases could explode. There had always been an option in the form of the flooring loaded with conductive carbon black but such floors had a depressing, unattractive all-black finish. Marley was able to combine safety with aesthetic appeal. The innovation was a process whereby Marley took PVC chips and tumbled them in conductive carbon black and pressed them into sheets. When cut into tiles they provided a finish of a predominantly light green or grey but with the individual chips surrounded by a fine black carbon border; this border provided the conductive path for the static electricity. Additionally, Marley developed an epoxy adhesive which also contained carbon. Thus, if there was an electrical charge, it passed through the tile via the carbon path and was dissipated through the carbon based epoxy adhesive.

In the early years of the floor tile, the builder or local authority was the primary sales target. However, by the late 1950s, the retail customer was being identified as a separate market. Although Marley later developed a general do-it-yourself retail business, the first involvement in retailing was solely within the confines of flooring. The Boardroom debate was clearly underway in 1956: 'Mr R H Aisher queried the wisdom of the Company opening its own retail shops, the suggestion of which was discussed at some length'.[5] Next month, a proposal was submitted to John Lewis for the installation of a Marley shop in their do-it-yourself department. The first "Shop within a Shop" was opened in Birmingham with all the Marley products sold by Marley's own staff. By the 1957 accounts Marley could report that 'Now established in numerous stores throughout the country, the "Marley Shop" idea is much sought after by store managements. A wider role was played by Marley Retail Supplies, a division of Marley Tile and later a Company in its own right, which had the specific responsibility for selling Marley products into the retail trade and played a particularly important role in broadening the range of selling outlets stocking Marley's flooring products. Sir Owen argues that the existence of a retailing presence lay behind Marley's ability to promote Consort so rapidly: 'Our shops selling Consort made it necessary for others to sell it – otherwise you could not get it into a lino shop for it killed everything they had'.

Cushioned flooring

It was the retail customer that also provided the impetus for the next generation of product – cushioned flooring – but in this instance, the running was made not by Marley but by Nairn. Cushioned flooring virtually describes itself: it is a thicker, spongier product than the solid resilient floorings which had preceded it and was designed to give a more luxurious feel underfoot to the floor, taking the fight back to the carpet industry. Cushioned flooring was invented in the USA in 1963 by Congoleum-Nairn where it sold under the trade name Cushionflor. To put the names in perspective, Congoleum of Philadelphia was one of North America's leading producers of felt base floor covering and in 1924 Nairn pooled its North American interests with Congoleum to form Congoleum-Nairn; the British firm's interest in the American joint venture ceased in 1968. After the war, Nairn continued with its linoleum business, only belatedly diversifying into thermoplastic tiles in 1953 but without achieving a major presence.

Cushioned flooring marks such an important development in the history of resilient flooring that it is worth dwelling on the technical background. The thick, foamed or "cushion" effect which gives the flooring its name was achieved by the addition of a chemical agent to the PVC formulation which caused it to "blow" or expand. The blowing agent decomposes at a high (and controllable) temperature, releasing tiny nitrogen bubbles into the PVC, thereby making a foam. This in itself was neither difficult nor patented: the breakthrough was what could be done to the surface of the flooring and this was patented by Congoleum-Nairn. The "ink inhibition process" offered a

5 *Marley Floorings minutes, June 1956.*

method of producing a contoured or relief texture on the surface of the sheet with perfect colour alignment. The texture was created by the use of inhibiting inks which retarded the action of the blowing agents. The solvent of the printing ink incorporates an agent which alters the blowing temperature of the blowing agent by raising the temperature necessary for it to expand. Thus, when the final clear PVC wearing surface is laid on, the sheet is passed through the oven, the foam blows but the part which is covered by the ink, i.e. the line in a tile pattern, is inhibited at that temperature and does not rise as much. The beauty of the process lay in the fact that both the colour and the relief were created by the inks at the same time; the inhibition process therefore allowed perfect alignment, or "registration" between the colour and whatever texture or relief had been designed into the system. Complicated relief patterns could be created with a perfect colour registration. A trade view outlined the attractions of the new cushioned product to the customer: 'the most important are a marked reduction in noise level, as compared to other types of "hard-surfaced" floor coverings; a comfortable feel underfoot; and an excellent ability (particularly in embossed designs) to camouflage and resist heel and furniture indentations.'[6]

In 1965 Nairn reached agreement on the use of the patents and in 1967 became only the second company in the world to manufacture cushioned vinyl using the ink inhibition process. By the end of that year, Marley itself had entered into negotiations with Congoleum-Nairn for a manufacturing licence. One appears to have been offered but Marley decided against it in the belief that they could engineer an equivalent product themselves at a lower cost than paying royalties. In December 1973, Marley attempted to buy into Nairn & Williamson (as it then was) when a block of just under 30% of the share capital became available but Tunnel pipped Marley to the post.

Going it alone was a difficult choice for Marley, giving Nairn the lead for the 15-year life of its patent. Nevertheless, Marley successfully developed its own cushioned flooring on the spreader at Harrietsham, launching the two-metre wide Vinylaire in the South of England early in 1969 (a more economical range was later marketed as Softstep); by the end of the year it was available nationally and internationally and was obtaining significant export orders. It was made in six-foot rolls with a range of 24 designs and colours.

The foaming process, or the creation of the cushion, was no problem, but unable to use the ink inhibition process, Marley ran its sheeting through a four colour rotary silk screen printer; this process applies a thicker layer of print than gravure rollers and with the addition of some blowing agent to the specially developed ink, a relief effect was obtained but these were never able to match the designs achieved by Nairn; eventually, when the patents expired, Marley

---

6 Anon, 'The new wave in vinyl flooring', Modern Plastics, December 1967, pp 98–100. This article also provides a more detailed technical description of manufacturing processes.

adopted the inhibition process itself. Devising its own process had given Marley some advantages. For example, Marley believed it was the only manufacturer producing cushioned flooring in one continuous process: 'The good thing is you've no work in progress but if you have a break, or a fault, the whole thing stops'.[7] That may be so but it must be accepted that the decision not to take out a licence, to take its own independent line, so often successful in Marley's history had, on this occasion, made manufacturing more difficult for a while.

Changes were also taking place in the commercial flooring market. Industrialised building techniques were increasing their hold in local authority housing and to serve the industrial builder, Marley launched another felt backed vinyl in the summer of 1965, Vynatred, a flooring which incorporated sound insulation and which could be manufactured and laid very quickly. It was made on the spreader at Harrietsham and consisted of a tightly needled hessian felt base coated with a PVC paste; after passing through the oven it was embossed and then the embossing was filled with another coloured paste to give an inlaid pattern. 'Whole floors of Vynatred can be fabricated on the building site in a small temporary workshop. Since the living space in factory-built homes generally conforms to a standard pattern, a floor laying team can move from apartment to apartment fixing areas of standard section very speedily.'[8] Vynatred had outstanding sound installation qualities and as a result of field tests carried out by the Building Research Station, Vynatred had an official Grade 1 classification when installed on a 6-in. concrete subfloor.

By the end of the 1960s, resilient flooring had assumed the characteristics of a fashion business; manufacturers offered an ever widening range of products, patterns and colours supported by press and television advertising. A brochure accompanying Marley's 1969 Annual Report displayed a dozen different ranges:

> **Consort** – *"No-scrub" vinyl flooring from 13/- a yard*
> **Vinylaire** – *embossed vinyl flooring with foam backing and insulating qualities 24/- a yard*
> **Vynatred** – *felt backed vinyl flooring reduces impact noise 19/11d a square yard*
> **Marleyflor** – *vinyl flooring in sheet and tile. From 14/11d sq yd 1/1d per tile*
> **Econoflex** – *floor tiles, inexpensive, in many colours. From 9/4d sq yd*
> **Heavy Duty Vinyl Tiles** – *Hard wearing and elegant. 26/3d sq yd*
> **Marleyflex** – *vinyl tiles. From 16/- sq yd*
> **Consort tiles** – *easy to clean with their locked-in-shine. 1/3d per tile*
> **Tuscan** – *a vinyl reproduction of marble. From 24/- sq yd*
> **Travertine** – *a vinyl reproduction of travertine marble. From 20/- sq yd*
> **Heavy Duty Vinyl Sheet** – *a hard wearing and attractive sheet flooring 23/- sq yd*

7 *Geoff Barrett interview.*
8 Plastics Today, *no 29.*

> **Simplay** *at 8d and* **Peel and Stick** *at 11d a tile. The easiest tiles for the amateur to install*

Despite the growing competition, both from British and imported product, and the entry of the cheap mass produced carpet, the natural growth in the market place continued to have a positive effect on Marley's flooring profitability during the 1960s. Both Marley Floors and Wallington Weston made over a million pounds profit for the first time in 1968; the former through its domination of the tile market and the latter still benefiting from volume sales of Consort sheet vinyl. With Group pre-tax profits no more than £4½ million in 1968, these flooring contributions were as significant as they had ever been. But the directors were well aware that there was a major challenge on the horizon: the tufted carpet.

A diversion into carpets

Just as vinyl flooring had taken the market away from linoleum, so the resilient flooring manufacturers were being pressured by the introduction of cheap tufted carpets. A natural response was for them to enter the carpet business themselves. The commercial logic was not so much driven by the manufacturing side of the business but by distribution and contracting where the ability to offer a complete range of floor coverings was an important commercial advantage. In North America this had led Armstrong Cork Canada to acquire Brinton Carpets, one of Canada's largest manufacturers, in 1966; in the following year Armstrong's UK subsidiary took on the exclusive marketing arrangements for a tufted carpet manufacturer. By then, Marley had already decided to take the manufacturing route and in July 1965 the establishment of a carpet venture was minuted, with Tom O'Sullivan and Peter Wilson as its first directors. Reporting to the shareholders, the Chairman stated: 'Your Board considered that to take full advantage of all aspects of this large and important market [flooring] we should start production of carpets. Plans are well advanced for this and the most up-to-date plant has been purchased. We have already created a satisfactory market and through our own Marley shops and retail division confidently expect to enlarge the sales of this type of floor covering... we shall be extending the sale of this type of product which is already available through our shops. To deal with this, future shops will have a larger sales area.'[9]

Marley wanted to build a carpet factory in Lancashire but could not obtain planning permission and resisted efforts to push it into Merseyside. In the end, Marley sidestepped the planning constraints; in April 1966 it bought

---

9 *Marley Tile (Holding) Company Accounts, 1965.*

the West Country textile business of Alfred H Tucker for £130,000; it was then able to convert its cloth mill into a carpet factory. The manufacturing continued under Alfred H Tucker Ltd with sales being handled by Marley Carpet. At that stage, Dennis Knight became a director and assumed responsibility for running the factory, barely a stone's throw from Wallington Weston. 'This created a conflict of interest and Dennis never really had his heart in carpets, if only because it was in direct competition to the plastic flooring he was producing nearby at Wallington Weston.'[10]

The importance of carpets to the total contracting strategy is clear from the holding company reports of both 1966 and 1967: 'The first stage of our plant is now completed and... there is little doubt that we shall be able to provide a wide range of tufted carpets for a market which has prospects of providing a healthy growth... will help to create more work for our contracts division.'[11] 'On the contract side we are securing a growing volume of business in servicing new houses with carpet. Sales of this product will show a substantial improvement in 1968, and it is hoped that the factory will reach break-even point by the end of the year.' Unfortunately, the optimism proved misplaced. One of the problems was that instead of installing the two or three machines that would have satisfied Marley's own requirements, as many as nine machines were installed producing a high volume of carpet that needed to be sold outside. Eric Cook reported on the difficulties of securing the necessary sales volumes: 'It is difficult enough to secure the business in the first place and it has become more and more obvious that we need special representatives to tackle the job.'[12] Marley was also having problems with its product quality and then, on top of all that came the Cyril Lord collapse in November, flooding the market with cheap tufted carpets.[13] A year later the carpet strategy was being publicly questioned: 'As an investment our carpet manufacturing business has proved anything but satisfactory... we are... actively engaged in seeing how we can continue to fit ourselves into this market.'[14] The decision to withdraw from carpet manufacture was announced in January 1970 and a year later the plant and buildings were sold to US Concept Industries.

At the time Marley was seeking to protect its position in the flooring market by diversifying into carpets, the Company was also trying to extend the use of its plastic laminates upwards onto the roof. On April 1st 1967 Marleydek was launched to service the flat roof market. It was a calendered sheet backed on paper and looking back on it today, Robin Aisher still regards it as being 'ahead of its time in development but' – and there was a big but – 'we didn't do enough work on the method of fixing it'. The adhesive was

10   *Colin James interview.*
11   *Marley Tile (Holding) Company Accounts, 1966.*
12   Marley Board Report, *68/34, June 1968.*
13   *See Cyril Lord,* Dictionary of Business Biography.
14   *Marley Limited* Annual Report, *1969.*

supplied by Shell: 'it seemed to stick very well but what happened was that the adhesive completely disappeared and you then had a sheet flapping around in the wind. We suddenly found ourselves, sales having taken off tremendously with the single layer roofing system, with almost a horror show, but we managed to recover quickly enough.' It had taken two or three years for the adhesion problems to materialise and in October 1970 the Marley Tile minutes sombrely recorded: 'With large areas of roofing now completed, it was recognised that the potential liabilities could be enormous'. Production of Marleydek was stopped the following month and Marley seemed to have disengaged itself without too much difficulty.

Salaries, mergers and dividend cuts

The highest paid Director

Although 1973 is conventionally regarded as the end of the period of post-war economic growth, for Marley it was 1969 that brought a period of acute financial pressure. It all looked so unlikely in 1968: housing completions in that year reached an all-time record of 414,000 and Marley similarly recorded its best ever profits, at £4.5 million. In the press, of course, 1968 was the year which produced the first revelations from the new Companies Act. The 1967 Companies Act required additional disclosure including directors' share-holdings. The Chairman reported in the 1967 accounts that '... it will not come as a surprise to find that the Aisher family holds a large stake in Marley. Let it be said that the Aishers have a large holding in Marley and I like to think the evidence is overwhelming that a proprietary interest in a business is the most dynamic managerial incentive.' Out of a total number of shares in issue of 37,085,000, Aisher holdings were given as O A Aisher and family 3,840,000 (10.4%); Jack Aisher and family 3,321,000 (9.0%); O A A Aisher 298,000 (0.8%); and Allgoods (a family company with overlapping interests) 4,162,000 (11.2%). This would exclude shares held by the family of Dick Aisher and sisters of Sir Owen and Jack.

The 1967 Companies Act also required disclosure of directors' salaries and that proved infinitely more interesting to the press and, at the next Annual General Meeting, to some shareholders. Tables of the top earning directors led with Sir Owen on £91,722 followed well behind with three others on £50,000 (Sir Maurice Bridgeman of BP; John Davis of Rank Organisation and Sir George Harvie-Watt of Consolidated Gold Fields). That £92,000 largely derived from the 2½% profit sharing arrangements established for Sir Owen and his father in 1935 prior to the flotation; today it would be the equivalent of three quarters of a million pounds.

When the controversial remuneration details were published, Sir Owen could justifiably look back with pride on what he had created. The pre-tax profits of £4.5 million that Marley was heading for was not far short of the £6 million or so being earned by other leading building materials companies such as BPB Industries, Ready Mixed Concrete, Redland or Tarmac, and ahead of London Brick and Taylor Woodrow's £4 million. Marley was the leading UK roof tile manufacturer; its flooring business, started from scratch after the war and augmented by Wallington Weston, accounted for nearly half the domestic trading profits; and Extrusions and Foam had become substantial businesses in their own right. The following year Sir Owen stood on the threshold of creating one of the largest building materials companies in the country when, on the 14th October 1969, merger talks with Redland were announced.

The Redland merger

A merger between Marley and Redland would have brought together largely complementary interests. Redland would have contributed its successful overseas roof tile companies, especially in Germany and its portfolio of domestic building materials – bricks, aggregates and concrete pipes. Marley had the wide range of plastics companies where it arguably had the leading position in Britain. Somehow, the participants thought that the incidental merger of the two dominant producers of concrete roofing tiles could be justified to the Monopolies Commission on the greater good. Admittedly, the original business of the erstwhile partners was going through a difficult phase and therefore represented only a small part of combined profits. To the extent that it was thought about at that early stage, it was assumed that undertakings on pricing would be acceptable to the Commission.

Personalities were to prove a more immediate problem. Initial talks were held at the Dorchester Hotel between Sir Owen, Jack Aisher and Fred Hardy from Marley, and Alec Young, Tony White and Colin Corness from Redland. While some progress was made it was not long before the inevitable question of the top position had to be addressed. Looking back on the discussions Jack Aisher commented that 'It got to the point where Alec Young [Chairman of Redland], I think, was more interested and keener to do it than Owen. Owen saw the advantages and, encouraged perhaps by me, the discussions went on to the point where it was agreed, yes, we would do it. What made people cool off was the fact that neither Alec nor Owen really could reach a decision as to who was going to run the joint organisation. Not at the Dorchester but subsequently, without Alec or Owen saying what they had at the back of their minds, it became clear that it really wasn't going to work. When it was abundantly clear to them that Owen wanted to run the show and when it was also abundantly clear to us that Alec could not agree to that, or wanted to do it himself, it was Alec who thought, well I must find a compromise.'

The first attempt at a compromise was Sir Owen suggesting Jack Aisher as Chairman. 'Alec knew it wasn't the solution. Then Alec came through with the thought of Dick Beeching [late of ICI and British Rail]. I remember Owen coming back and saying "Look, I met Alec, what do you think?" We all sat round and said, "Well, what do you think Owen?" – "I don't think much of it at all. And that really was that." On the 18th November 1969 it was announced that the talks had been discontinued. Sir Owen stresses that his objection was to the concept of a "City man" rather than a Chairman from within the building industry, but it seems unlikely that any compromise could have been agreed between two such forceful parties.

Dividend pressures

The merger proposals had come at a time of growing competition in the building industry but few felt it as as hard as Marley, with a high exposure to the new housing market in its domestic base. Between 1967 and 1970, housing starts fell by 29% and completions in 1970 were some 15% below the 1968 peak. The plastics businesses held up relatively well but there was a collapse in the returns from the original roof tile and contracting company, exacerbated by losses in the new carpet venture and losses in Germany and South Africa. Group profits more than halved to £2.1 million in the two years to 1970 and Marley now had to pay the price for the high rate of capital spending on its new businesses. In 1969 the final dividend was cut from 14% to 11½% making 17½% against 20% for 1968, but there was worse to come for shareholders the next year. For the three months to April 1970, Marley (which then published its results on a quarterly basis) announced a pre-tax profit of only £36,000 and a post-tax loss. In July, Terence Burton, the Company Secretary, circulated a confidential report on the Group's financial position to the Directors. Borrowings at 30th April were £20,059,000 against the maximum legally permitted £20,621,000 – the size of the shareholders' funds. The borrowings were expected to deteriorate even further the following spring. The profit forecasts in the document were worrying with a fall to only £1.6 million expected in 1970 and a further reduction predicted for the following year. (Fortunately, profits actually trebled in 1971!) The message was stark; '... it is time to adopt a policy of financial retrenchment. We should over the next two years reduce borrowings down to safer levels, using this period to make the most of the capital we now employ. If overdrafts are sufficiently reduced, we could agree with our bankers that a funding operation be indefinitely postponed... The question of dividend reduction is the most important factor in obtaining the banks' agreement to the postponement of a funding operation... Marley's high financial gearing emphasises the company's vulnerability in periods of economic recession and allows no elbow room for intelligent diversification or expansion.'

The previous month the interim dividend had been cut from 6% to 2½%. John Pollard (later Finance Director) had also taken a tough line: 'Our borrowing margins with the bankers will certainly see us through to the end of the calendar year. The financial position will not be so comfortable when we hit our high payout period between January and April of 1971. During this time we pay our taxes, debenture interest and final dividend (if any). Our two main bankers, Lloyds and Barclays, have loaned us about £10 million between them and are looking for a funding operation of some sort which will repay at least a major part of this. Against all of this background, it is clearly prudent not to pay dividends until profitability improves, and certainly not to pay a final dividend this year. In the event, the outcome for 1970 was not as bad as had been feared and trading in the opening months of 1971 began to improve; the final was reduced from 11½% to 3½% making only 6% for the year against 17½%.

The financial pressures which emerged with unexpected suddenness at the end of the 1960s may have resulted in part from a practice of expanding first and financing later but a contributory factor was the individual structure of the finance function within Marley. Since the war, Jack Aisher had acted as the Finance Director. When John Pollard joined the accounts department in 1955, it was under the control of a 'clear minded' bookkeeper, Fred Baker. As a qualified accountant, fresh from working on City prospectuses, John Pollard was surprised to find himself reconciling inter-company balances. Wally Green, another qualified accountant was recruited in the same year, and he eventually became Marley's Chief Accountant. Soon after, John Pollard was given a year's practical experience of manufacturing by being put in charge of the Bridgend and Poole factories; he then moved over to work on special assignments as personal assistant to Jack Aisher and in effect became his deputy. They were later joined by Bill Gard to form the Financial Controller's department with responsibility for banking, the City, and the Group budgets. This was quite separate from the Chief Accountant's department, which prepared the monthly accounts and the group consolidations. The two functions co-existed and the budgets were not always prepared on the same basis as the group accounts. (That separation of function existed until 1985 when Mike Armstrong, then Finance Director, took over all responsibility for the first time.) Marley's ability to foresee, and therefore react quickly to, sudden changes in the financial climate, was less than ideal.

Part 7
The pressures begin

The boom conditions at the opening of the 1970s came just in time to avert John Pollard's worst fears; with the wind behind it, Marley could demonstrate what it was capable of earning. Although the public sector housing programme was declining, the private housing market experienced one of its most active periods since the war. Private sector housing starts (Great Britain) jumped from 165,000 in 1970 to 228,000 in 1972; building society commitments for loans on existing houses, so important for refurbishment demand, rose by 59% between 1969 and 1972.[1] Marley's profits rose from £2.1 million in the year to October 1970 to £15 million in 1973, well over treble the previous record profit; even allowing for inflation the peak to peak profits growth was in excess of 130%.

Something had to prick the inflationary bubble of the early 1970s; in the event it was the international oil price that was cast as the villain though it came at a time when domestic policy considerations anyway would have necessitated action to restrain credit growth and price inflation. Neither was the public sector, still a substantial buyer of houses, immune from those same financial constraints. More particularly for the building industry, these pressures came at a time when the secular demand for housing had already peaked. The crude gap between the housing stock and the number of

1   Source: *Building Societies' Association.*

The Marley Board 1974: sitting, from left *Jack Aisher, Sir Owen Aisher, Fred Hardy;* first row standing *Bill Courtney, Richard Aisher, Peter Wilson, Eric Cook, Owen A A Aisher;* second row standing *Trevor Aisher, Robin Aisher, John Pollard, Tom O'Sullivan;* back row standing *T P Burton, Peter Winfield*

households had been eliminated: for what it was worth, there was now a statistical surplus of housing stock. Moreover, household formation, which had been averaging 220–230,000 a year during the 1960s, began to fall rapidly, and averaged no more than 120,000 a year in the ten years to 1981. The immediate impact on the housing market was dramatic as private housing starts collapsed from 216,000 to 106,000 between 1973 and 1974. Although there was a partial recovery during the mid-1970s, the decade finished with private housing starts back down at the 100,000 level. Even more serious was the reductions in the public sector housing programme where starts fell from 146,000 in 1974 to only 56,000 in 1980 – and still falling. All in all, the decade after the oil price shock was an exceptionally testing time for those serving the housebuilding industry; Marley had to trade against a background in which housing starts halved (from 351,000 in 1972 to 153,000 in 1981).

Marley faced the challenges of the 1970s with a substantially enlarged top Board. In 1963, two intermediary holding companies had been created to give senior executives a broader role immediately below the main holding company: the old Marley Tile Company had been given responsibility for the domestic business with a counterpart, Marley (Overseas) was created under the Chairmanship of Owen Aisher Junior. In 1971, the new generation of executives were appointed to the parent company Board (by then called Marley Limited): Robin Aisher (Floors); Richard Aisher (Transport); Trevor Aisher (Roof Tiles); Eric Cook (Sales); Bill Courtney (Buildings); Dennis Knight (Wallington Weston); Tom O'Sullivan (Retail); John Pollard (Finance); Peter Wilson (Extrusions) and Peter Winfield (Foam). The Board increased in size from five to fourteen. The appointments brought all the specialist operating expertise to bear at main Board level but this was not without its drawbacks.

Robin Aisher   *Richard Aisher*

Trevor Aisher

Tom O'Sullivan

Peter Wilson

Peter Winfield

Interviews with those executives suggest that many regarded their role as protector of their individual fiefdoms.

If there was conflict between individual operating entities, or between Directors, then it centred on the inter-company trading, the style and control of selling and marketing and the extent to which Marley was thought to compete with its own customers. These are issues which are intertwined with the history of the individual Marley subsidiaries and are best covered in the discussion of those entities which follows. The issues involve the centralised role of the original Marley Tile contracting division which, in the late 1960s, still handled a significant proportion of non-roofing tile business; the concept of maintaining a large contracting force in competition with their customers' business; and the role of a merchanting and retailing business within a manufacturing structure. Main Board directors were questioning the very nature of the marketing principles which had driven Marley for nearly half a century – and while their progenitor was still in charge.

"The Last Supper"

It was a debate which led to "The Last Supper" – as it was irreverently termed by those not present – a dinner at Faygate, Sir Owen's house, with most of the senior Directors attending, where operating companies sought to establish more control over their own selling function. Marley's traditional approach, which had served the Company so well, was strongly defended by Sir Owen and Eric Cook who ran Marley Tile's contracting business. Even they, however, had different views, with Sir Owen arguing that the selling and contracting function served only to support factory throughput, whereas Cook believed that they were independent activities which should be profit centres in their own right. Whoever was right, it is a matter of record that the last twenty years has seen Marley gradually change from a Company that made its own markets, put its own product in place as a contractor, and had its own merchanting and retailing outlets, to a Company which is now predominantly direct sale, possessing no merchanting or retail outlets and with its residual contracting businesses at arm's length.

To the end, Sir Owen still believed that the traditional Marley approach should have been adapted and not abandoned. Indeed, it is possible to argue that if Marley had integrated even further downstream, increasing its merchanting with, say, the acquisition of UBM (as was once considered), and keeping its retailing chain, Marley could have controlled its own market place. Possibly, but it would have been a very high risk strategy in the face of the structural changes which took place in the housing market. Marley had been built before the war and in the immediate post-war years on new building, the times of 300,000 houses a year with little repair and maintenance work and do-it-yourself not yet invented. Give Marley a contract for 100 houses and it could roof them or floor them without a competitor to touch it. But when the new housing market declined, and the typical contract became a replacement roof here, or a new floor for Mrs Smith there, the organisational problems multiplied. It became the age of the small man, the local roofer, the do-it-yourselfer, and to reach him Marley increasingly needed to have the local contractor and the small man on side.

It is also fair to say that the rationale which lay behind Marley's original supply and fix policy, the need to establish a market for new products eschewed by the traditional distribution channels, no longer remained valid. In the post-1960s world, Marley no longer had to fight for the acceptability of its new substitute products; they were recognised in their own right and, indeed, many of the younger customers, even installers, would have to pause to recollect just what it was that the concrete roofing tile, the vinyl floor and the plastic drainpipe had actually replaced. Marley's fight now was not with an unknowing marketplace; it was with an increasingly strong body of competing manufacturers, all seeking to erode Marley's hard earned position as market leader. How the pressures of that competition led to change within Marley is discussed in more detail in the chapters that follow.

Roofing

The market changes – strip and retile

Within the roofing industry, the nature of the demand altered significantly in the 1970s, producing an entirely different customer profile – and one to which Marley was not ideally suited. As already indicated, it led to radical changes within Marley Tile's marketing and contracting business, changes which were not fully effected until the mid-1980s. The roofing industry faced a co-incidence in the collapse of the new housing market (completions fell by 55% between 1972 and 1980) where Marley's strength lay, while at the same time re-roofing work, or strip and retile as it was commonly called, grew rapidly. Patently, roofs have always been repaired and it is difficult to argue for re-roofing as a new concept – one of the first issues of *Marley News* (December 1954) has a photograph of Marley re-roofing Storrington Abbey with plain tiles. What changed was the scale of this re-roofing and its consequent recognition and targeting as a market segment with different characteristics and requirements from new housing.

Strip and retile originally started on the South Coast and then moved through the South East – particularly into the London market. The pre-First

World War roofs began to give trouble in London during the 1960s and 1970s. If roofed with Welsh slate, the nails rusted and the slates broke away; if European, then the slate itself had a tendency to break up. At the same time, the clay tiles put up in the inter-war period were de-laminating.

Figures for the growth of re-roofing work are rough and ready. Marley records first mention strip and retile increasing in 1969. By 1973 the subject features in the Group Annual Report: 'An important factor is the rapid growth during the last three years of the work we do in replacing the roofs of existing homes. The point may best be illustrated by looking back to 1964 when 435,000 homes were started. In that year we delivered no more tiles than we did in 1973, when starts were about 100,000 houses less, which emphasises the importance of roof renovation or "strip and retile" work.' Two years later the Group accounts reported that strip and retile accounted for 40% of sales in some areas. By 1980, the proportion of Marley's roof tile deliveries accounted for by strip and retile had reached 55%.

Apart from the increase in renovation work, other changes were also taking place in the roofing industry to the benefit of the concrete tile manufacturers. In the local authority market, the high-rise blocks had succumbed to a new generation of sociologists and, albeit in a falling market, a given number of dwelling units now had a higher number of roofs; pitched roofs increased their market share. Apart from that, flat roofs generally were going out of favour not only on low-rise housing but also on commercial and public buildings. Pitched roof advocates will argue for the aesthetic appeal of their product, but the maintenance problems of flat roofs laid in the previous two decades were probably more relevant. The smaller commercial projects effectively became a new and important market for the tile industry and by 1977 Marley estimated that non-housing use accounted for 30% of its tile deliveries.

As was indicated earlier in the text, the growth of the re-roofing market challenged the domination of the large tiles. This partly reflected the size of the original clay tiles being replaced but the smaller tile blended in more naturally on the Victorian and Edwardian terraced roofs; this was particularly true of the London market. The acquisition of Sawston had brought in another 15 × 9 in. (380 × 230 mm) tile suitable for the London strip and retile market, but Marley did find itself a little short of the smaller tile in its range. The Ludlow had been down to one line at Beenham and this was reintroduced towards the end of the 1970s with a revised design as the Ludlow Plus.

The role of the Contracting Division

The growth of strip and retile work served to heighten a division which was already beginning to surface within the higher reaches of the management.

Marley owed its existence to an ability to create its own market; the product was not simply a tile but a finished roof. Supply and fix was not just a marketing aid but an integral part of the process whereby Marley delivered a roof to the builder. By the early 1960s it had been in use for nearly 40 years; employees had started and finished their working lives knowing no other system. Marley's newer products – flooring, extrusions – were all absorbed into the supply and fix approach and, indeed, used Marley Roof Tile's own sales and contracting organisation. Yet the market place was changing and the Marley Tile contracting division was increasingly seen as monolithic and unresponsive. Throughout this period, two separate but interconnected strategies were being challenged: the concentration of virtually all Marley's marketing, distribution and installation of manufactured goods through The Marley Tile Company which led to organisational diseconomies of scale and conflicts of interest; and the very concept of Marley as the prime customer of its factories and the resultant competition with its customers. But abandoning a philosophy that had served the Company so well since its formation was not to be lightly undertaken and it was a full two decades before the dilemma was fully resolved.

Trevor Aisher, then in charge of roof tile manufacturing, describes the organisational problems that were increasingly apparent during the 1960s as the scale of the business grew and the range of products widened. 'The whole business had been built up very successfully on the basis that we had one large selling force selling all the manufactured output. All the manufacturing companies were therefore relying on a core contracting business. During the 1960s, as the Company expanded and developed more products, one large contracting operation could not efficiently control all the administration and provide the right selling effort for all the new products. Not only was the contracting business a most expensive business to administer but, in addition, the really critical problem was that one area salesman was responsible for selling maybe 15 different products ranging from roof tiles to plastics. Human nature being what it is, he tended to concentrate on the easiest products which, not unnaturally, led the other companies, particularly in plastics, demanding control of their own sales and marketing forces. In other words, they had reached the point where they wanted to control their own destinies.'

The Sales and Contracting Division was under the control of Eric Cook (who had joined Marley in 1948, becoming a director of the Holding Company in 1971); he had a natural interest in preserving the structure which had served Marley so well in the past. Equally supportive was Sir Owen who was able to look back at over forty years of success with the supply and fix approach. Supply and fix had first been questioned in the early 1960s when the concept slowly began to come under scrutiny; the Board minutes during 1961 contain frequent references to discussions on Jack Aisher's memo on supply and fix or merchants but no changes resulted. Suggestions for change were no doubt tentatively put. Jack Aisher: 'I wouldn't put it as strongly as a disagreement. Owen stood alone in wanting to make the supply and fix part predominant in the marketing of our products. Nobody else felt as strongly as that. Let's face it, it was the cornerstone on which Marley was built; it was created by Owen.'

Those outside the roof tile division became the strongest critics: they were running factories but forced to sell their output to Marley Tile and had no control over their own marketing. A Board sales report prepared early in 1969 recognised the problems being created by Marley's marketing structure: 'The present organisation does not allow us to maintain sufficient drive behind individual products and we have got to find a way of overcoming this difficulty'. It went on to discuss the balance between supporting the depots, marketing the range of Marley goods and the need for separate product sales forces. Later that year the minutes record a decision to transfer a number of representatives across from supply and fix to direct selling to roofing contractors. Labour shortages were putting added pressure on supply and fix as Marley's own subcontractors turned to stripping and re-tiling on their own account on an ever increasing scale. This not only forced Marley to increase the rates it paid to its subcontractors but also accelerated the trend to supply only sales.

In the summer of 1970, Marley began to break up the monolithic contracting business operated by the Marley Tile Company. Marley Extrusions, for example, took over responsibility for its own marketing and selling in August 1970. At the same time, a separate sales force was established within the building and contracting division to sell tiles directly to the roofing contractors. For the first time, Marley produced a comprehensive price list for roofing contractors, and Eric Cook, the Sales Director, undertook 'to report separately on the increasing supply only roofing business'. The supply-only activities were now entities on their own but it was still not a complete separation. 'It must be remembered that this part of our business operates under the umbrella of our supply and fix activities. Any low priced jobs are generally taken on a supply and fix basis to allow us to maintain our supply only margins.'

But what made the pressure for change so strong within Roofing was the swing away from new building towards strip and retile, discussed earlier. This was fundamental to Marley because the repair and re-roofing work was ideally undertaken by the small contractor who typically turned to the merchant for supplies. The merchant, of course, had little cause to prefer Marley and turned to Redland; thus, Marley found itself with a low market share in the fastest growing segment of the market. Redland made a virtue out of its own limited fixing business by making a public declaration in 1965 that it would undertake no more fixing at all.

The economic advantages held by the specialist roofing subcontractor were accelerated by the growth of strip and retile, but there were other powerful forces at work. The progressive abandonment of a local authority building programme diminished the importance of a customer who could offer a standardised flow of work. At the same time, the private housebuilder was moving away from the use of a main contractor to subcontracting the whole of the building work. Capital became more expensive, variety of design more important, and any building method which gave the developer greater flexibility became standard practice. Housebuilding gradually changed from the construction of a standard product by a main contractor, or housebuilder acting as its own main contractor, to the increased use of subcontractors co-ordinated by the developer's own site agent.

Social changes, too, played their part. Retired Marley executives invariably look back with satisfaction at their early days in supply and fix – out at seven in the morning to organise the tilers; on the road all day; the home as the office; their wives as unpaid secretaries taking telephone messages. It is one of the economic facts of life that people now prefer to work in that manner and for those hours on their own behalf. Thus, Marley's large contracting organisation not only became harder to organise but was increasingly finding itself in conflict with Marley's need to develop its supply only business.

With the establishment of parallel selling systems in place, Eric Cook turned his attention to the reorganisation of the contracting business. The managers were to be taken out of their houses and given their own depots. In August 1975 Eric Cook reported to the Board: 'Over the past 18 months, we have carried out a major reorganisation of the Contracting operation culminating in the restructuring of the Sales force in April and May of this year. We still have 9 regions, but each region now has its own estimating department and control is exercised by the Regional Manager operating through a simplified management structure. The Sales & Marketing people are responsible for selling to the major customers – builders, local authorities, architects etc whilst the contracts personnel control all site work and sell to the remaining medium and small customers. Most of the estimating is now done centrally... The results, so far, have exceeded our expectation. Turnover per man has risen substantially due to increased business and the reduction in the number of salesmen employed.'[2]

Indeed, the first recorded financial breakdown within Marley Tile did show an increase in contracting profits from the previous very low levels (see overleaf).

In 1977, Marley Roof Tile's contracting division was established as Marley Contract Services, trading as MCS, though still a part of the Tile Company; it was then installing 150,000 roof tiles and 15,000 square metres of flooring every day. In October 1978, Marley Tile held a national conference for its sales force: '... the Management have been given the task of setting up

---

2 Marley Tile Board Report, *75/142, August 1975.*

		1973/74	1974/75
			£000
Supply only	Turnover	7,449	8,773
	Profit	1,267	1,440
		17.0%	16.4%
Contracting	Turnover	16,703	19,329
	Profit	560	1,089
		3.3%	5.6%

Source: Marley Tile Board Report, 75/202, December 1975

local roofing and flooring contractor units with all possible speed... I am quite sure that once the initial teething problems have been overcome, Supply and Fix profits will increase sharply'.[3] In February 1979, the Group Accounts described the progress at MCS: '... fundamental changes are being made to the structure of the business by the creation of a national network of more than 70 key centres over the next 12 months, each of which will become the local base for our contracting operations and each under the control of its individual management.' The following year, Marley was able to report that MCS 'have continued to make progress with our plans for establishing our contract services on a local basis and, having already opened 20 units this year, a further 50 are planned over the next 18 months throughout the UK. We will then be in a unique position to service the many small builders and local authorities whose needs cannot be met through large centralised organisation.'

The *Monopolies Commission Report on Concrete Roofing Tiles* gave a clear picture of the substantive swing away from supply and fix during the 1960s and 1970s:

Marley sales by type of customer

	1960	1970	1971	1980
MCS	75	57	49.4	28.3
Roofing contractors				47.9
Builders' merchants				12.9
Marley builders' merchants	25	43	50.6	5.0
Roofing centres				3.3
Others				2.6

Note: Accurate figures available for the first time in 1971.

3   *Ibid, 78/153, October 1978.*

The roofing centres

To reach even further down to the small roofing contractor and builder, Marley next developed the concept of the roofing centre. Trevor Aisher describes their genesis: 'We could all see that there was going to be a tremendous amount of business in inner city refurbishment; the problem was trying to deal with that business via the normal factory outlets'. Structured to service bulk loads, it could not cope with the little man in a pick up truck waiting for 20 tiles or 50 ridges. 'He didn't get the service, so he went to the chap who gave him the service. We said what we have got to do is to have these depots strategically located where he can just come in and he can buy Marley, Redland, slates; we are providing him with a total roofing service, felt, nails, battens, everything for cash on a daily basis because he has nowhere to store the materials.' To some extent this could be regarded as filling a gap in the builders' merchants service; the general merchants did not typically stock a full range of roofing products for space reasons. Marley argued that it was not competing as they were providing a specialist roofing service to the roofer and to the merchant.

The concept was treated cautiously to start with. In June 1974, Eric Cook reported to the Board that 'an experiment would be carried out involving two or three roofing depots'. Fulwood Roofing Centre near Mansfield was opened in September 1976 'being the third in a planned programme of expansion... extending the policy of making all forms of roofing materials available'.[4] Marley continued to feel its way towards the right formula and in 1979 there was no more than £1 million turnover coming from the centres, though with a healthy 14% added margin. Once they could see the emergence of a good distribution margin, as well as the additional support for the manufacturing base, Marley then moved rapidly; there were five roofing centres in full operation by the end of 1980 and twelve a year later. Turnover in 1983 rose to around £13 million with profits approaching £2 million; by the end of 1984 there were nineteen roofing centres.

Despite the restructuring of the marketing effort in the 1970s, Marley continued to suffer a decline in market share. Marley's strength was proportionally greater in new housing, where it had around 55% of a declining market, and it was weakest in the growing strip and retile markets. The Monopolies Commission Report showed the position of the four largest companies in the latter half of the decade, indicating that Marley had lost its position as the largest UK manufacturer of concrete roofing tiles in 1979.

---

4   *Marley Limited* Annual Report, *1977.*

Volume (million square metres) and % market share of the four largest manufacturers

	1976	**1977**	**1978**	**1979**	**1980**
Marley Tile	12.24	11.02	11.99	11.48	10.34
	43.4%	42.8%	42.0%	39.7%	38.6%
Redland Roof Tiles	11.79	10.63	11.58	12.33	11.70
	41.8%	41.2%	40.5%	42.7%	43.6%
Sandtoft Tileries	3.31	3.31	3.96	3.94	3.58
	11.7%	12.8%	13.9%	13.6%	13.4%
Anchor Building	0.88	0.83	1.04	1.15	1.19
	3.1%	3.2%	3.6%	4.0%	4.4%
Total	28.21	25.79	28.57	28.91	26.82

Source: Monopolies Commission Report on Concrete Roofing Tiles, 1981

"Privatisation"

At the opening of the 1980s the manufacturing operation had control of its own direct selling but the roof tile contracting was still under separate management. Eventually, on the first of November 1981, The Marley Roof Tile Company was formed as a separate entity with Trevor Aisher responsible for the totality of the business. 'I was quite clear that our real destiny was getting the independent roofing contractor on our side if we were really going to build up our market share... We set out to privatise our contracting operations.' Even then the contracting business was responsible for flooring as well as roofing and it was by no means clear whether one was subsidising the other – and if so, which one. Flooring contracting was transferred to Marley Floors and much of the central administration was closed. 'We suddenly discovered that we could actually run the contracting business a lot cheaper than we thought. Within a year Flooring found that contracting was very expensive and then had to privatise it later on.'

Following the creation of MCS as a trading name, apparently distancing it from Marley the manufacturer, the next move appeared to be a step backwards in that Marley bought an independent roofing contractor, Furlong Bros in 1982. It was a calculated risk but it was bought to act as the role model for Marley's existing contracting operations. Ironically, Furlong was run by Gordon Lee who had once been a regional sales manager with Marley at Leighton Buzzard; he joined Furlong in North London and helped build it into the largest roofing contractor in London. In Trevor Aisher's words: 'The sooner we bought Furlongs, the better, to prove that they were running their business in a more efficient manner than our own contracting business. On paper, the results certainly proved this.' Furlong was not used to provide a captive outlet for Marley tiles; it was allowed to keep its contracting independence selling and fixing clay tiles, slates and even Redland tiles.

After the acquisition of Furlong, and the rapid growth of the Roofing Centres, Marley sought to strengthen its position with the builders' merchants, which it did through a system of Allied or Accredited Roofing Merchants who offered a service similar to that of the Marley Roofing Centre, though usually on a smaller scale. 'At the Builders' Merchants Exhibition from 5th-8th September, 1983, we will be launching our A.R.M. packets to Builders' Merchants... our aim by the end of 1984 to have established a number of A.R.M. stockists throughout the country who will complement our network of roofing centres and factories providing a large stock-holding of Marley Roof tiles. The A.R.M. package has been introduced as a result of market changes, in particular the growth of refurbishment and the growing use of Builders Merchants for daily provision of roofing materials by the smaller roofing contractor/builder.'[5] By the end of 1984 Marley had 129 of these Accredited Merchants.

Once Furlong was established (its pre-tax profits approached £1 million a year), two more small contracting acquisitions followed, primarily to provide a base for new roofing centres: South Western Tiling of Salisbury in March 1984, and Strathclyde Building & Roofing Supplies in March 1985. Bracknell Roofing, bought for an initial £1.6 million, added another significant contracting operation in May 1987. The next step was to give MCS the trading independence that Furlong enjoyed, a policy that was not without its risks. 'The first was that they were not going to sell as many Marley tiles. No, but the purpose is that they will make more money. How many less will they sell? If they sell 10% less can we get that 10% back from the independent contractors because they now see us as a friend. We were able to convince them that it was probably better overall in the market place and they were all together, no-one had any major advantage and that is really how the business is today.'[6]

The final stage with MCS was to reorganise its operational structure. David Trapnell: 'One of the very first things I did when I became Managing Director of the Marley Roof Tile Company was to say that we were basically a manufacturing company, not a contracting company and therefore we needed to somehow separate out the contracting part of the company and just become a manufacturing company. We did this by setting up two separate companies, one was called MCS, which traded in the Midlands and the North and the other was called Mastercraft Roofing, which was the Southern half of the original MCS business. They became separate subsidiary companies within the group which then enabled the Marley Roof Tile company to be solely a

5   Marley Roof Tile Board Report, *August 1983.*
6   *Trevor Aisher interview.*

213

manufacturing and direct selling business and nothing else.' (In Scotland, however, the old structure persisted as MCS Scotland remained an operating part of Marley Roof Tile. Scotland had a history of employing its own tilers, rather than subcontracting them and they had 90 men on their books, often with over 20 years service.)

The advantages of this final reorganisation of the contracting structure were not just that it allowed the roof tile company to specialise in manufacturing and selling but 'it also would enable these newly formed contracting companies to be much more efficient because they were concentrating on contracting only; they could also undertake re-roofing work and use other roofing materials like slate, clay and even Redland tiles. We therefore had a saving in the administration, much more in line with the way Bracknell and Furlong ran their businesses, whereas when it was all part of the Marley Roof Tile company we had a considerable administration organisation all over the country; we took the advantage and slimmed them down at the same time and indeed they moved off the Roof Tile Company sites and rented office accommodation and yard space elsewhere.'[7] By 1987, Marley had a contracting unit with an annual turnover of £50 million and today, Marley sells around 40% of its concrete roof tiles to the merchants; 40% to independent roofing contractors, and 20% to Marley's own contracting business. A mark of both the size and independence of Marley's modern contracting business is that it claims to be the largest customer for Redland tiles.

Automation: from factory to site

One of the features of the building industry in the 1970s was the development of mechanical handling and packaging for heavy goods, improving productivity at the factory and, no less important, facilitating easier site delivery. Marley sought to be one of the leaders and its first experiments were undertaken at Poole and Riverhead in 1972: 'Development of mechanical loading and unloading at Poole is progressing satisfactorily and the majority of the plant will be installed during the Bank Holiday. Initial trials with the Atlas lorry mounted crane will be carried out at Riverhead.'[8] Two months later the minutes record that 'Mechanised clamp handling of tiles in the yard has now commenced at Riverhead and Poole, and we foresee that this system of handling will be extended to other factories during 1973'. During 1972 and 1973 the demand for palletised loads continued to increase, and the majority of major customers were 'continuing to adopt the use of fork lift truck handling on sites'. That, however, proved a premature assessment.

7   *David Trapnell interview.*
8   Marley Tile Board Report, *72/129, August 1972.*

A year later, in July 1974, Marley began trials on a shrink-wrapping plant, this time at Burton. The plant itself worked well and was introduced to Poole and Ebchester within twelve months, but again Marley had moved faster than its customers. Thus, in April 1975: 'at the present time we are only shrink-wrapping to order, where customers are in a position to accept palletised loads or are prepared to off load the packs by hand, the remainder of the production off these lines being hand stacked. Manual off-loading of packs on sites has not been met with much enthusiasm as it does take longer. It is quite clear that until all building sites are in a position to provide mechanical off-loading facilities, shrink-wrapping in its present form cannot be progressed a great deal further. The installation of lorry-mounted cranes on our own lorries which can clamp off-load packs on to sites will improve the situation but the lack of such facilities on sub-contract vehicles in this country does pose long term problems. There is no doubt that some form of packaging and economic off-loading system must be adopted fairly soon in this country, and I am convinced that we as a Company are proceeding along the right lines. We are not likely to succeed until we can convince the majority of our customers that it is in their interests also.'[9] Unfortunately, one of the side effects of the new handling equipment was a higher degree of damage to the tiles, which no doubt contributed to the customers' attitude and Marley's new delivery systems had to be abandoned for the time being.

In 1979, a working party was established to look again at the automation of post-production tile handling. Marley was manually stacking the tiles into packs on special purpose tables, then taking the packs to the stacking yard using fork lift trucks with clamps. In 1980, the Bandapak clamp unloading system was introduced by Marley Transport. Tiles came off the line 60 at a time and were banded together with metal or plastic strapping. Fork lift trucks with clamps were used to load lorries with 6 banded packs at a time. The lorries unloaded the individual packs on to the building site by means of a lorry mounted hoist. Transport was then being run by Richard Aisher, the only son of Dick Aisher. (Richard Aisher joined Marley in 1958 after graduating from Cambridge, the only one of that generation of Aishers to go to University. On the death of his father, he assumed joint control of sales and contracting with Eric Cook but later moved to take charge of Marley's transport and distribution. As a non-executive director, he remained the only member of the Aisher family on the Marley Board.)

The Bandapak system was introduced at, literally, the low-point in the housing market, and was heavily supported by Marley with training and a free introductory service. Its great advantage was that it got the tiles to the site in good condition and with a saving in unloading time; however, there were

---

9 *Ibid*, 75/65, April 1975.

limitations. The Bandapak system needed a flat surface to pick up from and if the building site was uneven (a not unusual feature) subsequent handling could be difficult. The eventual solution, which was adopted around 1985/86, was for all the factory output to be palletised. Automatic palletisers were introduced into the UK factories although they were not new to the Group – they had been in use in the French factories since the mid-1970s. Once on the pallets, the tiles could be handled on the site by fork lift truck – and sometimes even up the building.

Investment and rationalisation

The restructuring of Marley's marketing did not preclude changes in the manufacturing base and, indeed, the 1980s were years of substantial investment and rationalisation as Marley strove to reduce its cost base. The last distribution of roof tile factories we listed was at 1954; the table below shows the position in 1980, with indications of any subsequent closures.

Roof tile factories as at 1980

| | Year closed | Capacity in millions | | | |
		Plain	Ludlow	Large/ Anglia	PTE Tiles
Leighton Buzzard	1986	12.0	–	8.0	56
Riverhead	1989	12.0		9.0	66
Burton		15.0		16.0	111
Poole	1990	12.0	–	9.0	66
Glasgow				9.0	54
Delamere		12.0		12.0	84
Ebchester			–	12.5	75
Beenham		12.0	5.5	15.5	124
Dewsbury	1987			6.5	39
Sawston			5.0	4.0	41
Total		75.0	10.5	101.5	716
Standard Tile Equivalent		12.5	6.0	101.5	120

Source: Monopolies Commission Report on Concrete Roofing Tiles, 1981

In 1980/81, Marley installed its first chain machine for trials at Leighton Buzzard. This was the successor to the drum machine referred to earlier. The 'chain', described as like the track on a tank, was physically more compact than the drum machine and was able to push the pallets in a completely continuous motion: 'the whole development over the 60 years was one of going from a reciprocating type of machine, pushing one tile through at a time, to becoming a completely continuous and smooth action which enables you to go up to 120 tiles per minute plus'.[10] The success at Leighton Buzzard was followed up with the installation of a new fully automated 15 × 9 inch line at Sawston in 1982, and chain machines were gradually introduced at other Marley factories as they were modernised. A new automatic plain tile line was also installed at Riverhead in 1983, with a capacity of 500,000 tiles per week, incorporating 'the latest continuous curing, automatic, low cost plant'.[11] With the help of smaller scale investment elsewhere, Marley was able to report capacity up to 3.75 million tiles per week or around 190 million large tiles a year. The substantial increase over the 120 million capacity given in the 1980 Monopolies Commission Report reflected a combination of the investment in new higher speed plant but also the introduction of multiple shifting during the 1980s. That increased capacity was fully required due to the most generous present ever given to the roofing industry: The Repair Grant, about which more later.

Extrusions meets roofing

One of the more important innovations that Marley brought to the roofing industry came about as a result of co-operation with the Extrusions company: its Dry Verge and Ridge System. Geoff Marsh explained the logic from the Extrusions side of the partnership: 'We could see that with claddings, soffit, fascia, gutters and rainwater pipes, Marley Extrusions were beginning to encompass the perimeter of the roof, but a lot of the roofing know-how is with Marley Roofs. When one looks at how you put on roof tiles, they are really dry fixed until you get to the ridge and the eaves. If you can cut out the cement and mortar, which is always a messy job and labour intensive, then there could be products for Marley Extrusions.' A small development team was set up between the two companies to see if Marley could produce uPVC fittings to take the place of the cement mortar fixing and, by 1980, the product was ready and tested. 'On Wednesday, 10th September, we are launching our new patented dry verge and dry ridge systems at the "Rooftec 80" Exhibition, New Horticultural Hall Westminster... The dry verge system will be available for sale in the very near future with the dry ridge system following in 2–3 months' time. The 2 systems have been patented in each of the countries where we are likely to have an interest in roof tiles in the foreseeable future.'[12] The advantages of the PVC verge and ridge fitments were speed of fixing, particularly in adverse weather conditions, the secure fixing of the verge tiles

---

10 *David Trapnell interview.*
11 Marley Roof Tile Board Report, *August 1983.*
12 Contracting Board Report, *September 1980.*

and ridges and a maintenance free finish. Initially, the system was introduced for use with Smooth Grey Modern and Ludlow Major tiles but was gradually extended across the range. The system was well received in the trade and by the end of 1982 Marley was unable to meet the demand. Productive capacity was increased and sales in the following year reached £4 million.

There had previously been a plastic dry verge system since Redland introduced one in 1967; Extrusions made Marley's under licence. However, that was a continuous piece of extruded plastic fitted to the barge board and, as such it lacked flexibility and aesthetic appeal and was not extensively used. What was unique about Marley's system was that it comprised individual plastic injection mouldings each of which interlocked together, in conjunction with the tiles. 'The advantage is that it that it is a much more efficient and flexible system for keeping the tiles in place; it is a much neater system and it is more robust as well. [The Marley System] can be used with all the different interlocking profiles and sits equally well with all these different shapes.'[13]

Marley had its new system well covered by patents. Redland's response was to adopt the concrete cloaked verges which for many years had been traditional on the Continent as a dry method of finishing the roof.[14] These had the advantage of appealing to the traditional elements in the industry who did not like the use of plastic on the roof. Marley was producing a similar product at its French associate, TMB, and now offers a dry concrete alternative. Both systems have eaten into the traditional wet finish mortar finish.

Marley's Dry Fix installations were to be thoroughly tested by the severe gales which hit Scotland and the North of England in January 1984. They came through virtually unscathed and within months the system received notable public recognition. On May 1st 1984, The Duke of Edinburgh presented Marley with a Design Council Award for its Dry Fix roof system: 'The panel considered the system's design to be reliable, easy to use, cost effective and to solve a common problem in the building trade'. The Award was accepted by Chris Cooper of Marley Roof Tile and Geoff Quinell of Marley Extrusions. At the same time, the Dry Fix system also received The Building Centre Trust Award for the most innovative product of 1984, presented at Rooftec by the President of the RIBA.

The re-roofing boom

Demand for concrete roofing tiles had fallen to a low of 22.7 million square metres in 1981, some 27% below the peak of 30.9 square metres reached in 1973; this reflected a fall of a third in new housing completions compensated

---

13   *David Trapnell interview.*
14   *It comprised a concrete roof tile with an integral concrete shoulder extending down about six inches.*

by growth in the strip and retile market. Although private housing was beginning to recover, at the beginning of what was to prove an excellent decade, local authority building was still in decline and the overall size of the housing market changed little in the first half of the 1980s. However, what had a more immediate effect on the roofing industry was the improvement in the terms of the existing, but little used, Repair Grants in the March 1982 Budget.

On March 9th, Geoffrey Howe announced that 'The value of grants given for major repairs... under the home improvement grant system, will be increased for a limited period, to a maximum of 90% of the eligible cost, instead of the 75% currently available'. The grants were specifically available for 'substantial and structural repairs to pre-1919 houses' and as such were peculiarly suitable for the re-roofing industry... 'For a limited period only' is a well recognised marketing ploy within the private sector. Whether the Government knew what it was doing in telling the public the offer was only good until the end of the year, it produced an explosion of applications. House owners complained that demand was so high, they could not get their surveys completed and applications processed. In November, the time limit for applications was extended to the end of the 1983/84 fiscal year and the local authorities were told that they could spend without limit on improvement grants that year. For the roofing industry, it was a present without precedent. The table illustrates the dramatic growth in grant expenditure.

Repair Grants paid: England

	1980	**1981**	**1982**	**1983**	**1984**	**1985**	**1986**
Number of Grants (£000)	0.5	5.1	28.7	113.1	116.1	54.4	42.3
Amount paid (£m)	0.4	6.7	54.2	271.3	341.9	166.4	115.3
Average Grant (£000)	0.7	1.3	1.9	2.4	2.9	3.1	2.7

Source: Department of the Environment

The re-roofing boom increased concrete roof tile deliveries by a remarkable 44% in two years producing a new peak of 32.8 million square metres in 1983. The normally restrained Board Reports could barely conceal the roof tile management's astonishment at the impact of the repair grants which had, '... created a demand for re-roofing far in excess of anything we have experienced in the past'. In November, deliveries hit a record 16 million tiles. Marley was additionally helped by recouping some of the market share it had lost over the previous decade, attributed to its 'more integrated and aggressive marketing.'[15] The 1983 accounts were able to claim once again that the 'Company is the largest manufacturer of concrete roof tiles in the UK', a

15 Marley Roof Tile Board Report, *August 1983*.

position it continues to hold. It is worth stating that market share figures have not been universally agreed between the participants; in view of the different covering areas of the individual tile profiles, it is perhaps not surprising.

Marley certainly enjoyed an exceptionally profitable period in its roofing business. Roof Tile profits had fluctuated around the £4 million level in the 1970s hitting a peak of just over £5 million in 1978; the collapse in the housing market at the end of the 1970s had taken profits down to only £2 million in 1981 and 1982. From that low point, Marley Roof Tile enjoyed a phenomenal recovery. Tile volumes alone rose by 45% to a record (and never since exceeded) 150 million in 1983 compared with an industry increase of 26%; market share had climbed to around 45% compared with a low point of 40% at the beginning of the 1980s. Profits jumped to almost £9 million and, although those record volumes could not be sustained, a carry forward of strong pricing into 1984 created a record profits contribution of £13½ million, with another million pounds coming from Furlong. By then, however, the repair grant boom had passed its peak and the warning signs began to appear in the second half of 1984.

During the late 1980s the concrete roof tile industry found itself in an unusual position – on the defensive. Its market share began to fall in the face of a modest revival in clay tile demand and little short of a boom in the slate market. The natural slate industry was able to enjoy some of the benefit but most of the growth in demand for slate (primarily a re-roofing phenomenon) was satisfied by fibre cement slates and a new product – the reconstituted slate, based on crushed slate. By 1989 concrete's share of the total roofing market had dropped down to 75%, the balance being natural slate 6%, fibre cement slate 11%, and clay 7%. Marley entered the reconstituted slate market in 1987 with its Monarch interlocking slate, made at Delamere. The Monarch was a product of Marley research which had started around 1980. The eventual formulation was almost a standard concrete mix of cement and a crushed aggregate, in this case crushed slate rather than sand; combined with a small amount of an acrylic polymer. That enabled Marley to produce a strong material relative to its weight and thickness; it could therefore easily be used on the roofs that had originally been designed to take slate. As well as widening its range with the Monarch slate, Marley also supplied the clay market from its Bisch factory in Strasbourg.

The high profitability created by the re-roofing boom attracted new competitors into the industry. A joint venture between ARC and Tarmac announced its plans for two new tile works in 1984 and this was followed by the Irish CRH commissioning a new plant at Gravesend in 1985. Despite the powerful parentage, the new entrants proved less troublesome than feared. In 1986, Tarmac sold its half-share to ARC who in turn sold out to Redland in September 1988. A fire destroyed much of CRH's Gravesend factory in that same year and in February 1989 Marley purchased the undamaged plant, which was later to replace the old manual plain tile line at Burton. Marley's response to the new entrants lay in further investment. Plans were approved for a new high speed large tile line at Beenham, at a cost of £1.5 million, followed by a similar line at Burton; these were both computer controlled and used Swedish ABECE Tank Track Chain machines run at over 120 tiles per minute. These came on stream during 1985 and 1986, at output levels well beyond the original plants. This was followed by a new fully automated plain tile plant at Beenham in 1987. The increase in Marley's capacity, coming at a time when the re-roofing boom was abating and new entrants coming into the industry, allowed Marley to rationalise its older works. Leighton Buzzard, Dewsbury and Riverhead were all scheduled for closure though Riverhead was kept on until 1989 due to demand for the plain tile.

Roof tiles get the concrete pavers

Marley Concrete had suffered from the inexorable decline in the prefabricated garage market; the hard fact was that no one wanted a prefabricated garage if they could afford a new house with a brick built garage. Marley Buildings (as it had by then been renamed) tried to increase sales in the rapidly growing home extension market but without a great deal of success and even as recently as 1980 garages accounted for half Marley Buildings' turnover. Gradually, Marley Buildings began to retrench. In 1982, Marlith was sold to RMC Panel Products ending an operation which dated back to the war, and the kitchen furniture manufacture was run down in 1983 and 1984. Greenhouse manufacture was transferred from Storrington to Cheltenham, freeing the former site for development, and the Cheltenham concrete factory was closed to increase throughput at Guildford and Carluke. In 1985, greenhouse manufacture ceased and the Marleymix dry concrete business was sold to British Fuels. Steadily, Marley Buildings was cutting back on its fringe activities but, unfortunately for Buildings, the most promising new concrete product of all was being introduced elsewhere – by the Roof Tile Company!

The decline in the traditional concrete products business, which was eventually sold at the end of 1990, can be ascribed to Marley's commitment to a product which was in long term decline; it looked more serious because it was identifiable in a self-contained company. But there was an inability to introduce successful replacement products in areas of the market which were growing. In many ways it was market driven but by a form of marketing that was not found, nor required, in any other part of the Marley organisation. Bill Courtney: 'I think it always needed somebody who, rather like Owen Aisher was to the roof tile business and the flooring business and Derek Robins was to Banbury. If you were not innovative and driving constantly, very much aware of the changing market place and what your competitors were doing you would gradually die and I think that was the story of many businesses in concrete.'

As already indicated, the one growth product was not made available to Marley Buildings. In the late 1970s, the roof tile company prepared to enter the paving block market. In part this reflected a view that future growth in roofing tile demand would be limited but there was also recognition of the rapid growth which was being achieved in continental markets by the intersett paving product. The product was by no means new; indeed it had long gone out of fashion. During the industrial revolution, granite setts had been used for the new roads and fast became the conventional road surface, only to be replaced in turn by the smoother and cheaper macadamised or 'black top' roads. The concrete interlocking sett appeared in the British market in the early 1970s in response to the need for a harder wearing surface in areas of high traffic and where a more aesthetic finish was sought. Thus, they began to appear in shopping centres, local authorities' inner-city pedestrianisation and residential cul-de-sacs.

By 1979, the market was approaching one million square metres of paving a year. Fast growing though the British market had been, it was still small in absolute terms compared with even Denmark and paled into insignificance compared with the 35 million square metres a year produced in Germany, where the concrete sett had been introduced in 1956. Although there were by now a group of established UK manufacturers, led by Marshalls of Halifax, Marley rightly perceived that the natural growth in the market during the 1980s would permit one more and it installed its first plant at Aveley in 1978. Perhaps to differentiate itself from the existing manufacturers, Marley's entry into the paving market utilised the supply and fix concept. Capacity was steadily increased and in 1985 paving plant was put onto the sites at Burton and Poole.

Although Marley achieved the sales growth it had expected, with a 25% market share by 1986, profits proved more elusive. The paving business was separately constituted as a part of Marley Building Products in March 1985 and then, after continued trading losses, it was established as a separate company, Marley Paving, with a new management team. One of the surprising features of Marley's entry into the paving business had been its adoption of the supply and fix concept at the very time when the roofing and flooring companies were trying to limit their competition with their customers. The 1987 Marley Annual accounts duly reported that 'Marley Paving by directing more sales effort into "supply only", became less dependent on contracting. In addition, initiatives taken to market the product through builders merchants have opened up a previously underdeveloped sector of the market.' During 1990, the remaining supply and fix operation was closed.

The writing is on the floor

The resilient flooring market had proved an exceptionally profitable second leg for Marley complementing the roofing company and by the early 1970s Marley Floors and Wallington Weston were making nearly £3 million profit between them – over a quarter of the Group's UK profits. But by then the signs of a radically changing trading environment were already becoming evident: changes which Marley Floors would only overcome with intense effort, which were to push Wallington Weston into losses and force some of Marley's long-standing competitors to leave the business.

The rapid growth in the resilient flooring market in the 1950s and 1960s had attracted new capacity, predicated as always on the assumption that demand would continue to increase; this occurred both in the UK and continental Europe. Competition from the continent became increasingly troublesome after Britain's entry into the EEC – with decreasing tariffs in the EEC the margins available in the UK market are becoming very attractive to European competitors accustomed to working on narrower margins'.[16] But there were greater challenges to come. The rising consumer incomes which had supported the introduction of more expensive ranges of resilient floors also responded to the new availability of cheap tufted carpets which could be fitted wall to wall; the private householder now had new aspirations to satisfy. At the same time, the local authority housing programme had reached a peak. In both 1975 and 1976, public sector housing starts exceeded 170,000; by the early 1980s they were averaging no more than 50,000 a year. This was especially damaging to Marley as the local authorities were bulk purchasers of the cheaper Econoflex and Standard floor tiles where Marley had its greatest market share.

This collapse in the local authority housing market not only impacted on factory production but it also reduced demand for Marley's contracting services: the average private house used only 30 yards of flooring compared with 80 yards in multi-storey flats. This was exactly the opposite to roofing tiles where the switch from local authority housing (predominantly using flat roofs) to private housing (pitched roofs) was a positive benefit. It would, however, be a mistake to imply that the customer base was a choice between private or public housing. Marley had long been committed to a whole range of commercial and public service contracts, ranging through schools and hospitals to shops and hotels. This was becoming an increasingly important source of business and in August 1976 the *Marley Contracting Board Report* noted that 35% of flooring turnover was in non-housing. Sample contracts included one nuclear submarine base, one torpedo store, one court room, one remand home, one castle, the Royal Albert Hall and a scrap yard.

---

16   *Marley Limited minutes, February 1975.*

Just how skewed Marley's market shares were at the beginning of the 1970s was revealed in a routine sales report to the Marley Floors Board in October 1969; this pointed to Marley's success in the latter half of the 1960s in further increasing its share of the cheaper ranges but its comparative lack of success in establishing itself in the newer generation of flooring products: '... there is little doubt that we have increased our share of the overall market for Standard, Econoflex and Vinyl Asbestos tiles'. In the first half of the year, the market share on Standard and Econoflex tiles improved from 54% to 57% and on Vinyl Asbestos from 27% to 30% of the market. In effect, Marley had half of the rigid tile market with Nairn, Dunlop, Armstrong and six or seven overseas manufacturers sharing the balance. However 'we are still unhappy with our position regarding flexible vinyls where we have a miserable 13% of the market'.

In part, Marley's weak position in flexibles reflected Nairn's retail strength in cushioned flooring but Marley also had a lower share in the contract market where the two main competitors to Marleyflor were then Semflor and James Halstead's Polyflor. Halstead has not yet featured in the story, but it was incorporated as a textile company in 1915 specialising in rubberised fabric which it used to calender. The Company did not move into flooring until 1954 but it gradually concentrated on the contract, rather than the retail, market and worked closely with the contractors; Halstead now claims to be the leader in the UK contract market. Robin Aisher attributed Marley's weaker position to its distribution structure. 'We were not geared up to sell that product because our selling system was selling through Roof Tile to builders and they were not into [industrial flooring]; it was the flooring contractor who was selling that on to his customer and at that stage only 10–15% of [Marley's output] went through contractors'.

What to do with Wallington Weston?

Despite this critical assessment of its own market position, Marley Floors proved a survivor in what became an increasingly difficult decade for the economy in general and the flooring industry in particular. Unfortunately, the same could not be said about Wallington Weston. Although Wallington Weston achieved record profits in 1973, problems were on the horizon. In its heyday, it had been earning more than Marley Floors and for one reason only. Of all Marley's flooring products, none had been more successful than Consort and, as already mentioned, in 1964/65, six years after its launch, it achieved its peak sales of 11,165,806 square yards. Although still a major seller for many years after, Consort sales declined steadily as newer products were introduced in the flooring market. By 1971, Consort sales had halved and Dennis Knight reported that 'the resultant lost margin is far in excess of our total current yearly profits'.[17]

At first, the decline of Consort seemed to provide other opportunities: 'Prior to 1965/66 we had to restrict sales of Sheeting because of the ever increasing sales of Flooring. Since this time it has been a question of selling more and more Plastic Sheeting to make up for the fall off in Flooring. This has not always been easy due to the fact that each Calender is really only satisfactory for one thing or the other... We are now, however, in a position where not too many calenders are tied up on Flooring and this has made it possible to take a different point of view so far as sheeting sales are concerned.'[18] Wallington Weston achieved an impressive success in reorienting its business: in 1965, industrial plastics represented less than a quarter of sales; five years later it was over a half. The profits followed; in the mid-1960s the major part of the profit was earned from Consort whereas by 1974 around two-thirds of profit came from industrial plastic sheeting – the original basis of the operation prior to its acquisition. The customer base was widely spread but stationery accounted for 30%, the printing trade 12% and the furniture industry a further 12%.

Wallington Weston's range of plastic sheeting was still confined to flexible plastics in the early 1970s but in 1974 preparations were made to enter the market for rigid and semi-rigid clear and opaque plastics, sometimes referred to as unsupported PVC sheeting. As well as complementing the existing stationery business, the purchase of a new £1 million Krauss Maffei calender took Wallington Weston into new markets, especially imitation wood veneers for laminated chipboard. This presented another very competitive market, the three leaders being Storeys, British Xylonite and Commercial Plastics.

Wallington Weston also made strenuous efforts to increase the export sales of Consort. These were handled by Marley Floors International (later within Marley Floors itself) and the rewards were not, therefore, fully reflected in Wallington Weston's own accounts. Some broadening of the product line was undertaken although there was never a range to match Consort. Consort was being replaced by cushioned flooring and if Wallington Weston had been an independent company it would have introduced its own cushioned product. One even wonders whether a management structure which incorporated the whole of flooring under the control of one Director would have produced a different balance of products.

Although the restoration of its traditional industrial plastics business sustained Wallington Weston's profits for some years that market gradually became more competitive; in effect, it turned from being speciality production

17 Marley Board Report, *71/37, June 1971.*
18 *Ibid, 72/217, October 1972.*

PVC sheet production at Wallington Weston

to a commodity market. 'The vast majority of our production capacity is involved in single ply calendered and embossed sheeting and these products... are very much standard materials available from a number of suppliers throughout Europe.'[19]

When the decline came, it was rapid. Profits peaked at £1.42 million in 1974 but only the next year the Board was warning of the inroads that cushioned flooring was making into Consort sales: 'It does seem that the solid printed vinyl market is now decreasing fairly rapidly and even if, as seems possible, we are eventually left with the vast majority of it, it may still not be a very interesting figure for the factory at W W.'[20] In 1979, Wallington Weston incurred its first losses since joining Marley; by that point, Consort production

19 *Ibid, 78/135, September 1978.*
20 *Ibid, 75/124, 1975.*

had fallen to 4 million square yards and it was considered no longer economic to keep the line in production. The closure of the Consort line contributed to 500 redundancies but despite that, the loss increased to £2.2 million in 1980 with a further £2.5m of exceptional charges; Wallington Weston was now completely out of flooring and its number 5 and 6 calenders were offered to the South African company. Although there were further strenuous attempts to reduce costs, Wallington Weston remained in loss as intense competition drove prices down. The October 1981 Board report typified the mood, reporting a 'price war in most sectors of our activity with the general pricing structure totally collapsing and customers auctioning off any business they have'. Even when Wallington Weston was producing flat out, as in the following year, pricing still prevented the Company returning to profit. Finally, on February 2nd 1983, Marley announced that Wallington Weston was to merge with ICI Hyde Products to form Weston-Hyde Products. Hyde, which was based in Manchester, manufactured wall coverings and coated fabrics as well as PVC products, and the product range of the two companies was largely overlapping. Marley's contribution to the capital employed of the new associate was £6.6m compared to ICI's £19.4m; with a £9m loan from Barclays, Weston-Hyde's total capital employed reached a substantial £35m. Like Wallington Weston, ICI Hyde had also been losing substantial sums and although extensive rationalisation eliminated £3 million from combined overheads and returned the company to profit, the joint venture never prospered and it was sold during 1987.

Lay-Flat Stay-Flat

Marley Floors, still operating from Harrietsham and Leighton Buzzard, proved, if the word can be used, more resilient than Wallington Weston and, indeed, than most of its large British competitors. Marley's achievements in just staying alive in this market should not be underestimated. It was the contract market that saw the greater pressure on volumes:

Resilient floor covering volumes (million square metres p.a.)

	1977	1979	1981
Contract	24.0	23.0	17.6
Domestic	13.8	15.8	15.8
Total	37.8	38.8	33.4

Source: Marley Floors

The intense competition resulted in Dunlop and Armstrong (Marley's two original competitors) and Nairn incurring substantial losses; Dunlop ceased production, Armstrong reduced its product range and Nairn found new owners.

How then did Marley Floors not only survive the 1970s but come out of it so strong? Part of the answer lay in sustaining a low cost base, both in the formulations and in capital expenditure. Marley also maintained its very strong position in the basic floor tile: 'we have made very good money out of a very boring product, rather like Hanson and bricks'.[21] Marley also fought back successfully in the sheet market. Growing over-capacity and the broadening of consumer tastes had increased the pressure on the manufacturers to differentiate their ranges. While attractive design played its part in attracting the consumer, technical innovation was a vital ingredient in the development of new products and during the 1970s Marley's research effort was directed towards the use of fibreglass based material as the flooring base.

It is worth restating the problems which Marley's research efforts were seeking to overcome – shrinkage and curling. Shrinkage arises from the molecular structure of PVC which has a memory; if distorted, it remembers its original form and tries to return to it. Part of the technique in making calendered vinyl flooring is avoiding distortion of the vinyl sheets during calendering or subsequent lamination processes. However, it is impossible to avoid all deformation and various "relaxation" processes are employed during manufacture to remove as much strain as possible from the flooring but this could never be wholly successful. Overcoming this natural tendency by use of a fibre backing only brought out a different symptom; the vinyl would still shrink and therefore pulled against the backing material with the result that the sheet flooring curled at the edge.

The enthusiasm for a product that would "lay flat" and be stable was understandable: 'A new generation of floorings appears to be possible based on the work done so far which we think will enable us to offer materials which will be free of strain and curl and could be offered to the retail trade as loose lay materials without the problems of shrinkage experienced with Consort... will incorporate gravure printing ... [also looking at] the general use of fibreglass carriers which could be used as a substitute for paper which despite its general acceptance has its problems regarding long term curl and age hardening.'[22] Just as Nairn had led the entry of cushioned flooring into Britain, so Marley took the lead in 1978 with its introduction of its Lay-Flat Stay-Flat cushioned flooring marketed under the Supasoft name. Marley experimented with a variety of backing materials in its search for a flooring that the do-it-yourself enthusiast could lay down himself, without sticking and which would not creep or curl. There seemed no solution for as Denis Moss pointed out: 'If you put a

21   *Robin Aisher interview.*
22   Marley Board Report, 75/106, 1975.

rigid layer on the back of the flooring, it will curl because as the vinyl top shrinks through molecular memory, or plasticiser migration into the base material, the base layer will have stayed to its original dimensions'. The solution, like so many successful ideas, now looks obvious: the "backing" was put in the middle of the floor. In 1966, Denis Moss filed a patent for Marley describing the use of non-woven fabrics incorporated within the flooring to stop it from curling, though the patent proved less watertight than the flooring. Glass was found to be the most suitable woven material because of its strength and dimensional stability.

An early problem was that non-woven glass was then made by a process which put a slight ripple in it which could be seen in sheet flooring. 'I cut it up into tiles and put them in my office at Riverhead. Every week Sir Owen used to come over and inspect it to see whether the tiles had shrunk. Eventually he said "We've got to do this" and then they brought out a glass that didn't have the ripple in it and we could make sheet flooring using glass, and from then on it just grew and grew – everybody making this type of flooring uses a glass layer now.'

As Marley was establishing its new lay-flat range, it faced potentially the most serious challenge to its market position. Demand was beginning to increase for widths wider than the conventional 2 metres. Sums of money not easily within Marley's reach were being committed to investment in 4 metre wide sheet – potentially up to £20 million for a single line!

The fate of the competition, however, showed that capital backing was not to be conclusive. As early as 1970, Armstrong had drawn up a plan to build a 4 metre wide cushioned rotogravure sheet vinyl flooring at Teeside: 'probably the largest single investment the company had ever made'.[23] Construction started in 1975 and eventually finished in 1977; by that time the market had moved on and competitors were already marketing the newer glass fibre backed floorings. A final recognition of Armstrong's problems: 'It was now reluctantly agreed that North American rotovinyls with felt backings had little future there. It was also painfully clear that Armstrong did not immediately have the technology necessary to produce the lay-flat cushioned floor on a glass-encapsulated back that was flooding the market.'[24] The British company lost $15m in 1977 and the US parent came close to closing the UK factory. The decision to stay was made and a new range of cushioned vinyls was introduced in the 1980s.

Despite the tremendous advantage that the Cushionflor patents had given Nairn, that company was also facing problems at the end of the 1970s. In 1975, Nairn had been acquired by Unilever and it, too, went for a large scale capital investment programme opening a new £17 million factory to make 4

23 *William A Mehler Jr*, Let The Buyer Have Faith: The Story of Armstrong, *1987, p 68.*
24 *Ibid, p 190.*

metre widths. As with Armstrong, this proved unprofitable and in 1979 and 1980, Nairn Floors was losing around 10% on yearly turnover of £23 million. At the end of 1979, Nairn withdrew from the production of vinyl floor tiles and the marketing of contract vinyl sheet to concentrate on cushioned flooring. In 1985 Unilever eventually disposed of its investment in Nairn to the European Forbo floorings group, and it now trades as Forbo-Nairn.

Dunlop had not chosen to go the 4 metre route but by that time it was finding the marketplace particularly difficult and was steadily losing money at the end of the 1970s. During 1980, Dunlop withdrew from contract flooring, but that was insufficient and in 1981 the company began to organise a total withdrawal from flooring manufacture and in 1982 the Brynmawr factory was closed. Total losses since 1980 were almost £10 million.

Marley was having to pay careful attention to its own capital spending proposals and the Holding Company Board viewed the introduction of 4 metre widths by the competition with considerable misgivings. These wider floorings offered the consumer a continuous surface the width of his room and threatened to push the traditional 2 metre product to one side. As we have seen in the earlier comments, the sums expended by Armstrong and Nairn would have severely tested Marley's financial resources. Working with Dornbusch, Marley 'devised a possible method of manufacture at reasonable cost' for a 4 metre wide plant; this would have enabled Marley to produce 5.5m square metres a year at a capital cost of £2 million which the directors carefully contrasted with Armstrong's 10m square metres costing £15 million.[25]

Marley's eventual response was characteristically innovative – and cheap; they went for 3 metre widths yet managed to make them on the Company's existing 2 metre machinery. Robin Aisher: 'We recognised that we had to have a wider flooring than 2 metre and at that time we were beginning to have the shop opening programme. We had other developments in train like the automotive and extrusions business and we felt that we couldn't afford the £20 million necessary to do it, if that was what it was going to take, and we had to make a decision that we either abandoned making cushioned flooring for the retail side of the business or we compromised. We did some quick homework and found that actually 3 metre was the right size for most things. Geoff Barrett got his engineering team in and the printing people and, between those two, we found we could strip down the whole line, stick in a metre and make 3 metre with the existing plant. So that seemed to us to be a first class compromise at a time when we didn't have much money.'

Marley Floors' budget of £378,000 was approved in November 1980; the plant provided the base for the introduction of a new 3 metre range, sold as

25 Marley Board Report, 77/5, 1977.

Vinylaire Super Sprint and Vinylaire Nova. Marley found that its competitors were now suffering under the cost disadvantage of trying to produce 3 metre widths (now half the market) on 4 metre plant. The new plant was operational in 1981 and although the lead may have been short-lived, it was enjoyable while it lasted. In isolation, Marley Floors' static profit record during the 1970s looks unexciting: against the standards of what was happening elsewhere in the industry it is arguably one of Marley's most creditable achievements. After peaking at £1.6 million in 1973, pre-tax profits fell no lower than £1.3 million and actually finished the decade earning a steady £1.6 to £1.7 million a year; with the competition in disarray, Marley Floors then proceeded to treble profits, reaching an all time peak of over £5 million in 1982, albeit these figures were not subsequently maintained. Only James Halstead of the major domestic manufacturers appears to have prospered.

Marketing and contracting

Important decisions were not only being taken on manufacturing; there were crucial changes taking place in Marley Floors' distribution channels though with less immediate success. The contracting division of Marley Tile Company (that is, the original roofing Company), had run a supply and fix operation for flooring in parallel to roofing and this continued to absorb virtually all the flooring output into the 1960s. During that decade, Marley Tile also began to operate a supply only service to the Approved Flooring Contractors – the AFC Division. It was not until 1972, and after intense internal negotiations, that Marley Floors finally gained control of its own direct selling to the trade. At that point Bill Moffat (then Sales Manager and later Managing Director of Flooring) stopped reporting to Eric Cook, head of the contracting division, and instead reported to Robin Aisher. Supply only sales rose dramatically and ten years later they were taking some three-quarters of the factory output. In 1980, Marley Floors assumed control of the selling to the retail market (previously with Marley Retail Supplies). Eventually, on January 1st 1983, the rump of the old supply and fix operation was brought over from Marley Tile and put under Bill Moffat's control leaving Marley Contract Services concentrating solely on supplying and fixing roof tiles. Marley immediately recognised that the re-launch of its floor contracting business as a separate entity, under the name Florstyle, was a public reminder that it was competing with its customers. In the autumn of 1982, Marley held a conference in Nice for the 40 flooring contractors and 40 wholesalers who constituted 85% of its UK custom, to launch its new product range and to explain Florstyle: 'contractors, although a little wary, were prepared to go along with the proposals'. Unfortunately, customer reaction turned out to be the least of Marley's concerns.

Although Florstyle was now seeking new contracts in its own right, it had also inherited the existing contracts from MCS; separately constituted for the first time, the cost of executing these contracts was now fully visible – and not helped by subsequent price increases imposed by its sister supplier. Administration costs proved higher than expected with the new computer system the villain of the piece. Losses in excess of £2 million were identified in 1983 but although these were reduced in 1984, Marley decided to withdraw the following year. 'Although the contracting operation has been an important part of our flooring business for many years, it has become increasingly costly in recent years, so much so that we decided to close it down during 1985. To arrange this cost effectively Marley helped a number of its contract managers, who wanted to continue as flooring contractors, to set up their own businesses.'[26]

Further product improvement came with Marley's introduction of the "scratcher", a machine which despite its name, does far more than scratch. Tiles had long been made in America using the "scratching" process which was designed to introduce a more consistent marbling effect into the floor tile. On the conventional floor tile the marbling effect was created by dropping small pieces of a broken, and different coloured, vinyl carpet into the nip of the calenders where they would be pressed into the tile carpet. However, the marbling could not be added consistently and some tiles would always come out with little or no marbling effect. What the scratcher did was to take the two separate vinyl carpets, the base and the marbling, and "scratch" them into small pieces; these broken bits where then mixed together and re-calendered to produce a consistent marble finished tile.

Marley had installed a scratcher at Leighton Buzzard in the 1960s. 'We put it on the production line but we couldn't make it without getting bubbles on the tiles. Eventually we pushed the plant to one side and abandoned the project. When we closed down Leighton Buzzard [1985] we put it in at Harrietsham and off they went at it again. We didn't get so many bubbles and when we stopped using asbestos we got no bubbles at all and it worked as sweetly as anything.' In view of its history, one could understand the feeling behind the Board Report of December 1983: 'The scratcher at Leighton Buzzard was started with, much to our surprise, no difficulty'.

By the mid-1980s, competition was once again increasing, this time from the European manufacturers who by then had secured a 35% market share; the French Gerland and Sommer, the Dutch Krommenie, the Swedish Tarkett, and the Norwegian Rieber were all regular suppliers to the British market, though Marley in turn was re-entering the European markets on the base of its low production costs. Marley had been able to rationalise its manufacturing base

---

26   *Marley plc*, Annual Report, *1985.*

further by moving the one line left at Leighton Buzzard down to Harrietsham, which by then had five lines. This released 15 acres for development and took Marley from the site that had first come into the group in 1927. More subtle changes took place during the 1980s in the industry's marketing of resilient plastic flooring. Functional utility was assumed and the product was now primarily sold on design. Like the wallpaper industry, patterns were changed every two years and the biennial Harrogate Floorcovering Fair became the most important event in the calendar – especially in 1988 when Marley's Image pattern in its Connoisseur range carried away the design award. That same year saw an honour which brought equal satisfaction to the manufacturing arm of the business when the British Safety Council judged Marley Floors one of the safest employers in the world, awarding the Company its Sword of Honour.

Extrusions: the search for new products

By the time the housing market collapsed in 1974, Marley faced the need to widen the base of its extrusions business it it was to continue its rapid expansion. It had introduced plastic to all the cold water related functions in the house – rainwater off the house, cold water services into the house, and waste products out. It had admitted defeat in hot water plumbing and its only significant non-water extrusion, cladding, had progressed as far as consumer taste would allow. A breakdown of deliveries in 1974 and 1975 is shown here (the figures understate the importance of underground drainage where, of course, the pipe diameters are much larger).

Deliveries by product (million feet)

	1974	1975
R.w.g.	19.8	19.5
Soil pipe	4.2	3.9
Waste pipe	8.6	7.5
U/G drainage	3.6	3.7
Cladding	8.7	10.8
Hand rail	0.5	0.3
Fencing	0.4	0.9

Source: Marley Board Report, 75/200, December 1975

Marley had long had a record of experimentation with new products but the successive development of its rainwater goods, cold water services, and drainage products had monopolised management energies. Moreover, the early product ranges, particularly rainwater goods, had almost completely replaced the traditional materials. And Marley itself could hardly hope for a larger market share; surveys in 1975 and 1976 showed the Company had over 50% of all plastic plumbing in the UK,[27] and over 60% of the total internal drainage market.[28] The Directors therefore recognised that it was now time for a concerted effort to widen the base of the Company: 'A heavy programme of development is underway on a variety of new products and the static situation on rainwater goods does underline the necessity of keeping ahead of the competitors with new ideas'.[29] Marley had already been working on the plastic window and more effort was put behind the existing fascia and soffit systems.

Into the bathroom

The natural choice of a new product range, especially for a Company nurtured on water-related products, was the bathroom, and in March 1974 Marley took delivery of vacuum-formed equipment to manufacture the domestic bath; production was "in full swing" by May 1975. Plastic had been making the same inroads into the baths market (by then over 50%) as Marley had experienced with its own rainwater goods a decade earlier, but this time Marley was following, not leading. Nevertheless, Marley's sales growth was rapid: 1,400 baths were sold in 1974/75, 7,000 in 1976, 17,000 in 1977 and 22,000 in 1978. In comparison with the traditional extruded products, the production of baths was space consuming, the one thing that Harrietsham did not have in abundance. To further the expansion of Extrusions it was decided to build a new factory at Catterick in Yorkshire. One of the reasons for moving so far away from Harrietsham was the increasing production of larger diameter drainage pipes which had proportionately higher transport costs. Land had been purchased in February 1974 as a precautionary move but it was not until December 1975 that the decision to build the factory was accepted in principle. Production began in late 1977 and the plant was running at full capacity in 1978. A reduction in the product range and a need to reduce overheads eventually led to Catterick being closed as a manufacturing unit in 1986; it continued as a distribution centre for another year.

Although volumes were not insubstantial. Marley's share of the bath market was never much more than 5%. It was, however, a sufficient base to move into other bathroom products and in 1978 Marley began producing an acrylic washbasin, together with an extensive range of injection moulded accessories including a Hardy Amies range. In May 1978 the Directors were

27 Marley Board Report, *75/200, December 1975.*
28 *Ibid, 76/67, April 1976.*
29 *Ibid, 73/103, July 1973.*

able to report that 'The total programme on the viability of the sanitary ware operations is now virtually complete... the initial figures look reasonably encouraging although we must work very hard to achieve the market penetration in the first and second years'.[30] Unlike its competitors, though, Marley did not produce a WC, and a significant proportion of the washbasin market also remained ceramic; Marley could not offer a comprehensive range of bathroom products. Attempts were made to secure complementary ceramic products. Manufacturers were approached to produce sanitary ware to Marley's design and one set of negotiations in 1981 advanced far enough to merit minuting, but no satisfactory outcome could be agreed. A greenfield study was undertaken to consider own manufacture but after a detailed financial appraisal it was decided not to proceed. Talks were also held with potential acquisition targets but, again, satisfactory arrangements could not be achieved.

Production of baths eventually ceased in January 1986; although the operation never lost money, it was not particularly profitable either. If part of Marley's skill lay in its ability to compound the PVC then, for baths, they came too late in the cycle: '... you're going to take a part-processed material in the form of acrylic sheet from ICI, who fixed the prices absolutely. You couldn't go anywhere else, then you were only as good as the chap down the road with a small shed, except that you had great overheads to carry.'[31] However, it is arguable whether Marley could ever have succeeded in the bathroom without being able to offer a complete range of products. Without the range offered by the market leaders, Twyfords and Armitage, Marley was always going to face an uphill marketing struggle.

Marley was also meeting resistance in other new areas, in particular its soffit, fascia and bargeboard systems – the design was complicated for the average builder to put together and the Company was 'not able to reconcile the price differences with conventional materials.'[32] One bright spot was the acquisition, in August 1979, of the Southampton Company, Phetco, manufacturer of Multikwik – 'The fastest way to connect a WC'; bought for only £1.5 million, it made profits of £400,000 in the ten months to October 1979 on turnover of £1 million. Multikwik was a range of self-sealing WC pan connectors, bends and extension pieces designed to join the WC to the soil pipe system and the building drain.

Plastic windows

A plastic window project had been underway for some years at Central

30   *Ibid, 78/87, 1978.*
31   *Peter Wilson interview.*
32   Marley Board Report, *79/138, September 1978.*

Research, often working in conjunction with the German subsidiary with a view to Marley positioning itself in the wider European market. Mouldings were first manufactured in 1977 and field trials undertaken but it was not until the end of the 1970s that Marley finally determined that it was time to break into the replacement window market. A new factory was built at Sittingbourne and in November 1980 it produced its first window sections. Reflecting the influence of its German partner the product was the European style "tilt and turn" window. Trading as Marley Windowline, Marley sold direct to the house owner (advertising, mailshots, etc) and provided an installation service. Demand for the new product was encouraging and at the end of the year the Company was able to report that 'The product had been well received and with very few problems regarding installation and we are satisfied that we should continue to develop this division.'[33] A new range of outward opening windows was to be designed for launch in the following spring. This was perhaps a recognition of the fact the German influence had been too strong: 'This system will conform to the standard window style that the UK has been specifying for a number of years, as against the present Windowline 300 system which is very much influenced by European design which ultimately may be better suited to commercial applications than domestic.'[34]

The new product range was a success and in 1983, with sales running well ahead of budget, two new lines were laid down. Even that was insufficient to cope with demand and later that year a second factory was acquired on the other side of the road, doubling capacity. Although a substantial flow of business was sustained, it never appeared to be a particularly profitable operation. By 1984, problems were beginning to emerge. The whole industry received a blow when the Chancellor imposed VAT on residential improvements with effect from June, but even prior to that Marley had its own difficulties. 'As activities increase, our major problems are the surveillance of installations, the quality of workmanship [and bad debts].'[35] The production side posed no special problems but the nature of the market was such that Marley operated through a commission only sales force and this proved less easy to manage than elsewhere in the organisation. Alistair Vearonelly, now Managing Director of Extrusions remembers one occasion when a rival Company sent over a coach from the West Country to poach one of the senior sales executives and twenty salesmen: 'they wined and dined these people overnight, persuaded them to join for apparently better terms, and we lost 21 people overnight!' Early in 1989, Marley established a joint venture with the Danish firm Inter Primo to manufacture cellular plastic building products (typically used for timber replacement) and uPVC window profiles for direct

33 Marley Extrusions Board Report, *December 1981.*
34 *Ibid.*
35 *Ibid, February 1984.*

sale to window fabricators, and Marley therefore ceased the production of uPVC windows on its own account. Marley sold its shareholding to its partner in 1991.

The development of the traditional product range had not stood still. In rainwater goods, still its leading profit earner, Marley benefited from the 'overwhelming success of our Deepflow system, which has considerable advantage over its competitors'. Deepflow was a 110 × 75 mm semi-elliptical gutter designed for better self-cleansing characteristics, with greater strength and capacity than the traditional half round gutter. The underground drainage range was gradually extended by the manufacture of larger diameter pipes: 10 inch pipes, for instance, being added to the 4 and 6 inch range in 1974. And in the waste pipe systems, Marley had achieved leadership through its high temperature chlorinated PVC material; by then Marley had also introduced a polypropylene ring seal system. Thus, by 1980, the traditional water related product ranges still accounted for around 90% of Marley Extrusions' turnover; rainwater goods being 25%, internal service and waste 40%, and underground drainage 25%. The overall share of the building extrusions market had fallen to around 30% but Marley just about retained market leadership, closely followed by Key Terrain, and then Bartol (owned by Hepworth) and Osma (Wavin).

One new product caused Marley particular satisfaction in that it brought Extrusions and Roof Tiles together – the Dry Verge and Dry Ridge systems. Roof tiling is a dry fix system until you reach the eaves and ridge where the tiles were fixed by cement and mortar; messy, labour intensive and difficult in the cold weather. A small development team was formed between the two companies to see whether Marley could make uPVC fittings to replace wet fixing and the result was the Dry Verge system which provided Extrusions with an extra product range and Roof Tiles with a marketing advantage. This has been discussed in more detail earlier in the book.

The ten years from 1973 saw substantial growth in Marley Extrusions' turnover and profits, albeit by assisted by inflation. Sales rose from £7.7 million in 1973 to £32 million in 1983 and profits rose from the then peak of £1.7 million to a record of over £5 million. The performance was remarkably similar to Key Terrain who also ended 1983 making profits of around £5 million.

From manufacture to merchanting

The selling of the extrusion products had remained under the control of Marley Tile's contracting division throughout the 1960s, under the name of Marley Plumbing. The growing dissatisfaction of the Extrusions management finally came to a head in 1970: in August, new moves to increase selling effectiveness gave Marley Extrusions the Marley Plumbing title. In Peter Wilson's own words: 'There was a tremendous fight... eventually there was sufficient evidence that something had to be done so Extrusions was then allowed to go off and do its own thing, become an autonomous subsidiary. 'The sales emphasis continued to be based on direct sale to the builder rather than to the merchant. Peter Wilson was clear on the logic: 'If Wimpeys or New Ideal Homes were building 1,000 houses, there was no room for a merchant to take his cut. We might as well deliver direct to the compound and do the deal with them and service the whole contract. Rainwater, roof treatment, cladding, underground drains, soil, you do the whole deal which is what we did and this is another aspect of the strength of the business, because we were able to deal with the very large building groups. We had a very good relationship with them. They knew that we were able to service them because we had very good technical background, we could give them advice, we could provide design service and so on. We had a very strong based business there.' This strategy, while it went to the heart of the large contract market, did cause some alienation amongst the merchanting community, some of whom would not stock Marley products. Marley had already begun to fight for the smaller trade customer by opening its own merchanting depots; increasingly, these depots were steered towards the plumbing market.

In February 1977, Peter Wilson had expressed his concern to the Holdings Board over 'the reaction in the plumbing distribution industry generally when a manufacturer such as Marley increases its investment in the distribution side of the trade.'

The first Marley depot had been opened in 1964 with the twin object of stocking Marley products whilst also supporting the contracting units. In the 1966 *Annual Report*: 'Our selling organisation is being further strengthened by the opening of depots specifically designed to serve the building trade and to provide a centre for our contracting activities.' The Chairman was able to report a total of twelve depots in operation, a number which more than trebled to 38 by the spring of 1969. However, by then the profitability of the dedicated depot system was coming into question and in 1970 a decision was taken to allow the depots to stock complementary products, effectively turning them into general builders' merchants; Marley then had some 45 depots, a sizeable force in the merchanting industry at that time. 'With the transfer of direct sales to the Extrusions company, it has become obvious that we need to generate more throughput if we are to make profits and we are, therefore, selecting depots to experiment with sales of additional bought out products except that we are aiming at the small builder and plumber first and the general public second'.[36]

In 1974, Marley Building Supplies Limited was formed as a separate company; reflecting its roots as the depot division of Marley Tile, around half of its £10 million turnover was still derived from Marley products. But now

36 Marley Board Sales Report.

MBS had become more closely linked to the Extrusions Company, which accounted for almost 60% of its sales. In turn, MBS was taking 17½% of Extrusions' own sales. The merchanting industry was beginning to notice. MBS now pushed further along the plumbing route and boasted in its 1978 *Annual Report* that 'Our kitchen and bathroom showrooms offering a complete sales and planning service to the trade and public have been highly successful'. In 1979: 'Our policy of concentrating in depth on sanitary ware, kitchens and PVC products, is proving increasingly successful and we are now one of the leaders in these fields. Marley supported this concentration by the acquisition of Bimits, a specialist distributor to the plumbing trade, with three branches and plans for two more. The financial performance of MBS proved disappointing and in 1981 the business was restructured 'with the purpose of improving the position of Marley plumbing products in the market place. Future policy will be geared to specialist merchanting operations in plumbing, heating and sanitary ware; introducing the trade name Plumb-Center'.[37] Plumb-Center was a brilliant choice of name, selected unerringly out of a selection which included Plumb Shop, The Weather Station, Plumbers Mate and even Plumbers Parts. In the reconstruction that followed, two of the five regional offices and 11 depots were closed, leaving Marley with a chain of 33 Plumb-Center units, but in direct competition with Extrusions' principal customers.

There was little that the Extrusions management could do about the impact of its fellow subsidiary which, by its Plumb-Center renaming, had visibly become one of the leading plumbers' merchants in the country. At least one large plumbers' merchant had made it clear to Marley that they would not be significant stockists of Marley products while it remained a direct competitor. In August 1985, Marley bowed to the inevitable and sold its Plumb-Center business to Wolseley who then used the acquired brand name for the whole of its national chain of plumbers' merchants. Subsequently, Extrusions also cut back on its direct sales to builders. 'We used to cherry pick the good ones, we went direct and denied the merchant the business; when it wasn't quite so convenient, we tried to put the business through the merchant – and he didn't like it. So we have done a complete circle and now we are manufacturers only.'[38]

There had been another approach to the merchanting conflict of interest, which was to minimise the Plumb-Center presence in areas of greatest sensitivity, and instead to open depots which had no recognisable connection with Marley. The plan was to open an initial four depots with plans for a further six, trading under the name of Pennine Services. The first depot was opened in Huddersfield in November 1984 with other Yorkshire depots following in 1985 but these, too, were sold.

37   Marley Limited Annual Report, *1981*.
38   *Interview with Alistair Vearonelly, Managing Director of Marley Extrusions.*

The outsider threatens

Clarification of Marley's stance as a pure manufacturer came none too soon, for the established producers were having to face up to a determined new competitor, Polypipe, controlled by Kevin McDonald. McDonald had formed Bartol Plastics in 1964 which was later acquired by the clay drainage pipe manufacturer, Hepworth. In April 1980, Polypipe's Doncaster factory began producing a limited range of standard products, sold extremely competitively. Within three years, Polypipe was having a serious impact on the industry's pricing structure; Marley Extrusions' Board Report in February 1984 referred to 'severe competition from Polypipe offering systems considerably below market price'. An estimate presented to the Board later that year suggested that the industry's profits in 1984 would be some £15–18 million lower than they would otherwise have been due to the actions of "the newcomer" in securing a 10% market share.[39]

Even then, because of its limited product range, there had been a presumption that Polypipe would remain a peripheral player, but in February 1985 Polypipe purchased a suite of tooling and related patent rights from Courtaulds; with that, Polypipe became a major force in the industry and Marley recognised the need to reduce its own manufacturing costs. The mid-1980s was a period of intense pressure on Extrusions' profitability, falling to little more than £1 million against a record of almost £5 million two years earlier. The ending of the repair grants had a more serious effect than expected and, with 65% of the business depending on repair and maintenance work, the fall in demand for rainwater goods was the most severe on record. To make matters worse, as Polypipe began to look for the benefits from its newly acquired market share, the Dutch-based Wavin began to compete for business even more aggressively.

Marley had to work hard on its cost structure. In 1986, Catterick was closed and production consolidated at Harrietsham, which in turn received heavy investment in automation. This was rewarded in 1987 by a substantial increase in profits as 'Further benefits came from substantial reductions in manufacturing costs and lower overheads.'[40] Alistair Vearonelly spells out the importance of cost reduction: 'The last three years has been a continuation of the policy of getting costs out of the business. We have to recognise that most of the plastic plumbing range is now becoming a commodity product and therefore the emphasis is on cost control. The focus in terms of development of Marley Extrusions in the short term is to regain the technology leadership in plastic plumbing and drainage.'

39 *Marley Board minutes, November 1985.*
40 *Marley plc, Annual Report, 1987.*

Plastics in the motor industry

The early 1970s marked a broadening of Marley Foam in more than one direction. The earlier Davidson agreement restricted Marley's export rights, and in 1972 this was renegotiated to give Marley full freedom to export to the EEC. In August 1972 Marley gained its first continental order – a small armrest for Simca worth all of £50,000, but the forerunner of a growing export business. (By the end of the 1970s, exports exceeded £2 million a year, accounting for around 15% of Foam's total sales.) As well as revising the old agreement for interior foam, Marley also negotiated a new agreement with Davidson to cover the manufacture of urethane exterior motor components. The addition of an exterior car trim to the product portfolio was a resounding success giving a whole new dimension to Marley's role as a motor component supplier. In contrast, the third leg to Marley's expansion plans, rigid components for the car interior, known as the Triform project, proved a disappointment. The new interior products were considered important enough to justify a separate company, Marley Triform, another factory. 'A new company, Marley Triform, has acquired a site of 10 acres at Aylesham... to manufacture injection and blow moulded components for a wide variety of domestic and other uses.'[41] The objective was to look for opportunities in large mouldings such as steering wheels and radiator grilles. Triform started by taking over small contracts for blow moulded parts (windscreen washer bottles and ventilation ducts) supplied by RTZ Pillar Plastics to Ford Motor, in practice, it was the steering wheels which found the ready market and the first ones were delivered in late 1972. They were a new alternative to the traditional wood or the painted hard rubber wheel supplied by the major competitor, Clifford Covering.

Triform's sales experience was encouraging and production facilities were doubled in 1977. The Chairman reported with some optimism the following year: 'We have been particularly successful with regard to steering wheels. Here our growth has been very rapid with turnover doubled for the third successive year. We anticipate sales will again double in the coming year. Significantly more than half our production of steering wheels is for the export market. Technology we have developed for the manufacture of polyurethane steering wheels is opening up a wider product range.'[42]

Marley Foam's move into exterior components was the basis for sustained growth through the 1970s and 1980s. In March 1973, Peter Winfield reported to the Holdings Board 'on discussions with Davidson and the prospects for attractive, but capital expensive, expansion into the production of foam products for the exterior of cars'. The first order for urethane foam

---

41 *Marley Limited Accounts, 1972.*
42 *Ibid, 1978.*

bumper over-riders for Standard Triumph was obtained during 1973 – a start, but only a small one with an estimated sales value of £50,000 in 1974. Of greater significance were the negotiations which had taken place in 1972 and 1973 'for a series of full size bumpers which will be the first such items to be used in full production by any British motor manufacturer'.[43] Davidson had first introduced an elastomeric bumper on the Pontiac Firebird around 1970 and by 1972 urethane bumpers had grown to account for 40% of Davidson's sales; the potential for Marley in the UK was plain. At the end of 1973 Marley Foam had achieved its breakthrough; it was awarded the contract for the complete front and rear energy absorbing bumpers for the MGB and the MG Midget. It was the US safety regulations which had again proved a stimulus with their requirement for bumpers to withstand even minor damage at a contact speed of 2½ and later 5 miles per hour; inevitably that had an immediate effect on export specifications. The 2½ miles per hour impact standard was later adopted in the UK. Marley began delivery of the sports car bumpers in September 1974 at an annual rate in excess of £1 million. In June 1975, Peter Winfield told the Holdings Board that the MG bumper was the most successful new product ever introduced by Marley Foam. The tooling costs were on a larger scale than had been the case with the much smaller interior foam products, amounting to £200,000 on this one contract – and British Leyland paid for the tooling cost, an arrangement which became standard practice for Marley Foam's exterior trim contracts throughout the motor industry.

The MG bumper was the first of what is now regarded as a standard product and the model range proceeded to widen – in 1976 Marley obtained its first significant order for exterior trim from Ford when Ford Fiesta production started at Dagenham. The urethane bumpers were also supplemented by a new energy absorbing block system for bumpers which had also been developed by Davidson as a substitute for hydraulic shock absorbers. Marley began producing in August 1978 for the Triumph Spitfire.

In the mid-1970s, Davidson developed an injection moulding technique for bumper manufacture called reaction injection moulding (RIM). This technique uses liquid raw materials that are mixed just before being injected into the mould; the reaction between the chemicals fill the space and the heat generated cures it, producing a better quality product. The RIM bumpers could be painted to match the body work of the car, enabling the bumper to be designed almost as a fashion accessory on sportier models.

Figures given earlier demonstrated Marley's position as the leading independent producer of foam products for the UK motor industry. The only substantial independent competitor for interior moulded foam components at that time was British Vita, and at the end of 1975 they withdrew leaving

43 Marley Board Report, 73/32, March 1972.

Marley with virtually all the non-captive market. In the polyurethane bumper market, Marley had a share of around 75%, with only one major competitor, Miles Redfern (a BTR subsidiary) although there was strong competition from bumpers made from injection moulded polyproplene. Marley's market strength was far from being a recipe for making easy money, however, for the motor manufacturers had the options of sourcing in-house or overseas. In 1979 British Leyland brought some of the interior product business back into its Pressed Steel subsidiary. Ford threatened to dual source head rests from Spain but Fred Hardy said that he would close Marley's production down if necessary. Bluffing or not, Marley was able to show Ford that it was a quality supplier at competitive prices and, in 1991, Marley Foam received Ford of Europe's Q1 award.

During the 1970s Marley Foam also had to contend with the steady decline in UK car production, down from a peak of 1.92m in 1972 to 1.07m in 1979. Despite this, and the cost pressures coming from the manufacturers, sales more than doubled and Foam was regularly earning profits of around £1½ million a year. However, the further fall in domestic car production to only 924,000 in 1980 could not be offset; Marley also lost the MG bumper contract when the model ceased production, and the Escort crashpad. Sales fell from an annual rate of £15 million in the first half of the year to only £11 million in the second half and Marley Foam's profits halved. To make matters worse, Triform was now in deep trouble. Despite the rapid growth in sales, tough competition and the costs of expansion prevented Triform moving into profit. Matters were made worse in September 1979 when Ford refused to accept Marley's price for its injection moulded instrument clusters and re-sourced, leading to 60 redundancies. The following month Marley acquired the steering wheel business of one of the principal competitors, Creator, a subsidiary of Imperial Tobacco, giving Marley entry to Vauxhall and Ford of Europe – an additional 6,000 steering wheels per week.

Despite the acquisition of the Creator market share, losses in 1980 rocketed to over £1 million and the totality of the motor components business lost money. 'The major depressing factor is the largest steering wheel manufacturer, Clifford Coverings, who admit to making heavy losses over the last 2–3 years, and whose openly declared policy at the present time is to hold on to market share at any price.'[44] Marley tried to rationalise its production facilities to cut its cost base; the factory at Aylesham was closed and the plant transferred to Harrietsham in July 1980. That autumn a further 100 redundancies were announced taking the total numbers down to 445 compared with over 900 at Foam and Triform together in June 1979.

The final blow came in November 1982 when British Leyland notified

---

44 Triform Board Report, *December 1979.*

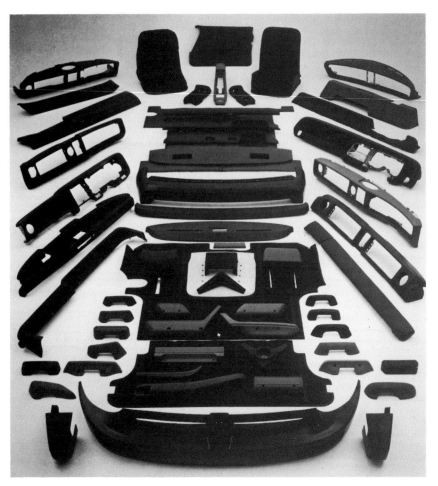

Marley Foam products

Marley that it intended to single source its steering wheel business with Clifford Coverings. This lost Marley 60% of its budgeted 1983 steering wheel turnover and there was little alternative but to withdraw from the business, which it did in 1983. Fred Hardy, who had remained Chairman of Marley Foam after he retired from the Holdings Board, believed that the problem was undue pressure on prices from the car companies and that eventually Marley had to make a stand. 'There was always a struggle with the buyers in the car companies. Triform had a good product but it went wrong just on pricing. We gave Ford and the other companies 6 months to increase their rates and when they didn't we closed the factory and moved the equipment to Harrietsham and then eventually closed it down. We were asked to come back as a producer but said "no".'

Competition from moulded fibres

Other changes in the structure of the market place were also taking place. For instance, Marley was beginning to feel increasingly nervous about competition from a cheaper product – moulded fibre panels. At the bottom end of the car market, some models had switched from moulded polyurethane foam to moulded wood fibre and by 1978 Marley began to examine the alternatives. The solution was the purchase of British Moulded Fibre in October 1980, following a year of investigation and negotiation. BMF had factories at Bristol and Reading but, as a prelude to the acquisition, the Reading factory was closed. British Moulded Fibre was formed in 1955 at Spencers Wood in Reading by the Burrows family and the first components for the motor industry were supplied in 1957. Since then, BMF has developed a range of products for the motor industry including door panels, armrests, rear parcel shelves and seat backs.

The traditional crash pad market also began to decline, being replaced by all inclusive instrument panels, often injection moulded by the car manufacturers in house. Marley's response offered substantial economies compared with the conventional vacuum formed, foam filled crash pad. This was first featured at the 1979 European Automotive Suppliers Exhibition in Geneva and formed the basis of a new generation of padded fascias in the 1980s.

Perhaps more significant than anything was a gradual change in the relationship with the motor companies, from combative to co-operative. At the 1983 Davidson Licencees Conference, Ed Blanche, President of Ford of Europe, spoke of the need for closer relationships with suppliers, taking the form of nominated preferred suppliers undertaking design and development work for vehicle manufacturers and then receiving the production order without open tender. Marley Foam already had one such contract from British Leyland. This closer relationship derived in part from the increasing complexity of the components (which in turn had their own sub-assemblies) that Marley was required to provide. The business had gradually changed taking its activities from relatively low technology interior trim to more advanced techniques required for manufacturing exterior trim and integrated dashboards; this required a much higher level of capital commitment which would not readily be provided if contracts could subsequently be withdrawn on the whim of an annual pricing review. Marley spelled out its view of the changes in the 1986 Group accounts: 'Motor manufacturers are now demanding that component suppliers take increasing responsibility for design, research and development and sub-assembly work to become more technically able to provide higher quality components. Marley Foam continued to evolve the business successfully to meet these changing customer demands and is now involved in a number of large design and development projects.' That was the second successive year that Marley Foam was given the Pursuit of Excellence Award from Jaguar.

Freed from the Triform losses, with new bumper assemblies to replace the lost MG contracts, and gently rising domestic car production, Marley Foam showed what it could do. The average use of polyurethane rose from 11 kg per car in 1980, to 15 kg in 1985;[45] Foam sales doubled over that period and in 1985, otherwise a very depressed year, Marley Foam's pre-tax profits exceeded £4 million – 20% of the Group total.

Increased internationalisation of the business has also been a feature of the last decade and will become even more so over the next. As model ranges are increasingly designed on a European or even worldwide basis, so the component suppliers have recognised that their domestic order book is being determined by executives outside the UK. One of the best examples was Marley's long courtship of Nissan in Japan even before the Sunderland site had been chosen. In 1981 Nissan announced that it expected to go ahead with the construction of a 200,000 car a year plant in the UK. As luck would have it, that year the Annual Conference of Davidson Licencees was held in Japan and Peter Winfield took full advantage to open contact with Nissan and, five years later, the first trim was supplied to Sunderland.

Since the late 1980s, the motor industry has seen the development of the world car concept. Marley has responded with the rationalisation of the existing business and the formation of a series of strategic partnerships, giving Marley a manufacturing presence on the Continent and a closer relationship with Nissan. At home, the original armrest business, now small relative to the fascias and exterior trim, had not been profitable for several years and was sold. Marley Foam was then merged with BMF, to form Marley Automotive Components, achieving considerable overhead savings. In June 1990, MAC further strengthened its relationship with Nissan with the announcement of a joint venture with Kanto Seiki of Japan (now Kansei) to manufacture automotive components in North East England; the new factory came on stream in May 1992 giving Marley the capability to produce the full range of Nissan's requirements. There have also been two important moves giving Marley a manufacturing presence on the Continent. In September 1989, MAC formed a joint venture with Davidson Investment Panel Textron in Holland which will give Marley access to Ford in Belgium; a new factory at Born began production of instrument panels in August 1992 – a specific response to the implications of the world car concept. To further strengthen its European presence, in February 1990, Marley spent £5½ million on the purchase of KKF Karl Fels, a German manufacturer of high-quality injection moulded plastic components with the objective of opening up supply to Volkswagen and Audi.

Marley's achievements in the automotive market have been further

---

45 NEDO Report, *1987.*

recognised by the Supplier of the Year Award from General Motors Europe in 1990 and 1991 and the Nissan Most Improved Supplier (Europe) in 1991.

The age of the superstore

The early superstores have long been superseded themselves by larger units but their size seemed awe-inspiring at the time. Sir Owen: 'Jack and I went and had a look at them with Tom O'Sullivan. In order to grow bigger we bought this place down in Exeter, terrified us, 7,000 sq.ft. and when we put our things in it was empty and we gradually built up from that.' In fact, two sites were chosen in 1972 as experiments – Exeter and Brighton. Early trading was encouraging with takings of around £20,000 a month and in October that year the Board was told negotiations were in progress for a further eight new large sites. The formula worked for Marley and for its competitors too. None of the major retailers could afford to move too slowly or business was immediately lost to rivals' larger premises. It was now a question of finding the sites as quickly as possible, financing them, and closing down the traditional small units. Looking back at the end of the decade: 'We have closed 150 shops during the 'seventies, as we moved from being purely an outlet for our own manufactured goods to a more or less straightforward retailer. This has cost us quite a lot of money, but should now be all behind us.'[46]

Marley Retail was run as a division of Marley Tile until November 1968 when it was constituted as a separate company. Apart from the shops, Marley Retail also included the wholesale distribution of Marley manufactured products to the independent retailers; this latter function was itself separated into Marley Retail Supplies in February 1976. By the time those first two superstores had been developed in 1972, Marley Retail had selling space of a little over 200,000 square feet, sales of £9 million (of which a third could have been wholesaling) and pre-tax profits of £400,000. The restructuring during the 1970s took selling space up to around 375,000 square feet but from only 31 superstores with a further 50,000 square feet in the remaining High Street shops. Sales grew steadily, to £21 million in 1979, and record profits of £1 million were achieved.

Competition for prime sites was intensifying and even when Marley found them, it no longer guaranteed a local monopoly: 'As a sign of more competitive times, we will be opening at Loughborough tomorrow, 7th March, just a quarter of a mile away from a large B & Q store, opening the day before'.[47] The pace of change was indeed rapid and it could not avoid having a

---

46 Marley Board Report, *79/80, May 1979.*
47 Homecare Board Report, *March 1981.*

Marley Homecare DIY centre

financial impact on Marley. The cost of closures and, in particular, the high costs associated with opening new superstores had always been a restraint on profits; this was particularly painful at the start of the 1980s.

In 1981, the management opened 20 new superstores increasing the physical size of the business by a remarkable 60%; exacerbated by the recession

Marley Homecare could do no more than break even. Some months were even worse and the Board must have wondered whether it had advanced too fast: 'losses shown in August are the cause of deep concern. It is unfortunate that... we have expanded far faster than ever before, and faster than any other DIY chain has ever done by opening 22 units since August 1980. They will stand us in very good stead in the future, but the burden in the short term will be heavy.'[48] Despite that disappointing return, store expansion continued at a frenetic pace and the rewards to Marley but three years later were to provide ample justification for all the investment and effort that had been put into retailing. Sales increased from £21 million in 1979 to £91 million in 1984, generating profits of £7.4 million – an exceptional pre-tax return for a retailer of 8.1%.

The Payless name

The naming of the stores had long been contentious and was a focus of the difference between those who saw the shops as an additional outlet and support for Marley's manufactured products, and the retailers who wanted their division to be a fully independent player in the market place. There had been an unsuccessful attempt to abandon the Marley name when the Exeter store had been opened but to no avail. The discussion reached main Board level when Owen Junior questioned 'the long term wisdom of continuing to trade in the shops under the name of Marley whilst it is known to discourage the customers of the Retail division and of other divisions. After discussion it was agreed that an experiment, on an area basis, to try out shops under the style "Homecare" only, would be acceptable.'[49] The experiment was not adopted and the Homecare stores continued to trade under the Marley banner through the 1970s.

The issue came to a head again in the early 1980s following consumer surveys Marley had carried out, not only of its own customers but also of customers in competitive stores who had never shopped at Marley Homecare. It was the answers of this latter group which were most revealing. Many of them thought that Marley Homecare sold only Marley goods and they also thought they would be more expensive because they associated the Marley name with quality, and therefore higher prices: this time the name had to change – but to what. Again America provided an answer. Tom O'Sullivan had seen the Payless name on Payless-Cashways stores; Ted Lansdowne suggested coupling it with do-it-yourself to give Payless DIY, and during 1982 the new name was adopted on all Marley's stores. At the same time it was coupled with a further change in the product emphasis. 'In January 1982, the decision was

48 *Ibid, September 1981.*
49 *Marley Limited minutes, April 1972.*

taken to go into building materials in more depth, and the store at Ramsgate was converted to a Payless store in both name and concept.'[50]

Soon after the Payless name had been adopted, the DIY retailers found themselves at the centre of a trading controversy which is still with us – Sunday opening. Tom O'Sullivan spelt out to the Marley Board just how important Sunday opening was to Payless: 'May 1982 saw the commencement of the company trading on Sundays. This has obviously had the effect of increasing turnover... and Sunday now represents our second busiest day of the week. It is impossible to assess how much of this business we would have achieved and how much we will lose if we are forced by legislation to close. The second reading of the Private Members' Bill is before Parliament of 4th February, and the outcome of this is awaited with keen interest. Although there is a strong anti-lobby, the most important thing is that our customers are in favour and it would be a pity if they cannot have their way.'[51]

Marley had opened as many of 39 of its stores on Sundays and with its competitors trading on a similar scale. Local authority opposition was restrained at first and Tom O'Sullivan was able to report at the end of the first month's Sunday trading that 'A fair amount of correspondence has been received from local authorities, but as yet no prosecutions have been made.' There were only a few months of grace (or lack of it); by the end of the year, the retail company was reporting fines in 13 towns. The local authorities, of course, were to find that fines were no substantial deterrent; average turnover at a Marley store on a Sunday reached £20,000. By the second half of 1983, the injunctions were beginning to fly and Marley had to close half a dozen of its stores and a distinction emerged between those authorities who took a hard line and those who were prepared to turn a blind eye; Sunday opening had become a matter of routine.

By the end of 1983 store numbers had almost doubled from four years earlier, at 59 giving selling area of over 1 million square feet. At the end of 1985 Marley announced the sale of Payless. It then comprised 65 superstores with a total selling area of 1.4 million square feet, third in the industry after B & Q and Texas. The suggested returns in that last year of ownership were sales of £110 million and profits before central charges of £9 million. Unfortunately, Marley's finances were becoming increasingly stretched and Payless was seen as the most marketable asset; a public announcement was made that it was available for sale. Optimistic estimates of the potential price went as high as £130m at one stage though the Company eventually achieved £93.6 million, compared with a book cost of around £20 million. (A sale of a package of freeholds to Courtaulds Pension Fund had earlier raised another £10 million.) It was a difficult decision for the Board to take. Payless had become one of the

50 Payless Board Report, *February 1982.*
51 *Ibid.*

Colin James

most successful parts of Marley but competition was intense and nowhere more so than in the search for new sites and the construction of ever larger stores. Marley estimated that it needed to spend £40 million on new openings in the succeeding three or four years, potentially starving fellow subsidiaries of capital for their investment programmes. Also on the horizon was the possibility that the do-it-yourself superstore market would reach saturation level at which point returns would fall away sharply. However, the overriding consideration had to be the deterioration in Marley's overall financial position following the losses incurred by Ingrid in North America.

Colin James remembers the effort needed to bring the sale of Payless to a conclusion: 'It was the most serious and far reaching decision the Board had to take; it took several weeks to achieve it. It was like selling the jewel in the crown but we knew we could never finance the future expansion of that business. We went to Ockenden Manor in Cuckfield for the weekend to thrash through the strategy for retaining or selling Payless. We still didn't make the decision: Bob Clark couldn't hide his frustration. At the next Board meeting, Bob said we were not going to leave the room until we had decided about Payless. After another discussion he said 'Now is the time when everybody has to stand up and be counted and we'll start with you – Colin James!' Everybody, including an understandably reluctant Tom O'Sullivan, then voted to sell before the market for DIY businesses declined.'

The pressure from the manufacturing companies to gain control of their own distribution and selling had concentrated on their trade custom leaving the distribution to the retail trade still centralised within Marley Retail Supplies. For obvious reasons, retail distribution had not been an issue for the Roof Tile company but for Marley Floors the retail trade was a critical element of its customer base. In 1980, Marley Retail Supplies, by then serving 10,000 retail outlets, was broken up. Although the logic of Floors taking responsibility for all its own distribution was accepted on both sides there were doubts as to whether all the manufacturing divisions had sufficient retail trade to merit their own independent distribution arrangements. In Retail Supplies' valedictory Board report, Tom O'Sullivan set out the position: 'During the last ten years it has always been a very profitable company on a very small capital base. It has purchased goods from the manufacturing companies at or above the prices paid by the biggest customers, leaving the factories with the real profit. Marley Floors are big enough to go their own retail way without too much trouble, but I fear that the split of the rest of the products three ways will damage our business with the retail trade. However, the deed is done, and we will do our best to make it work.'[52]

A residual business was retained of Marley goods that the manufacturing companies did not want to distribute, and this was placed within a newly formed company, Mayfield Distributors. Mayfield then began to take on a life of its own. In March 1981, Tom O'Sullivan and Richard Aisher reported to the main Board that Mayfield was 'still in the process of building up a range of products for the company'. Much of the range was coming in from North America and plans were made to search in the Far East for products which could be offered within Homecare and "further afield".

Another independent distribution business existed in Mayfield Ceramics, marketing ceramic tiles and kitchen furniture. Its origins lay in the purchase of the West London ceramic tile business of A W Baker for £534,000 in 1980, bought as an adjunct to Marley's substantial distribution function. After losses in 1982, ceramic tile distribution was transferred to the control of Marley Floors, where there was felt to be a greater identity of interest with the customer base, and kitchen distribution was transferred to a separate company. By then, Marley had withdrawn from the distribution of other manufacturers' kitchens and sold only its own Princess product.

---

52 Marley Board Report, *November 1980.*

Part 8
Marley abroad: the rationalisation of an empire

Marley's overseas investments almost rivalled its UK activities in size and by 1975 accounted for 44% of the Group total. Nevertheless, the rewards from that investment remained low. In the ten years to 1975, the return on capital employed averaged only 9% overseas compared with 27% at home; in 1975, as a result of poor performances in France and New Zealand, the comparison had worsened to 5% against 29%. During the 1970s, more lasting management structures were slowly implemented and earlier trouble spots either became more consistent performers, or were sold. The United States, unfortunately, continued to beckon and Marley became increasingly concerned about its lack of presence in the world's largest market. When it finally took the plunge in 1979, the damage inflicted by the purchase of Ingrid far outweighed the gradual improvement that was being achieved elsewhere in Marley's overseas empire.

Consolidation in Europe

France: from concrete to clay

In 1975, Marley estimated that the concrete industry's sales were around 100 million tiles compared with capacity of 180 million. There was only one answer to the industry's overcapacity and on December 2nd 1976 Marley and Betopan reached agreement for the merger of their respective concrete roof tile businesses to form Tuileries Marley Betopan. Sir Owen Aisher: 'they got fed up competing against us and we got fed up and said why don't we join together. It took about two years; they wanted to give us 30% and I said, "no, 50:50". I went down to Cannes and sat on the fence in the sun drinking champagne. I said you can stop here forever but it is 50:50 or we don't do it. Well in the end they agreed but it has never really been as successful as it ought to have been.' Even so, it looked a good piece of negotiating by Marley: the forecasts were for a Betopan profit of FF 650,000 for 1976 and a Marley loss of FF 16.2 million for the sixteen-month period.

The merger brought in Betopan's three tile factories at Ons-en-Bray, Vagney and Realmont; Fontenay was closed leaving TMB with a total of six factories. The enlarged business soon returned to profit and, with activity picking up, TMB's factories were working flat out in 1978 – a record FF 18 million profit was made. A new factory was acquired at Saulieu (Cote d'Or) in 1979; La Roque in Provence was built in 1981 and Graulhet (near Toulouse) replaced Realmont in 1982. Unfortunately, the concrete tile resolutely refused to increase its share of the total roofing market in the way that capacity dictated. Competition became more intense, not just from from Redland but also from the Dutch firm, SET (owned by St Gobain and Dutch State Mines) which was trying to expand into France. The scale of the overcapacity was enormous. In 1982, TMB had a productive capacity of 130 million tiles yet it sold only 72 million. 'The tragedy is that 3 concrete roof tile manufacturers have spent the year fighting each other and not increased their share of the overall roofing market.'[1] Returns remained poor and TMB rationalised back down to six factories in 1987. Eventually, in March 1990, Marley sold its share of TMB to SA Financiere Eternit for FF 17 million.

In the meantime, Marley was putting fresh resources behind the clay factory at Selz; a £3 million investment programme completed at the end of the 1970s took profits from below £500,000 to over £1 million and Bisch was steadily increasing its commitment to the German market just across the border. The Germans were particularly keen on Bisch's plain tiles, exporting over half the 4.5 million annual production of plain tiles; Bisch could not make

---

1 *Marley Board Papers, December 1982.*

Bisch factory, Harnes, France.

enough. Demand for plain tiles for vertical work in northern France was also on the increase and proposals were drawn up to double the capacity of plain tiles. By the autumn of 1983, Bisch's total tile capacity was over 20 million and then, following the completion of a 'major investment in modern highly automated plant' was raised again to 32 million by the end of 1985. Now Selz turns out around 40 million tiles a year and in the 1990 Marley Accounts, the Chairman was able to report that Bisch had 'achieved another impressive result to extend a long growth record. Its success since the major plant modernisation programme of the eighties has been based on the enduring popularity of its high quality, traditional clay tiles in a developing European market.'

Germany: a plumbing success story

Gradually, Marley Werke lessened its commitment to floorings. In 1970 the contracting business, a heavy loss maker, was shut; calendered flooring ceased in 1974 and the last floor tiles were manufactured in 1978 when the marketing of floor coverings in Germany was transferred to the UK. Turnover fell from over DM40 million to DM27 million in the mid-1970s and Riverhead gave serious thought to closing the whole German Company down. Slowly but surely, however, Marley Werke had been reorienting itself towards the extrusions market. New products were introduced, for example cladding in 1969 and plastic windows in 1973 although even by the mid-1970s the Spacesaver door still accounted for half domestic sales. In fact, even the rainwater goods had been slower to build up than in the UK, partly attributable to the transfer of the English designs into the German market: 'The first gutters

255

Marley Werke factory, Germany

that were made in Germany didn't look like German gutters. It may seem unimportant what a gutter looks like, but just half a pipe, which is what the Germans think the UK gutter looks like, just didn't sell.'[2] It was not until 1967 that continental style gutters were introduced and Marley Werke began to increase its presence in the German plumbing market. Slowly the business began to establish itself as a viable, though still small, national entity.

The end of the 1970s proved a turning point in Marley's efforts to build a business with real prospects of growth in Germany. The range of plumbing products was broadened to include soil and waste, and underground drainage systems and Marley Werke established itself as the dominant supplier of the fast growing do-it-yourself retail market. A new confidence in Marley's future in Germany signalled the start of a programme of investment in modern production and warehousing facilities, as well as tooling for the manufacture of

2 *Mike Evans interview.*

new products. Domestic ventilation systems and electrical ducting were added to the product range in 1983 and 1986 respectively.

Increasingly, Marley Werke was becoming the focal point for the group's European extrusion business with its exports ranging from the Benelux countries to Spain; sales into Austria had already been boosted by the closure of the small manufacturing operation in Linz in 1984. Despite the closure of the window business in 1989, Marley Werke's turnover in 1990 had exceeded DM100 million. Ahead of reunification in 1990, Marley Werke had been strengthening its position as a supplier to the refurbishment and DIY markets, in particular selling through the major out of town chains. These distribution links, now accounting for 75% of Marley Werke's sales, have enabled the Company to benefit quickly from the new opportunities in the East.

Ireland

The Irish economy has a substantial agricultural base and it was to benefit significantly from membership of the European Community. Combined with generous incentives for new manufacturing investment it created a favourable background for the construction industry throughout the 1970s. Strong

Chadwicks branch, Ireland

growth in the years immediately prior to accession had taken profits up towards the £1 million level in 1972 and, albeit helped by inflation, the rest of the decade saw CPI move from strength to strength, peaking at over £3 million in 1979.

The merchanting business became a substantial contributor to group profits but it had not been until 1967 that the first branch, at Kilkenny, was opened; following the success there, further stores were opened in the late 1960s and 1970s until, on the occasion of CPI's 50th anniversary in 1981, the Company could boast a national chain of 14 depots and a position as one of Ireland's largest merchants.

Grander schemes were mooted – gypsum manufacturing in 1967 and even a cement plant in 1978 (Marley had suffered badly from a national cement strike in 1970) but these were not pursued further. Possibly one of CPI's most notable achievements, resting as it did entirely on their own technology, was the introduction, in 1980, of hollow concrete blocks filled with Urea Formaldehyde foam.

In 1981, CPI celebrated its Golden Jubilee with record profits of 3.7 million punts, as they had then become. By then, however, the past excesses in the Irish economy were beginning to take effect and the building industry went into an ever deepening recession – by 1986, cement deliveries were down to little more than half the 1979 peak. The downturn was felt most acutely in the concrete block and tile business which had already reached maturity; the merchants provided a degree of stability. Nevertheless, the business as a whole moved into loss and in August 1987, Marley announced the sale of its 53% holding for £4.5 million to a consortium led by Michael Chadwick, a grandson of the founder and the then Chairman of CPI; Finton Chadwick and Tom O'Sullivan.

Africa

Marley might not have appreciated it at the time but the Government's refusal to sanction the sale of the African business to Abercom in 1973 was a fortunate turn of events. The main Board acted quickly to strengthen the management. Bill Courtney, soon to become a Group Deputy Chairman, was appointed to the Board and Denis Hunt was brought over from Rhodesia to become resident Managing Director: 'I was on holiday in Wales when an AA man flagged me down and asked me to ring Jack Aisher in Sevenoaks. He wanted to know whether I would take over as Managing Director in South Africa, and he wanted an answer there and then on the telephone. It was a Friday and when I said yes, he said he wanted me to start there the next Monday. They hadn't

Marley's South African factory

even thought through the regulations: I had to go as a tourist for the first three months.' The success of the new appointments, helped in no small way by an expanding marketplace, can be measured by the growth in profits; by the early 1980s Southern Africa was contributing a steady £7m or more to the group total.

The early years of the new management team were not easy ones for the South African economy but there was work to be done changing the organisation of the business. Like the main UK product areas, the South African company was divisionalised with a separation between manufacture, selling and contracting. Co-incidentally, both Hunt and Courtney had been running businesses which had not been large enough to divisionalise: they had been used to having complete responsibility for the whole of the business and they quickly put South Africa on to the same basis. This soon produced greater working efficiencies and, helped by a more sensible attitude to pricing, margins quickly improved. This was to produce the real rewards at the end of the 1970s when the gold price starting moving ahead and the economy boomed. African turnover moved from a plateau of around £15m to around £50m in 1982 and trading profits accelerated from a typical £1½m to a peak of £8m in 1983 – over 20% of the Group total.

Such rapid growth was only achieved by a continued programme of capital investment and introduction of new products. Illustrative examples taken from Marley's Annual Reports include one million pounds spent on new plant to introduce cushion flooring to South Africa (1974); a similar sum on an expansion of extrusions capacity (1976); the acquisition of Manifold Precision in 1978 taking Marley into water pressure control valves and the doubling of roof tile capacity in 1981. But above all, Marley benefited from the expansion of purchasing power in the black and coloured communities and the Government policy of assisted housing schemes. 'The increase in disposable income of the African population has resulted in a considerable improvement in our sales to them. This is a fast growing and potentially vast market. Vinyl sheet flooring, for example, which is mainly sold to our African customers, increased considerably during the year and the signs are that this will continue.'[3]

Unfortunately, Marley's hopes suffered a setback in the 1980s under the twin pressures of a falling gold price and increasing international pressure on the South African Government. However, unlike many other British companies, Marley did not withdraw from the South African market; although a less significant part of the Group, trading profits continued to average a steady £5 million a year, despite the fall in the value of the Rand. Rationalisation increased Marley's position in its main markets. In 1989, the five companies in the soil and waste market reduced to three, with Marley buying NIP to take its market share to nearly 50%; in 1990 Marley bought its long standing flooring rival, Krommenie to give the Company a market share of over 70%. Marley South Africa is one of the country's largest building materials manufacturers, and has earned good profits for its parent during its forty year investment; its future success clearly depends on political developments now in train.

New Zealand: sale and return

Marley had achieved a domestic market share of around 65% but unfortunately, the economics of the flooring business moved against Marley in the 1970s when tariffs were removed – a bitter blow in view of the original understandings. Peter Wilson, then the main Board Director responsible for New Zealand 'commented on the strenuous efforts being undertaken to combat the sudden impact of the ending of all protective tariffs, warning the Board of the difficult period that lies ahead'.[4] Imports from American producers came to dominate the New Zealand market; they were able to bring in a full range of modern roto-gravure sheet floorings from their low-cost production base in the States, whereas Marley's manufacturing base had included the vinyl tiles where demand was falling. In 1976, Marley ceased producing floor tiles but continued

---

3 *Marley plc*, Annual Report, *1979*.
4 *Marley Limited minutes, June 1972*.

to develop its sheet flooring – the only domestic producer. Despite the intense competition, Marley's sheet flooring, led by Vinylaire, had been recording 50% of the market. Extensive representations were made to the Government, Peter Wilson himself joining in on his 1977 visit. 'Very strong representations were made about the situation and a warning issued that if some protection was not forthcoming, in view of the dumping that was going on, Marley would have no alternative but to close its plant. We said that our export record into Australia particularly was good and that we had continued to invest in New Zealand, giving employment to over 150 New Zealanders. I think they understood the seriousness of the situation but indicated that with the Trade Agreements with America, they could not see their way clear to introduce a quota system to limit the quantity of flooring imports.'[5]

The outlook for an indigenous flooring manufacturer was naturally viewed with pessimism and the position was not helped by the fact that the newer extrusions division was operating below break-even levels. Additional finance was needed to keep the business operational; other solutions were called for. While he was in New Zealand, Peter Wilson made contact with New Zealand Forest Products, one of the largest companies in the country, who expressed an interest in extending their own building industry activities; and UEB Industries (United Empire Box), a carpet and packaging firm. Peter Wilson left the Marley Board in no doubt of his view: 'We cannot continue as we are in New Zealand. The market is too small and we certainly need a broader base. The country is likely to go through a very difficult period and a consolidating of Groups of Companies seems to be the only long term solution.'[6]

In September 1978, 60% of Marley New Zealand was sold to New Zealand Forest Products for $NZ1.8 million. Although some of those proceeds were subsequently absorbed in warranty claims, there was a clause in the sale agreement which gave Marley the right of repurchase in the event that control of New Zealand Forest Products changed hands. Almost ten years later, in March 1988, this right of repurchase was exercised at a cost of £3.3 million. 'After the sale, Don Wylie stayed and pulled the business round during our period of absence. He did a good job of rescuing it and handed it back to us in very good order.'[7] In April 1989, the scale of the business in New Zealand was increased by the acquisition of the plastics products business of Carter Holt Harvey at a cost of £7.6 million; and the acquisition of Dynex Extrusions in April 1992.

---

5   Marley Board Report, *77/183, November 1977.*
6   *Ibid.*
7   *Colin James interview.*

The Consortium

The Brazilian flooring market continued to offer volume growth and in 1975 capacity had to be increased from 2.7 million square metres a year to 5 million. Profits were now increasing regularly and in the Marley Holdings Annual Report for 1976, the Chairman was able to boast that the Brazilian associate (where Marley now had 36%) had reported its ninth consecutive year of improved profitability, and its profits now exceed £2 million. During that period, Fademac Brazil had diversified its operations by acquiring a small needlefelt flooring company (1972) and building a new factory. The needlepunch carpet market was far more competitive, however, as Marley was but one of four manufacturers.

Marley was now happier to put new money into the Brazilian company and in 1978 contributed its share of a new $14 million plant. It became operational in 1981 with a capacity of 7 million square metres a year of Lay-Flat, Stay-Flat 2 metre width cushioned flooring. By then, Fademac was a major supplier of a wide range of flooring products, from vinyl and rubber tiles, through cushioned vinyl to needlepunch carpet.

The success of its partnership with Eternit Belge encouraged Marley to seek further operations in Brazil and in 1978 Marley agreed to form a new company, this time jointly with Swiss Eternit, to manufacture concrete roofing tiles at Jundiai to the north of Sao Paulo; a $2 million loan allowed it to finance a 50% holding in Tegula. A year later Marley acquired a one third interest in Fademac S A (Argentina) at a cost of $579,000. It was Brazil, however, that was setting the pace, trebling the floor tile production capacity at Sao Paulo in 1979 with Tegula producing its first concrete roofing tiles in September that year. Unfortunately roof tile sales started slowly: 'Eternit admit that they have had more difficulties in launching the product than they had anticipated'[8] while, at the same time, the break-even level rose to over 5 million tiles a year. More capital was needed and in due course Eternit Brazil became an additional partner.

A year later the outlook was brighter and the minutes were recording agreement to purchase a site for a second roof tile factory, at Juiz de Fora to the north of Rio, though with building still to depend on the financial results of the first factory. In June 1981, Marley moved further into Latin America with the decision to build a roof tile plant near Santiago in Chile; on this occasion the vehicle was the French associate who had 40% of the new company, the balance being taken by Pizzareno, Eternit's Chilean subsidiary.

The potential returns from the large Brazilian market have attracted many European companies but not all have found the high, and fluctuating, rate of inflation easy to contend with. Marley was no exception and on more than one

---

8 *Marley Board Papers, May 1980.*

occasion the Holding Company Board examined the basis for staying in the country. Eventually Tegula was sold in December 1989 and Fademac Argentina in February 1990, both at book values. Fademac Brazil, however, continued to prosper and as recently as 1990 it increased its capacity for needlepunch carpet.

Marley continued to investigate other markets and other partnerships. For instance, a detailed survey on the Malaysian market was undertaken in 1981 and an agreement was reached with Sime Darby for a joint company to make concrete roof tiles, but the project was put on ice in 1982 because of political changes.[9] The Japanese market had also been examined in the late 1970s and in 1981 a proposal was put forward for a joint company to make concrete roofing tiles in which Onada Cement would hold 50%, Marley 40% and Swire 10%; like Malaysia, this was taken no further.

Gradually during the 1970s, Marley began to earn better returns from its overseas investments. A pre-tax contribution which had reached no more than £3 million in the early part of the decade was steadily pushed up in the later years until it exceeded £10 million in 1979 out of a group total of £22 million. Led by South Africa, those constituent countries produced even more, £12 million, in the next couple of years but, by then, a new loss maker had emerged to overshadow anything else Marley had achieved.

Problems in America

By the 1970s, Marley was once again ready to look at the prospects for manufacture on the North American continent but this time of extrusions. A study visit at the beginning of 1970 found low plastics usage in rainwater goods but perhaps better prospects in "sidings". A detailed scheme was prepared in 1971 for the construction of an extrusions plant in Toronto and existing businesses were also investigated. One of the attractions of the Toronto proposals is that they could utilise the existing Marley presence in Canada to provide a lower risk entry into the market south of the border. Indeed, the 1972 Holding Company accounts specifically stated that the Canadian management was looking for investment opportunities in the United States. However, as with earlier plans, it was not taken further. The McMahon business continued to prosper, achieving record trading profits of $1½ million in 1974 and serious consideration was then given to selling the company with a view to redeploying the funds in a manufacturing capacity. That the deal was not done probably owed as much to Marley being unable to find a suitable

9 *Marley Board minutes.*

acquisition as any particular belief in the long term future of carpet wholesaling. With hindsight, an early sale might have been the best decision for, a decade later, disposal was virtually forced on Marley after intense competition and a collapse in the market brought McMahon into loss.

In 1976, Marley came as close as it ever had done to a substantial US acquisition, that of the Whitlock Corporation, which operated 24 retail stores across the Midwest; 55% of sales went to the home improvement market with which Marley was well familiar, and 45% to the auto repair do-it-yourself motorist market. Full agreement on the acquisition of Whitlock by Marley was reached but, literally at the last minute, objections to certain of the contract conditions were raised by some of the younger Marley directors and the deal was pulled. Marley directors were now feeling a sense of frustration at the lack of progress in establishing a US base and the search for opportunities was intensified. At the December 1977 Board Meeting, a full discussion was held on Marley's attempts to find a way into the US market: 'It was agreed that, despite the cost, the employment, full time, of a person or persons to seek out business opportunities for Marley from a US base should be supported'. Jack Aisher, Bill Courtney and Trevor Aisher were left to report.

By then, Marley had decided that the opportunity existed for establishing its concrete roofing tile business on the American continent. Detailed studies were made of the Mexican market where there were a number of clay tile manufacturers but only one of concrete tiles, and those hand made. No substantial opportunities were seen and Marley soon turned to the southern United States. America, with its timber framed tradition of house construction, had a roofing market dominated by asbestos cement and asphalt shingles, and wood shakes. Apart from the unfamiliarity of the product, most roofs would not even have supported the greater weight of the concrete product. However, in the South, Spanish architectural styles had allowed a traditional clay tile and that had already provided the basis for a modest concrete roofing tile industry. By the mid-1970s, Monier Raymond, in which Redland had an indirect interest through its Australian associate, had three plants, and there were three other companies operating one plant each. During 1976, US Gypsum was considering entering the market but, by the beginning of 1977, they were negotiating with Marley to construct a roof tile plant at Torrance in Southern California. Reporting to the Marley Board in March 1977, Trevor Aisher was in optimistic mood: 'I am personally convinced that the time is now right to enter the American market and consider that it is highly unlikely that we will find a more suitable partner than USG'. Unfortunately for Marley, USG decided to stick to its last and Marley was looking for a new partner. Discussions were held with Swiss Eternit but, in September 1978, a joint company, Marley-Celotex, was formed with the Jim Walter Corporation of Florida.

Ingrid

In March 1979 a roof tile site was bought at San Bernadino; Marley at last had a physical presence in the United States. A month later a word was to appear in the Marley records that will still send shivers through those involved: Ingrid. There will be those whose first act on opening this book will be to turn to the index and head straight for Ingrid to see how much the author has been able to say. Let him merely say at the outset that the events are too recent to explore extensively; neither does he relish the prospect of a libel case on either side of the Atlantic.

Ingrid was owned by two Chicago entrepreneurs, David Rosenak and Stanley Berg; it owed its name to Berg's wife Ingrid, who herself had been responsible for much of the product design and selection. The 1979 Group Accounts, which introduced both Celotex-Marley and Ingrid to shareholders, described Ingrid as 'a market leader in the field of plastics, strong both in manufacturing and marketing. Ingrid operates in markets which are new to Marley, such as tableware, kitchenware and gardenware and is recognised as an innovator in these fields'. The products were sold to the large department stores, taking Marley into a market in which it had only a limited experience in the UK.

Ingrid had been brought to Marley by Hill Samuel, its merchant bank. Marley appears to have undertaken extensive preparatory investigation. Jack Aisher, Bill Courtney and Peter Wilson made repeated visits and Price Waterhouse of Chicago acted as reporting accountants. Bill Courtney looked at Ingrid's markets: 'We said "we want to go round the stores and we want to see your products" – we went round a lot of stores, most of the big cities, to talk to stores, buyers and customers and they all had very good shows of Ingrid. They had window displays – I always remember going to Marshall Field in Chicago and to Macey's in New York and San Francisco, Los Angeles and Philadelphia – they all had very good bright window displays of Ingrid. And of course not just one outlet in Chicago, because that is a big area, we went to half a dozen or more even going to garden centres where there were displays of the watering cans, pots and things. We really did a very thorough job and one could only be impressed by the penetration of the market place nationwide and the quality of the displays and the enthusiasm of the buyers.'

Peter Wilson, as the Marley Extrusions Director, reviewed the manufacturing; he identified the limitations of Ingrid's moulding processes but that was well within Marley's technical expertise. The accounting information and controls were also recognised to be limited but that was not unusual in a fast growing family controlled business.

At a main Board meeting on Tuesday, 8th May 1979, a facility letter from Barclays International was tabled making available up to US$6.8m for the purpose of financing the purchase of 80% of GPI Petrochemicals – the sole asset of which was the consumer plastics company, Ingrid. The 'report on the acquisition of Ingrid Ltd was approved indicating that agreement of terms had been reached and that the sale agreement would be signed of 11th May 1979'. Directors present were Sir Owen, in the Chair, Jack Aisher, Owen Aisher, Bill Courtney, Peter Aisher, Richard Aisher, Robin Aisher, Trevor Aisher, Eric Cook, Tom O'Sullivan, John Pollard, Peter Wilson and Peter Winfield.

By the time the Marley shareholders were being told of 'the strong foothold on which to build and capitalise when the American economy recovers' the main board minutes were already recording more worrying information.

September 4th 1979: $6m facility increased to $9m.

October 17th 1979: $9m facility increased to $12.5m – the extra being for working capital and bridging finance for the purchase of a new site at Lake Bluff in North Chicago.

December 12th 1979: $12.5m facility increased to $16m.

March 5th 1980: $16m facility increased to $18.5m. The additional $2.5m was to finance losses and provide extra working capital.

By the end of 1979 Peter Wilson was reporting on the poor results of Ingrid and warning that the move to new premises at Lake Bluff which had unexpectedly become available much earlier than planned, would be a further aggravation. Controls and management were strengthened. March 1980 had Jack Aisher reporting back to the Board; a profit of $103,000 in the three months to September 1979 had turned to a loss of $651,000 in the six months to December: Jack Aisher reported on the measures that had been taken to strengthen the financial reporting and controls of Ingrid. 'In the light of this experience, it was agreed that the well established financial disciplines in Marley companies be instituted immediately on the acquisition of all future companies.'

Move to Lake Bluff

Still the debt was rising and in May 1980 the limits were raised from $18.5m to $21.5m. It was also agreed to raise a Euro loan of $15m to increase the capital of GPI, using it to repay short term borrowings. Not surprisingly, relations with the original proprietors were deteriorating; Peter Wilson was having to spend significant periods of time in Chicago and eventually, in October 1980, Rosenak and Marley parted company leaving Stanley Berg as Managing Director. One of the problems faced by Ingrid, and recognised by Marley at the time of the acquisition, was that Ingrid was operating out of four separate, and cramped, premises and that a consolidation of the manufacturing facilities was always going to be needed. The new site at Lake Bluff had become available earlier than expected and was on a grand scale – 53 acres and a factory of 560,000 square feet, purchased for a consideration of $4.4 million. Marley made its move not only as the American economy was moving sharply into recession but before the British management had a true feeling for the business. It was easy to attribute the capital outflow to the demands of the relocation. When the Chairman came to report to the Marley shareholders in February 1981, he thought the worst was over: 'Ingrid... has grown out of its premises, so a very much larger facility was acquired; the move with all its dislocation was very expensive, but the company is now able to increase its production and has done so. It has, as from November, been trading profitably.'[10]

Peter Wilson had also identified difficulties of stock control arising out of the different locations, as well as the problems typically experienced by small growth companies. 'One of the major problems in Ingrid is the control of stock; at the two warehouses and at Maywood the control is extremely difficult and reconciliation of the figures problematical. The advantage of bringing it together under one roof is obvious... The Company exhibited all the symptoms of a small operation that has grown rapidly with the two owner/managers trying to do everything themselves. Again, this was a situation we knew when we purchased the Company.' Indeed it was. A pre-acquisition review of the financial controls of the proposed acquisition made it clear: 'My review of Ingrid's financial systems confirmed the view of everyone else who has visited the Company on behalf of Marley, namely that its strength lies first in its marketing skills and secondly in its technical and production abilities... With the eyes of the two main figures in the Company focused firmly on selling and production, it is perhaps not surprising that certain financial aspects of Ingrid's operation leave something to be desired. No budgets are prepared; no formalised costing system is in operation; production of financial statements is slow. Despite these shortcomings, however, the Company has operated very successfully up to now and has not been embarrassed, so far as one can judge, by the sort of unexpected capacity problem or inventory write-offs which might easily have resulted from the lack of financial controls that have been cited above. The abiding impression is of a "seat-of-the-pants" operation which nevertheless through a combination of good sense and a good knowledge of the business, works perfectly adequately.'[11]

The directors of Marley were aware of the weakness of the business they had bought and thought that they had brought it under control. Sadly, the profits which were being reported from Ingrid, and which had given the Board

10 *Marley Limited Accounts, 1980.*
11 *Marley Board Papers, 78/199, December 1978.*

some modest encouragement, proved to have been illusory. 'During the latter part of the year certain accounting practices, which had more to do with undisciplined marketing than anything, came to light in Ingrid showing clearly that the losses being sustained were considerably greater than we had previously thought. We took immediate action...'[12]

Eventually, Marley decided to make its own appointment as Chief Executive Officer and Dick Ryan was recruited at the beginning of June 1981, to start on July 1st; Stanley and Ingrid Berg departed at the end of the month. The Board view was that the 'main core of the business is sound but the management team is weak and divided and it requires a positive person to direct and control activities'.[13] Ingrid Berg went on to form Berg Plastics offering a similar range of products; she was joined by two of the Ingrid representatives. The true scale of the losses being made at Ingrid was now becoming apparent. A preliminary report of the 14 months to August 1981 was presented to the Board in September. Against a budgeted profit of $3.01 million was a loss of $3.41 million, and that without charging full interest and before year-end adjustments. The final results included stock write-offs of $3.6 million; provisions against debtors of $3.3 million; and a $2 million loss relating to under-provision of liabilities and plant write-downs, some of which dated back to before the acquisition of the company. The total loss for the year therefore exceeded $12 million.

The heart of the problem was that sales which Marley had assumed were firm were found to be subject to a number of deductions 'for which no written authorisation has been available'[14]; these included advertising and excess freight charges. There were also sales subject to sale or return clauses with major customers; and they were returned. 'The invoicing system presented the customer with a standard invoice price which was systematically reduced by verbal agreements undertaken by the previous Berg management, most of which were unrecorded and subsequently unidentifiable... Fortunately with the appointment of the new President CEO on the 1st July these practices have ceased.'[15] The table shows the sales which had been reported in the accounts and which had given Marley such early confidence.

Ingrid reported sales ($m)

1976	1977	1978	1979	1980	1981
7.3	10.8	15.1	17.4	24.6	34.2

12   *Marley Limited Accounts, 1980.*
13   *Marley Board minutes, June 1981.*
14   Marley Board Report, *December 1981.*
15   *Ibid.*

To begin with, Ingrid had looked to be a business which was growing rapidly, but just overextended. With hindsight 'We now know that, starting in 1978, sales numbers were overstated, either because some of the "sales" were in fact gifts to the customers or because credits granted for a variety of reasons were not recorded as sales reductions'.[16] An estimate of the amount by which sales should have been reduced was $1 million in 1979, $5 million in 1980 and $8 million in 1981. The true level of sales in 1981 was therefore only $26 million. The following year saw sales, more conventionally recorded, fall to $22.8 million, a full third below what Marley thought had been achieved in 1981 and less than half of the 1981 budget. The analysis was stark. 'The thinking in 1980 that Ingrid was a $25 million business growing at 35% per year caused management to take certain actions, including over-investment in plant and equipment and ballooning of marketing and manufacturing overhead costs... This resulted in burdening the business with high fixed costs, excessive debt and cash flow problems'.[17]

Marley's problems were compounded by the severity of the American recession in 1981 and the reaction of the major customers. 'The major departmental chains were quite unscrupulous in the way that they cleared inventory just by returning stock. They changed buyers round the departments so the people you were dealing with would say they knew nothing about it. The goods are going back: if you want to deal with us again, then you have to accept it.'[18] Action had to be taken to reduce costs at Lake Bluff ('we found when we closed it that it cost a million dollars just to heat the place'). The break-even point had reached $48 million which the management managed to reduce to $30 million but even that proved nowhere near low enough.

However, the scale of the changes that were required also affected the image of Ingrid in the market place. Dick Ryan's report to the Marley Board in 1982 spelt that out: 'Ingrid's market image was worse than any of us anticipated. The company's reputation for service, quality, pricing integrity and overall reliability declined rapidly from July 1980... The change in management signalled a tightening of business practices and concern about whether product innovation would continue.' Gradually Ingrid's customers were won back but the scale of the surplus capacity at the Lake Bluff factory was not going to be easily filled. One solution was to acquire other houseware manufacturers with a view to feeding some or all of their product lines through Lake Bluff. The first of these was Klein Plastic Products, based in Detroit but with its principal manufacturing plant at Baraboo, Wisconsin. Klein was purchased in July 1982 for a consideration of $3.75 million and, apart from broadening the range of products Marley could offer, brought with it

16 *Marley Board Report, March 1983.*
17 *Ibid.*
18 *Interview with Denis Rigden, Group Accountant.*

substantial business with the K Mart stores. It was, and remained throughout, a consistently profitable business and its initial five month contribution of $1.8 million was a welcome offset to Ingrid's $7.5 million loss in the twelve months to September 1982.

The problems associated with the original sales methods led Dick Ryan to completely rebuild the sales organisation. After a long search, a new Vice-President of Sales was recruited and Ingrid utilised manufacturers' agents working on commission. Old customers who had been lost during the earlier management upheavals were now being regained and K Mart took Ingrid products for the first time. Marley thought the worst was behind them and in February 1983: 'Following a massive... reorganisation under a totally new management team, the company is now operating under full control... right direction... exciting range of new products'.[19] The Board papers for May 1983 forecast that Marley Plastics (Ingrid and Klein) 'should show its first profit in April'.

Despite the wholesale reorganisation, sales could not be conjured up out of nowhere and the Lake Bluff factory was operating at only 40% of its moulding capacity; a voracious dragon requiring its regular supply of local maidens. To help feed it, another housewares company, Salton had been bought in September 1983 and arrangements were made to transfer some of Salton's assembly work to Lake Bluff. Dick Ryan continued to attack Ingrid's high cost base and, reporting to the Board in February 1984, he described how costs had been reduced from $13.9 million in 1981 to an estimate of under $10 million in 1984. The problem still remained finding sufficient work for Lake Bluff; additional product was switched from the Klein factory and, in April 1984, Republic Molding, another Chicago based manufacturer of food containers and microwave cookware was acquired. In a final attempt to raise the throughput, Dick Ryan, who had successfully brought down the cost base, departed and, to bring fresh emphasis to the marketing, Max Klein was appointed Chief Executive on December 18th 1984.

By the end of 1984, Lake Bluff was still operating at only 40% of capacity. The losses continued and although the forecasts were for these to reduce, patience was exhausted. On August 23rd, 1985 Marley sold its US housewares business to a consortium of private investors, led by a senior executive in another housewares company. The various companies were sold for $15 million plus a share of future profits; buildings with a value of around $5 million and the tax losses were retained. Including the costs of financing the investment, these businesses had given rise to losses of £12 million during the two years before the sales and we had, since acquisition, invested a total of £31 million. The sale resulted in an extraordinary loss in 1985 of £10 million but the trading position and indebtedness of these US businesses necessitated an

19 *Marley plc Accounts, 1982.*

immediate termination of our investment and we strongly believe this to have been in the best interests of Marley. This was an operation we could not continue to support.'[20]

Looking back some years after the disposal, Jack Aisher reflected that Marley had bought into the wrong product: 'We should have done over there what we had done here, plastic goods, rainwater goods'. Should Marley have known better at the time? 'Without any doubt, if you go and buy something, then you're the chap that's made the mistake, if there's a mistake going to be made. It's like buying a house or a motor car; you are perfectly free to investigate it thoroughly. If there was any blame to be laid, it had to be laid at our own door. In any successful business, and we are a successful business, you have great successes and you have the reverse.' Denis Rigden: 'If people had realised what they were buying – an up-market fashion plastics business capable of a turnover of between $12 and $15 million a year with a margin of about 10%, and quite capable of making $1½ million a year. The big mistake was, whilst it was essential to take the business out of the three clapped out factories that were in the Chicago suburbs, it could have been put into a building of 200,000 square feet [with] about 12 moulders. As soon as they put it into Lake Bluff, they were doomed.' And a final word from Bill Courtney: 'We did what we thought was a very good vetting job but in essence it was about a quarter of what we should have done with hindsight. Looking back it was all too good to be true but I suppose we liked what we saw and we believed what we were told and therein is the danger of buying American businesses – you don't ever believe what you're told.'

Back to roofing tiles

As the scale of the problems at Ingrid were beginning to dawn on the Marley Board, the management was also having to face a disappointing start in its roof tile venture. Management changes within Marley's Celotex partners and flooding by the Santa Anna River of the new factory site made 1980 a difficult starting year for the joint venture. Nevertheless, the factory was a good productive unit, one of 23 concrete roof tile plants in California at that time, and Marley-Celotex was soon looking for additional sites. By the end of 1980, the joint venture had identified a second site in California, at Ventura, and a third one at Houston, Texas; unfortunately, cash flow problems within the Jim Walter Corporation brought these proposals to a temporary stop. This also led to some renegotiation of the original partnership agreement which was now confined to the southern states; Marley was given the right to develop the concrete roof tile business in the rest of North America on its own. By then,

20 Marley Annual Report, *1985*.

Marley was already looking, but its partnership arrangements had cost it two vital years of development.

Eric Cook reported back to the Marley Board in August 1981 following his visit to North America. His view was that in every part of northern USA and Canada (where asphalt shingle is the dominant roofing material) there were enough expensive houses and commercial demand to support a concrete roof tile operation. A factory was proposed to the west of Toronto and the next month land and buildings were bought at Milton. To keep the costs down Marley used a second-hand low speed manual plant; although it had a two shift capacity of 10 million tiles a year, its break-even level was only 2 million. Production of Mendip tiles started on May 3rd 1982 but in a market which had little familiarity with traditional clay profiles, sales were hard to achieve. Marley worked hard at setting up authorised roofing contractors but the response was slow and Marley was drawn into running its own supply and fix operation, which it had to staff with tilers brought over from the UK. It was not until 1987 that Marley was finally able to convert to a supply only basis, many of its previous employees by then established as independent contractors. Its selling area was gradually extended through eastern Canada and into the United States.

In California, Marley was broadening its range. To the Mission tile, based on the Spanish clay profile, was added a flat tile; the concrete industry began to take the fight to the traditional wood shake and asphalt shingle. In 1982, most of the local and county authorities in Southern California were banning untreated wood shakes giving a welcome boost to alternative roofing. Pressure treated shakes began to cost significantly more than concrete and by the end of 1983 concrete had 30% of the roofing market. The transformation was dramatic: sales gradually overtook production and from October 1983 the factory was being operated 24 hours a day, 5 days a week and at that point the plant could have sold twice its capacity. The previous year's loss of over $1 million was replaced by profits of $100,000 a month. The joint venture was now prepared for its second factory and in December 1983 bought a disused concrete tile factory at Hollister to the South of San Francisco in Northern California.

The uneasy relationship with the Jim Walter Corporation was ended in July 1986 with the purchase of their shareholding in the joint venture for £1 million and the operating company was renamed Marley Roof Tiles Corporation. In December, the business was enlarged by the acquisition of the roof tile manufacturing assets of Carroll's Building Material Inc. at Clearwater, Florida for £2.3 million. The same year saw the introduction of Duralite, a lightweight tile designed for the re-roofing market. The Clearwater assets had been bought out of a Chapter 11 administration and needed substantial modernisation; it took longer to bring into profits than anticipated. Once the US housing market began to turn down (it virtually halved between

1986 and the beginning of 1991), Marley's lack of critical mass was exposed and in May 1991 the Californian plants were closed before being sold to Redland for $11 million in June.

In Toronto, the roofing tile plant was closed at the end of 1990, ending Marley's long-standing involvement with Canada. McMahon, so consistently profitable for Marley during the 1960s and 1970s, found the economic climate of the succeeding decade much tougher. The usual $1 million profit in 1981 turned into a $3.7 million loss in 1982; the Toronto branch was closed and McMahon concentrated on the western provinces. However, price competition remained acute, exacerbated by some of the carpet mills selling direct and bypassing the distributor. Marley eventually restored McMahon to profits but the old returns were no longer there and in September 1987, McMahon was sold at net asset value to a management buy-out team raising £6.2 million.

Part 9
After the family

If the first sixty years of Marley's history had to be characterised in just one phrase, then it would be as a family business. It was founded by the Aisher family; it was built up to become one of the country's leading building material companies by the Aisher family; the early technical and product innovations that made Marley a market leader were introduced by the Aishers; and individual members of the family could be found running some of the subsidiary operations. Although, well supported in the 1960s by non-family executives, the credit for Marley's achievements must largely remain with the Aishers, and with Sir Owen in particular. Without him, Marley would not exist.

But during the 1970s and 1980s, Marley certainly had more than its share of problems and the Company gradually slipped out of the first division of Britain's building materials industry. That is not to say that the Company made no progress; by 1984, pre-tax profits had reached a new peak of £43.7 million compared with its 1973 cyclical peak of £14.8 million, though all this could be accounted for by inflation. More to the point, Marley's peers in the industry had enhanced their position by strategic acquisition, supported by fund-raising, and a number of them were, by the mid-1980s, producing pre-tax profits of over £100 million (Blue Circle, Pilkington, Redland and Tarmac). If the Aisher family can be credited with Marley's undoubted successes, then it cannot be wholly absolved from its later weaknesses.

Marley suffered from capital limitations that were to a degree self-

Sir Owen's coffin on Marley lorry

imposed by the desire to maintain family control. Marley was a capital hungry Company; no organisation pursuing the new developments that Marley did could have been anything else. There was, however, a marked reluctance on the part of the Aisher family to raise new equity. There had been a rights issue in 1960 and the Aishers had borrowed from the bank to maintain their share of the Company. 'Later, all the expansionist ideas we had were definitely constrained by the fact that it had to be financed out of two sources; one was retained profits and one was borrowings.'[1] Ingrid, of course, was a serious cash drain and acted as a negative rights issue. From time to time, therefore, Marley had to turn down capital investment opportunities that it might otherwise have pursued. It was certainly not allowed to make substantial acquisitions for shares which might have taken it into new markets. The clay brick and tile industries had both been seriously considered and some thought had also been given to the aggregates market which would have represented a natural extension from the sand pits on which the roof tile works were based.

The conflict over marketing philosophies has been discussed at length in earlier chapters. One could argue that it did not matter who was right; there is often more than one answer to a problem. What does matter is that the preferred solution is carried out effectively. Unfortunately for Marley, the debate on marketing strategies, in particular Marley's position as a competitor of its own customers, continued for almost two decades, in one place or another around the group. It was divisive internally and frequently left the outside world unsure as to what precisely Marley stood for. But the length of time this dispute continued may, in itself, have been a symptom; the symptom of a management structure, rooted in the dynamism of a successful family business, unable to come to terms with the passing of the years. Interviewed by the magazine *Building*, in June 1978, Sir Owen had stated his views on the role of the family with characteristic force. 'One of the things we older people deplore is a lack of family. The invention of the word nepotism is all part of the academic idea of denigrating family. In other words, if you work for your family and create a job for your son, they suggest it's wrong. What do you live for really? If you're not living first to make your own family better, how the hell do you think you can do anything in this life to make the other family better? That's our philosophy. We look after ourselves first, on the basis that if we're strong and healthy, we can do something for the other fellow.' Re-reading that quotation in 1991, Sir Owen's view remained as clear: 'the most prosperous companies have been family businesses and in my opinion the most prosperous businesses in the future will be family businesses'. When asked if he thought that there had been too many of the family? 'On the contrary! Now, if you say, were the family as good as they ought to be? No, they never were. Were the others? Yes, some of them were, but they were each running [their

1   *John Pollard interview.*

own businesses] and doing it very well. What was the family doing? Well they were keeping their eye on it and getting out and seeing what was going on.'

By common consent, the outstanding non-family executive in the Marley history was Fred Hardy. In 1976, Fred Hardy retired after 41 years with Marley: he was 'undoubtedly one of the main forces responsible for our growth from the small beginnings of pre-war days. He will be missed but remembered with affection by the many employees, customers, suppliers and shareholders who knew him at Marley.'[2] His relationship with Sir Owen was often stormy and Fred Hardy's reminiscences of his early years are peppered with expectations of imminent dismissal. Little attempt was ever made to specify his responsibilities but his appointment as a Deputy Chairman was an acknowledgement of his role which was a cross between a managing director and a regimental sergeant-major sweeping up behind the officers. As the senior non-family executive in what was still regarded as a family firm he was the only person able to act as a counterweight to Sir Owen's powerful and imaginative personality. 'They had grown up more or less together and therefore they had a totally different relationship from anybody else... he knew how to deal with Owen.'[3]

No immediate replacement for Fred Hardy was made but the inside money was on Eric Cook, Tom O'Sullivan or Peter Wilson. In the event, two Joint Deputy Chairmen were appointed in 1977 – Owen Aisher Junior and Bill Courtney. However, whereas Fred Hardy had been a joint Deputy Chairman with Jack Aisher, the two new Deputy Chairman now ranked below Jack Aisher who had become Vice Chairman. If Owen Aisher Junior's appointment was the prerogative of the Chairman's eldest son, then Bill Courtney was seen as the successor to Fred Hardy. Although Marley Buildings was not one of the largest of the domestic operations, it had done well under Bill Courtney's control and he had also had the advantage of being able to run it as a self-contained business, unlike the other subsidiaries, always responsible for its own sales and marketing. Bill Courtney had also been closely associated with the revival of Marley's substantial South African business. He was not, however able to replicate the control and influence over the other subsidiary managing directors that Fred Hardy had exercised. 'They wouldn't call me MD or Chief Executive – I think... it is not their wish to give anybody a title of any sort. It was just one of those things which, I suppose, happened in a family business, but it was short-sighted and I found myself with a title of Deputy Chairman but without the powers to run the business. Most of the power resided with Sir Owen and Jack and of course the incidence of the family in the business was quite high. It wasn't a normal situation.' True, it was unrealistic to expect Bill Courtney to fulfil the Fred Hardy role without more clearly defined executive

2   *Marley Limited* Annual Report, *1976.*
3   *Sir Robert Clark interview.*

Sir George Russell

authority; indeed, it was by no means clear that the Aishers wanted him to.

Sir George Russell, currently Chairman, believes it was an inability to sort out the succession internally which eventually led to his recruitment. 'Why was I brought in? I think that is the first question I'd posed and everybody posed. There was an obvious unwillingness through the previous ten years to sort out the succession, and this doesn't mean that there weren't very able family members who could have done the job. Because there had not been a defined succession, it had drifted to the point of a non-acceptability of any succession. That is the point of an outsider coming in to a business that had been brilliantly built-up over a sixty-year period, leading in product innovation in this country in the building sector – a major figure running it, with a family structure, but not a management succession thereafter established to allow it to move from that one person dominance into what had to be a company that needed a broader professional management to grow.'

Sir Owen stood down as Chairman of Marley in October 1982, aged 82, becoming Life President. There had been a difficult Annual General Meeting earlier in the year and pressure had been growing inside the Company and also within the City. Asked if he felt he should have stepped down at an earlier age Sir Owen was characteristically forceful: 'No, certainly not. I never did. I was persuaded to let brother Jack run it. He thought he ought to and I was quite happy not to, or to let him.' Although he remained a director and continued to come in to the office, he no longer attended Board meetings. After he retired as Chairman, Sir Owen sold the majority of his Marley shareholding.

In 1982, the Marley Board also saw the loss of Peter Winfield who died at the age of 48, and Eric Cook who retired after 36 years with Marley. Mike Armstrong, who had been fulfilling the role of Finance Director since John Pollard's retirement was appointed to the Board on January 1st 1983. Sir Owen may have stood down but there was no pretending that the succession problem had been solved; indeed, the internal dissensions were growing. Amongst other things, the loose structure that had evolved had led to the individual directors acting more as representatives of their own businesses than as holding company directors. 'It bred a curious bunch of characters on the Board... it caused the fiefdoms, hardly surprising given the characteristics of the products and the way the responsibilities were split up. The fact is that they paddled their own canoes and there wasn't a great deal of control from the centre to make sure that everything was going according to plan, nor was there anything but resentment for any attempt to interfere. I remember one director saying in a discussion about internal audit and financial controls "I have nothing against financial control, so long as you don't try to interfere with my business" which was a very typical attitude.'[4] Looking back, Sir Owen himself considered it a mistake to have had all the Divisional Managing Directors on the main Holding Board: 'they just protected their own interests'.

There had in the past been pressure from the City, in particular the Prudential, for the appointment of a non-executive director. It had led to the possibly apocryphal remark from Sir Owen 'Who are the Pru? They've only
Sir Robert Clark

4 *Mike Armstrong interview.*

Sir Robert Clark

got 4% of the shares'. The pressures did not go away, however, and in July 1984 Jack Aisher appointed Sir Robert Clark to the Marley Board as a non-executive director. 'Bob' Clark had joined the Corporate Finance department of Philip Hill in 1962, after a partnership with solicitors Slaughter & May, eventually becoming Chief Executive (later Chairman) of Hill Samuel in 1980. He was a leading City figure with a string of directorships, including the Bank of England, and a long-standing associate of Jack Aisher. His appointment had not been a matter for Board discussion. At the end of that year, Bill Courtney's early retirement was announced; he left in 1985 after 38 years service, eight as Deputy Chairman, to become Chairman of the soon to be privatised Southern Water. Owen Aisher Junior had also advised the Board that he would be standing down as the other Deputy Chairman on reaching normal retirement age in 1985. Jack Aisher himself retired as Chairman at the AGM in May 1985 having fulfilled his lifelong ambition to head the Company he had joined as a young boy in 1926. Sir Robert Clark succeeded him in the Chair – the last unilateral decision of the Aishers.

Postscript

By agreement with the Company, the detailed story stops here. Although Jack Aisher remained on the Board as a non-executive director until May 1989, and the next generation of Aishers continued to be well represented, an era had drawn to an end. The unique character of Marley lay with the Aisher family – strengths and weaknesses – for it was not possible to have one without the other. The substance of this history is dominated by the Aishers and it is appropriate for it to end with the appointment of an outsider to the Chair.

As the new Chairman, Sir Robert Clark instituted a complete review of all the group's activities. Ingrid and its associated companies were sold in July 1985, bringing to an end a venture which had cost Marley in excess of £40 million. Plumb-Center was sold to Wolseley, raising £8 million and ending the conflict between Extrusions and its customers. And in the flooring business, Leighton Buzzard was closed and the loss-making Florstyle contracting business sold. The losses incurred by Ingrid had put extra pressure on group borrowings which reached a year end peak of £98 million net in 1984; seasonal factors helped raise this to £130 million the following spring. To make matters

David Trapnell

worse, operating profits fell sharply in 1985 and were completely eliminated by the extraordinary losses.

Sir Robert also needed to appoint a new chief executive and like Jack Aisher before him, he went outside. On the evening of December 12th 1985, the Marley directors met informally with George Russell and the following day he was formally appointed as Chief Executive Officer at the Board meeting. George Russell (now Sir George), a native of Northumberland, who had worked extensively in North America, and had previously been Managing Director of British Alcan Aluminium, took office in January 1986. He was given two main objectives: to keep Marley independent and to accomplish the transition from a traditionally managed family business. (Sir George became Executive Chairman in May 1989, only becoming non-executive in September 1993 following the promotion of David Trapnell to Chief Executive in the February of that year.)

At the December Board meeting that approved the appointment of George Russell, the policy priority was recorded as debt reduction. It was not believed that this could be achieved out of trading profits and a more radical solution was therefore required. Marley identified its core businesses as roof tiles and plastics within the building trade; after much soul-searching, new capital was found in the sale of Payless, then contributing almost £9 million of pre-tax profits. Despite the misgivings surrounding the sale of a business which had done so much for Marley it was an inevitable choice: its fast growth rate required its own capital expenditure programme; it stood to one side of Marley's predominantly manufacturing base; and it was the only asset which could readily produce such a large sale price. Payless was put up for auction and in March 1986, Ward White was announced as the successful candidate with a cash bid of £94 million (in addition to £10 million raised earlier from the sale of a portfolio of freehold properties). A pro-forma balance sheet showed a complete elimination of all group debt and an increase in net assets from £144 million to £208 million.

In the latter half of the 1980s, extensive changes took place within the Board and many of the names familiar from earlier chapters departed. Indeed, there was some external criticism of the number of departures and the length of time it took to establish a clear line of command under the Chairman. Perhaps it was unrealistic to expect that a management style that had persisted for sixty years, and which had left its mark in so many different ways, could be replaced overnight. Through all this, however, Marley's operational structure was being progressively tightened, peripheral activities eliminated and core businesses strengthened.

Under George Russell, substantial investment was directed towards the traditional manufacturing businesses to increase operating efficiency: 'the restructuring of the Group, which began in 1985, continued apace in 1986. The main thrust of this corporate rationalisation was towards improving efficiency and productivity. This meant considerable upheaval in the form of factory closures accompanied inevitably by redundancies and product rationalisation; this was followed, in several instances, by investment in the most modern production technology available.' In the three years from 1986 to 1988, Marley's capital investment totalled £123 million. That investment and the reorganisation of the existing businesses came just in time to enable Marley to benefit from the boom in private housing and commercial building and, in that three year period, Marley's pre-tax profits more than doubled to £70 million.

Acquisitions also played an early role in the reshaping of Marley. Thermalite, the leading manufacturer of aerated concrete blocks, was bought for £54 million in May 1986; General Shale, which has now been developed into the leading US brick manufacturer, for £63 million in June 1986; and Nottingham Brick for £44 million in March 1987. Judgement on the strategic value of those three acquisitions is clouded by the impact of the recession which had a particularly severe impact on the brick and block industries on both sides of the Atlantic. The long term arguments favour Thermalite and General Shale, respectively numbers one and two in their markets at the time of acquisition and now both the market leader. In contrast, Nottingham Brick brought no significant market share, leaving Marley only a minor player in the UK brick industry. However, in October 1993, Marley was able to announce that it was swapping Nottingham Brick for Tarmac's Hawkins Tiles, giving Marley capacity for 30 million clay tiles a year, thereby strengthening one of its traditional core businesses.

General Shale in particular gave Marley a sound manufacturing base in the USA for the first time. The subsequent purchases of Corbin Brick and Webster Brick made General Shale the largest brick manufacturer in the United States. One of the bonuses arising from the ownership of General Shale was the opportunity to purchase the neighbouring DG Mouldings in June 1990 for £27 million. Now trading as Marley Mouldings, the company is the largest producer of prefinished wood and plastic mouldings in the USA with a 40% market share; the 'Clearwood' process is patented world-wide, and the product is supplied for door and window edgings, picture frames etc. Opportunities are now being taken to transfer the technology into Marley's UK and German extrusions businesses.

There was further tidying up of the structure. In 1987, the Irish Concrete Products company and McMahon of Canada were both sold as was Marley Vehicle Leasing, the latter for a £12 million extraordinary profit. In turn, the former 60% holding in the New Zealand Marley (sold in 1978) was repurchased and there were bolt on acquisitions in roofing contracting and US bricks. Marley was increasingly concentrating on those areas where it believed it had reasonable long term prospects of influencing its marketplace. Between 1989 and 1991 Marley sold its flooring investment in Argentina and withdrew from concrete roof tile manufacture in France, Brazil, Canada and the USA, and from garages at home. Within the plastics business, automotive joint ventures were established with Davidson in Holland and Kansei near the new Nissan plant on Tyne & Wear, and Marley New Zealand bought out one of its major competitors.

The puncturing of the speculative property bubble at the end of the 1980s, first housing and then commercial, caused a recession in the building materials industry of a severity unprecedented in the experience of those managing the industry's leading companies. With its high exposure to housing related demand, Marley was early into the downturn but the management responded quickly and over £20 million was taken out of the UK cost structure by the end of 1990. However, demand continued to fall and, at the heavy end of Marley's range, industry deliveries of bricks, aerated blocks and concrete roofing tiles in 1992 were almost 40% below their 1988 levels. This necessitated further economies and early in 1992 the heavy end subsidiaries were merged to form Marley Building Materials, saving further overhead cost. In the USA, where housing starts had almost halved, General Shale remained profitable with a positive cash flow, a reflection of the underlying strength of the company, and a contrast to the results from some other brick manufacturers. Gratifyingly, Marley's capital investment, particularly in Germany, actually resulted in the world-wide plastics division achieving record operating profits in 1992. Even in that difficult year, the Marley Group was still able to earn profits, before tax and exceptional items, of over £18 million.

The ten years since the appointment of Sir Robert as Chairman have seen the full, though not always smooth, transition of Marley from an essentially family business to a more conventional management structure. Investment in the core businesses has underpinned the transition and, without the substantial investment made in the late 1980s, Marley would have been hard pressed to cope with the severity of the subsequent building recession. In the 1990 Report and Accounts, George Russell was able to draw comfort from that investment programme: 'We approached the current downturn from a sound base, following a critical five year phase in which the Group's manufacturing resources were substantially renewed.' At the time of going to press, the reduced cost base is benefiting from a modest revival in housing demand in the UK and US, and Marley's profits are beginning to recover sharply. As the building industry emerges from recession, so will the decisions taken over the last five years produce their full reward.

Bibliography

Books

Abraham, Herbert, *Asphalts and Allied Substances*, (3rd Ed), London, 1929.

Baumgarten, R H and Childe, H L, *Manufacture of Concrete Roofing Tiles*, London, 1936.

Beaverbrook, Lord, *Courage: The Story of Sir James Dunn*.

Bennett, Frank and Pinion, Alfred, *Roof Slating and Tiling*, London, 1935.

Bowley, Marion, *Housing and the State 1919–1944*, London, 1945.

Bowley, Marion, *Innovations in Building Materials*, London, 1960.

Briggs, Martin S, *A Short History of the Building Crafts*, Oxford, 1925.

Christie, Guy, *Storeys of Lancaster*, London, 1964.

Churchill, Winston, *The Second World War*, vol v, London, 1951.

Dennett, Laurie, *The Charterhouse Group 1925–1979*, London, 1979.

Dobson, Charles, *Roof Tiling*, London, 1931.

Dobson, Charles, *The History of the Concrete Roofing Tile – Its Origin and Development in Germany*, London, 1959.

Dobson, Edward and Searle, Alfred, *Bricks and Tiles*, London, 1936.

Elsas, M J, *Housing Before the War and After*, London, 1942.

Hartcup, Guy, *The Challenge of War: Scientific and Engineering Contribution to World War Two*, Newton Abbot, 1970.

Jeremy, David and Shaw, Christine (Eds), *Dictionary of Business Biography*, qv Sir James Dunn; Cyril Lord; Sir Hugo Cunliffe-Owen, 1984–86.

Jones, Geoffrey (Ed), *British Multinationals: Origins Managment and Performance*, London, 1986.

Lindsay, Jean, *A History of the North Wales Slate Industry*, Newton Abbot, 1974.

Mehler, William A Jr, *Let The Buyer Have Faith: The Story of Armstrong*, Lancaster, PA, USA, 1987.
Muir, Augustus, *Nairns of Kirkcaldy: A Short History 1847–1956*, Cambridge, 1956.
Postgate, R W, *The Builders' History*, London, 1923.
Richardson Harry W and Aldcroft, Derek H, *Building in the British Economy Between the Wars*, London, 1968.
Searle, Alfred, *Modern Tilemaking*, 1930.

Government publications

Annual Abstract of Statistics, CSO, various dates.
Central Committee Report on Slates, Standing Committees on the Investigation of Prices and Trusts, Cmd 1338, 1921.
The Distribution of Building Materials and Components, Ministry of Works, 1948.
Final Report on the Stone Brick and Clayware Trades, Standing Committees on the Investigation of Prices and Trusts, Cmd 1209, 1921.
Housing and Construction Statistics, Department of the Environment, various dates.
Housing: Needs and Action, Department of the Environment Circular, 1975.
Monopolies Commission Report on Concrete Roof Tiles, 1981.
Report on the Present Position of the Building Industry with regard to the carrying out of a full housing programme, Cmd 2104, 1924.

Articles

Anon, 'The Marley Tile Company', *Plastics Today*, no 29, Imperial Chemicals Industries Plastics Division.
Anon, 'The new wave in vinyl flooring', *Modern Plastics*, Dec 1967, pp 98–100.
Anon, 'The Halstead story', *Floors*, vol IX, no 5, Oct 1990, pp 8–9.
Desoutter, Gillian, 'Marley Tile – Maker of modern building components', *Financial World*, Nov 19, 1966.
Hodge, Major W J, 'The Mulberry Invasion Harbours: Their design preparation and installation', *The Structural Engineer*, Mar 1946, pp 125–192.
Madden, Len, 'Historical perspective', *Building*, 28 Jan 1983, p 43.
Whelan, Sarah, 'Building a tradition the history of Nairn', *Ideal Homes*, Jan 1990.
White, Sir George B, 'The Mulberry Harbours', *The Central*, Dec 1946, pp 58–66.

Other published sources

Marley: *Annual Reports*.
Marley Tile (Holding) Company: *Prospectus*, Jan 1935.
Marley News.

Marley Tile Jubilee Brochures, 1974 and 1984.
Concrete Products of Ireland: *Annual Reports.*
Concrete Products of Ireland: *Prospectus*, Feb 1965.
Redland: *Annual Reports.*
Redland: *A survey of the Company and its activities from 1919–1969.*
Polypipe: *Prospectus*, June 1985.
National Archives of Canada: *Sir James Dunn Papers*, vol 377.

Index